WALK THROUGH FIRE

WALK THROUGH FIRE

The Train Disaster That Changed America

YASMINE S. ALI, MD

CITADEL PRESS
Kensington Publishing Corp.
www.kensingtonbooks.com

CITADEL PRESS BOOKS are published by

Kensington Publishing Corp.
119 West 40th Street
New York, NY 10018

All Kensington titles, imprints, and distributed lines are available at special quantity discounts for bulk purchases for sales promotions, premiums, fundraising, educational, or institutional use. Special book excerpts or customized printings can also be created to fit specific needs. For details, write or phone the office of the Kensington sales manager: Kensington Publishing Corp., 119 West 40th Street, New York, NY 10018, attn: Sales Department; phone 1-800-221-2647.

ISBN: 978-0-8065-4218-8

First Citadel hardcover printing: March 2023

10 9 8 7 6 5 4 3 2 1

Printed in the United States of America

Library of Congress Control Number: 2022947428

ISBN: 978-0-8065-4220-1 (e-book)

For my parents, Drs. Subhi and Maysoon Ali, who were there for me and for Waverly in 1978, and for over 40 years since.

You can do what you have to do, and sometimes you can do it even better than you think you can.

—ATTRIBUTED TO JIMMY CARTER, 39TH PRESIDENT OF THE UNITED STATES

Contents

Author's Note

IN THIS BOOK, much of the story of the Waverly Train Disaster is told from the perspectives and points of view of those who were there to witness it firsthand. I drew upon my own extensive interviews, correspondence, and personal conversations with those involved in order to weave together all the different threads into one cohesive tapestry that presents the whole of the disaster. Dialogue, thoughts, and even narrative are often direct quotes from interviewees, and are therefore based on the interviewees' recollections. Wherever possible, I have fact-checked historical details against archival sources, and these sources are provided in the references. Descriptions of the deceased are taken directly from those who lived and worked closely with them.

Ball of Fire

FEBRUARY 24, 1978
FRIDAY
2:55 P.M.

THE WHOLE WORLD HAD TURNED upside down.

Police Sergeant Elton "Toad" Smith looked up to see what had struck him on the forehead. What he saw made his blood run cold in spite of the sudden, searing heat. It seemed as if the entire railbed had been hurled into the sky, in one giant whirlwind of rocks the size of golf balls. Debris flew everywhere. Beams from buildings, metal from train cars. Even a hard hat whirled above him, leaving him to wonder about the head that had been wearing it. And surrounding it all were the never-ending billows of smoke, streaked through with blinding flashes of white.

Toad had run no more than three steps from his patrol car in the center of Waverly's New Town section when he became aware that he was waist deep in an all-consuming blue flame that formed a wall for as far as he could see. This shimmering blue wall swept by and through him, engulfing everything in its path, marching all the way out to Commerce Street and passing in front of Slayden Lumber Company.

Oh, God, what a way to die, Toad thought. But then the blue flame simply disappeared, going out as quickly as it came, and Toad hoped that would be the end of it.

He kept running, picking up speed, knowing that he had to get out of there, put some distance between himself and the whirlwind of debris, or at the very least, get behind a building— preferably one that was still standing. As he ran, he became aware of a hideous noise ominously close to him, a sound he would never forget for the rest of his life. It reminded him of the sizzling sound a piece of raw meat makes when dropped into burning-hot oil. "Tshhh," hissed this awful noise near his ear, and he involuntarily turned his head to locate the source.

The sizzling seemed to be coming from inside his own ears now, and as he turned and looked around, glancing behind him while still running parallel to the large front wall of Slayden Lumber, he saw the far end of the wall spontaneously combust. He watched in disbelief as it went up in one big fireball.

He was now almost to the end of that same wall, nearly to the right front corner of the massive Slayden Lumber building, the left end of which was going up in flames behind him, and he just kept thinking to himself, *If I can get behind it, if I can just get behind this building, maybe I could stay out of it. Maybe I might have a chance.*

When he got to the remaining front corner of the building, however, he found that the fireball had beaten him to it. He stood stock-still, watching in horror as that ball of fire rolled out in front of him.

There was nowhere left to go, no place left to run. So Toad took one last look at the ball of fire, shut his eyes, and with the prayer "Lord, help us all" on his lips, ran right through it.

Introduction

MOST AMERICANS HAVE HEARD OF FEMA, the Federal Emergency Management Agency that coordinates the nation's response to disasters, both natural and manmade. But few know its origin story.

From floods, hurricanes, tornadoes, wildfires, and earthquakes to water contamination, Ebola, Zika, and COVID-19: FEMA has been there, as its mission states, "to help people before, during, and after disasters."

And while most of us take FEMA's existence for granted, a centralized, national agency for managing America's large-scale disasters has not always been around. Prior to 1979, disaster response was carried out by a chaotic hodgepodge of state and local agencies and civil defense forces. However, the 1970s witnessed a rise in the number of disasters resulting in loss of life and significant property damage. Calls for better emergency response training and coordination grew louder until, in the latter part of the decade, the need could no longer be ignored. Ironically, one of the primary events that finally catalyzed the formation of FEMA began in a way that hindsight might consider entirely appropriate: with a freight train.

AN EPIDEMIC OF freight train disasters and derailments has plagued North America in recent years, all of them devastating, many of them life-shattering. The July 2020 train derailment that sent a bridge to a fiery collapse in the Phoenix suburb of Tempe Town Lake, leaking hazardous material into the surrounding area. The July 2013 crash that destroyed the small town of Lac-Mégantic in the Eastern Townships region of Quebec, Canada, when a Montreal, Maine and Atlantic (MMA) Railway train carrying 7.2 million liters of crude oil jumped the tracks and exploded in the town's core. The propane and crude oil train cars that burned for days in January 2014 when a Canadian National Railway train went off the rails in New Brunswick, Canada. The April 2014 derailment that plunged nearly 30,000 gallons of oil into the James River in Lynchburg, Virginia. The explosion near Baltimore, Maryland, in May 2013 when at least a dozen rail cars on a CSX train derailed after colliding with a truck, setting hazardous chemicals, including sodium chlorate, aflame.

But before Tempe Town Lake, before Lac-Mégantic, before New Brunswick, before Lynchburg, before Baltimore—before any of the dozens of train explosions all across the continent in the past four decades—there was Waverly.

The Waverly Train Disaster of 1978 made news all over the world, as millions of television viewers, radio listeners, and newspaper readers literally could not avert their attention from the train wreck that consumed the heart of a small Southern town. It was the worst train explosion of its time, and most tragically, it was a disaster that never had to happen.

From the tiny epicenter of Waverly, Tennessee, the Waverly Train Disaster and its aftermath shook the globe, horrifying observers with the extent of its destruction and ringing alarm bells about train safety, hazardous materials handling, and disaster preparedness. Eventually, its aftershocks changed things for everyone everywhere, wherever there was an iron road, wherever train cars were made, wherever emergency preparedness officials drew up plans for disaster response.

The Waverly Train Disaster served as a catalyst for the establishment of FEMA, recommended by the National Governors Association just two business days after the disaster, and created by President Jimmy Carter's executive order the following year, in 1979. FEMA's origin story is included in the pages that follow.

A multitude of other changes in disaster management and training can also be traced back to what happened in Waverly. The Waverly Train Disaster has been labeled the "high-water mark of hazardous materials incidents in the United States" (*Firehouse* 2003), one that has since been used as a model to train firefighters throughout the country. The creation of the Tennessee Hazardous Materials Institute in the wake of the disaster resulted in the development of new standards for hazardous materials (hazmat) handling and containment; the training program created by the Institute became a model for the nation.

Fallout from the Waverly Train Disaster also led to the passage of the Staggers Rail Act of 1980, which deregulated the American railroad industry in what is widely regarded as a rare win-win situation, one that allowed the US rail freight industry to put itself on a more secure financial footing—which, in turn, led to implementation of much-needed safety changes for that time.

Additionally, the disaster led emergency managers to dramatically redesign training programs for emergency responders in order to place a focus on methods that reduce the risks to the responders themselves, thus protecting the lives of those who make the greatest sacrifice to help the rest of us when we need it most.

For decades since, the mere mention of Waverly has conjured memories of the train disaster for all who knew or heard of it and therefore associated the town with it, and for all who had learned the hard lessons of just how wrong things can go, and how fast, in the absence of correct safety measures and in the presence of faulty machinery. But at least as important as what went wrong that tragic day in Waverly was what went *right*—and therein lie the most promising lessons for the present. A number of infrastructural strengths existed in Waverly, and in small towns across America, that functioned as a counterbalance to the failings of the deteriorating railroads and the inadequate haz-mat handling standards of the time. This book highlights these strengths in detail, in addition to the aforementioned actions that were taken after the disaster to improve rail safety and haz-mat containment.

But in the end, after the tales of metal and machine have had their turn, we always, eventually, find that what it comes down to is the people involved. The people who lived, the people who died, the people who endured with uncommon bravery, who cleaned up the mess, and who were left to deal with the aftermath and all that entailed.

This book recounts a true story, told to me directly from the mouths of these very people—the ones who were there and lived it firsthand, who emerged from the wreckage with the scars to show and the stories to tell.

This is the first book to relate the entire history of the Waverly Train Disaster from beginning to end, while focusing specifically on the remarkable group of individuals from all walks of life who came together in the tiny, two-room Emergency Department of Waverly's Nautilus Memorial Hospital on that fateful day in February 1978, thrown together by the worst and most unexpected circumstances imaginable to them. They are people I have been fortunate enough to know all my life, because Waverly is my hometown. Two of them are my own parents, physicians who had emigrated from the Middle East years earlier and chose Waverly as their new and forever home—and had they not been there that day, many more lives would have been lost or permanently disabled due to the explosion and its aftermath. The narrative that follows draws upon more than ten years of interviews, local documentation, and primary-source research to tell the story of the train disaster and its consequences as experienced by the people who were actually there on the ground at the time.

Like so many who rise to the occasion when tragedy strikes, the people in this narrative are unsung heroes—true "small-town heroes"—those who toil endlessly, so often behind the scenes, to save life and limb. They ask for little, if any, recognition or reward, but they and all who know them remain forever changed by their bravery and selflessness. They don't expect honor or laud, but at some point, the time must come for their story to be told.

This is their story. This is their time.

WALK THROUGH FIRE

CHAPTER ONE

Derailed

FEBRUARY 22, 1978
WEDNESDAY
10:45 P.M.

FRANK CRAVER'S PHONE WAS RINGING.

A phone call at this hour could not be good news. Not for a senior captain of the Volunteer Fire Department in Waverly, Tennessee. When he picked up the phone, the voice on the other end was that of Police Chief Guy Barnett, calling from the City Hall dispatcher's office. Chief Barnett informed him that there had been a train wreck at the main crossing.

"I'll be right down," said Frank, not sure what to expect. Climbing out of bed and getting dressed, Frank tried to imagine what a train wreck would look like. He couldn't say that he had ever seen one.

As a jack-of-all-trades at the age of 37, Robert Franklin Craver had seen and done a great many things thus far, but working a train wreck was not among them. His father had died on the eve of Halloween, 1949, when Frank was just nine years old. When he was 25, he had joined the United States Air Force as a volunteer during the Vietnam War. He was an Airman Third Class from 1964 to 1965. He worked as an Air Policeman, and although

1

he had volunteered for a four-year tour of duty, he received a hardship discharge and went back home to work and help support his mother and younger brother.

Frank married Sue Sisk in November 1965. They had one child, a daughter, whom they named Susan; she was six years old and sleeping soundly in her bed when Frank stepped out of the house that night to meet the train wreck.

It was not unusual for Frank to hold several jobs at once. Most recently, he had served as funeral director and embalmer for Waverly's Luff-Bowen Funeral Home, and had been a county ambulance driver for the time that Luff-Bowen held the Humphreys County ambulance contract. When he wasn't busy doing either of those, he worked in the Luff-Bowen stores as a sales clerk.

One job—paid or unpaid—never seemed to be enough to occupy him; he was always wanting to be in the thick of any new adventure, and that was what had led him to become one of the 18 to 20 members of Waverly's Volunteer Fire Department, quickly moving up to fill dual roles of payroll clerk and captain. He enjoyed the camaraderie of the department and the awareness that he was being of service in times of greatest need. And now, with Chief Barnett's call, he had a feeling this was going to be one of those times.

When Frank got to City Hall, the Assistant Fire Chief, Francis X. "Dutch" Gisenhoffer, was already there, talking with Police Chief Barnett. Frank gathered from their ongoing conversation that the thing to do was to head on down to the derailment site, less than a mile away. He did not know what would be needed, but had all the fire equipment he possessed in his car with him. He just had to hope that would be enough.

LESS THAN HALF an hour before Frank Craver got out of bed, Jess "Cooter" Bowen III was the sole person responsible for the sole light emanating from the one illuminated building on Church

Street. He was there for one purpose, and one purpose alone: he had to refinish the upstairs floor in the two-story building Luff-Bowen had bought for their new furniture store, so the store could open on schedule.

Cooter was used to working around the clock; in fact, he had been doing so for 20 years already, since the age of 13, when his father, who ran the Luff-Bowen Funeral Home, would get him out of bed at night and on weekends to attend to the on-call needs of the funeral home and ambulance service. When he got his driver's license, he started driving ambulances. Those were the days before the state required medical certification or emergency medical training for ambulance personnel, and his first-aid training consisted of what he had gleaned from being in the Boy Scouts, learned from his dad, and picked up on the job.

The ambulances they were using in Humphreys County then were called "combinations," because they were both ambulance and hearse in a single vehicle. A special chauffeur license was required to transport the living—those who were ambulance patients—and when the vehicle was being used as an ambulance, the attendants' jump seats unfolded out of the floor and the stretcher lay flat, held in place by wall attachments. When the same vehicle was being used as a hearse, the stretcher was removed, the roller sides of the floor were up, and the jump seats were folded down.

The combinations had large glass windows down the sides and emergency medical equipment within. Usually there was a red light on top of the vehicle, and sometimes there were red lights concealed inside the grill. The vehicles did not have all the trappings of life support equipment found on even the most basic ambulances today, but they did have small oxygen tanks, basic first-aid supplies, and a bit of extrication equipment—typically a log chain, a fireman's axe, and a crowbar. When used as an "ambulance," the combination was basically an emergency taxi.

Luff-Bowen's ambulance and funeral services had grown organically from what today seems the unlikeliest of places: a general store on Waverly's North Church Street. Joseph Luff, the grandfather of Cooter's paternal grandmother, Maggie May Luff, founded the original L.J. Luff Company in 1879. When Maggie May married Jess S. Bowen, Sr., in the early 1920s, he joined the business and it became Luff-Bowen.

The general store started out selling farm implements and supplies, and as the store's stock expanded in volume and variety, coffins were added to the inventory. People would call in, sometimes from great distances, to buy a coffin when somebody died, and depending upon the distance, the store would either send the coffin by train or deliver it by horse and wagon. The general store quickly became L.J. Luff Furniture & Undertaking, with the funeral home as part of the store, and the embalming room in the very back. When motorized equipment became available, Luff-Bowen had the first motorized hearse in the county. In the meantime, the general store and furniture business also continued to thrive, and in the early 1900s the entire operation moved to the town square in the coveted McCracken Block on Main Street.

Jess Bowen, Sr., in turn, became the first licensed embalmer in Humphreys County after he went off to Christian Brothers University in Memphis, learned how to embalm, and got his license through the State of Tennessee. He came back to Waverly, where he would practice his trade until he died.

In the late 1930s, Mr. Bowen bought the Colonial Hotel on East Main Street when the hotel building was at auction, and turned it into the Luff-Bowen Funeral Home. The general store continued as a flourishing business across the street, and the new funeral home offered a dedicated location for funeral services. It was also where Cooter's grandparents lived and raised their five children, on the upstairs level, with just a bedroom, a bathroom, and a kitchen. Work was what they knew, it was what they thrived on, and its value was what they passed down to their children and grandchildren.

And so the cold, quiet night of February 22 found Cooter on his knees working on the floor of the furniture store. As he was in the middle of putting the floor finish down, an awful noise shattered the stillness. There was the loudness and harshness of metal scraping and banging together, again and again and again. It sounded like a multi-vehicle crash and pile-up down the street, but how could there be that many cars traveling through Waverly at that time of night?

If he hadn't been a licensed embalmer, following in the footsteps of his father and grandfather, he might have permitted himself to dwell on the thought that it was loud enough to wake the dead. But the noise died down quickly, and he was in the middle of refinishing that floor, and there were others in town who were equipped to take care of motor vehicle accidents. He figured if he were to be needed, he would find out soon enough.

SEEING THE LIGHT on in the furniture store building, Frank Craver knew that Cooter must be in there. He'd stop by and let him know about the derailment after he'd had time to check it out himself. He turned right off Church Street and drove over the Commerce Street bridge, which spanned Trace Creek.

Frank had hoped he would have what he needed with him in his vehicle, but upon reaching the site of the train derailment, he soon began to think that nothing would be enough, at least not anything that he or anyone else in Humphreys County, Tennessee, had in their possession. He had never seen anything like this before in his entire life. The headlights of his car revealed 23 train cars, all piled on top of one another in a jumbled heap, with two derailed tank cars among them. The rail cars may as well have been giant rocks that some monstrous hand had held above the ground and let fall all at once, resulting in a mangled mountain of twisted steel and fractured wheels. The two white tankers were connected to one another, and they had come to rest in a "V" formation, one on either side of the tracks.

"Whoo-whee, what a mess!" Frank said to himself. The pile of wrecked L&N Railroad cars lay at what was then the main crossing, just steps from Waverly's New Town section. The crossing sat at the end of Richland Avenue, to the east of the town's overpass (known to all residents of Waverly as the Viaduct, which they pronounced as "vaya-dock"). One of Waverly's two fire trucks was already on the scene.

Frank had a flashlight with him, and he got out of his car to have a better look at the wreck. His breath formed a fog on the cold February air as he surveyed the damage. The two tankers looked pretty banged up. He ran the beam of his flashlight in a steady line over the chaotic heap of boxcars. And that was when he noticed the two police officers crawling atop the wreckage. There, on top of it all, were the Frazier boys.

OFFICER WALLACE BERNARD "Buddy" Frazier had joined the Waverly police force three years earlier at the age of 22, which, in 1975, had made him the youngest police officer ever hired by the municipality of Waverly. At the time, Waverly's police department had only four patrol cars and eight police officers, two of whom were the Frazier brothers.

That Wednesday, Buddy and his younger brother, Joel, had been working the afternoon shift together as partners, assigned to the same car that night—the only one the city had available. On patrol together, they had been traveling east on US Highway 70 and had just passed the new Waverly Clinic building at the junction with Meridale Street when, a few minutes before

10:30 P.M., they noticed the westbound L&N coming into town, whistle blowing. Before they reached the city limits just a few miles farther east, they received a dispatch to report immediately for a train derailment that had occurred at the crossing near the downtown area.

The two young officers turned around and sped back to the Richland Avenue crossing, not knowing until they arrived what exactly had occurred, not knowing whether or not a vehicle with passengers might be involved in the accident at the crossing. Upon reaching the derailment site and seeing the mountain of wreckage, they still did not know what had caused the train to derail, and feared that a civilian automobile might be buried beneath the ruin.

So they got out of their patrol vehicle and began to examine the pile of train cars, climbing over and around them, unaware of the danger that lay beneath.

The train's conductor finally found Buddy, hailing him from the wreckage. He said that no motor vehicles and no passengers or other personnel were involved or injured, but he had lost all communication with L&N due to the wreck. Buddy told the conductor to get in the patrol car and he would get him to a phone. Buddy lived in a house nearby, only about half a mile from the crossing, so he took the conductor to his house where he could use Buddy's home phone to call his superiors at L&N Railroad and inform them of the derailment.

THE MAN USING Buddy Frazier's home phone was the latest in a long line of L&N conductors to come through Waverly. The famed Louisville & Nashville Railroad was chartered on March 5, 1850 by the Commonwealth of Kentucky to run between the two cities in its name; specifically, the charter allowed the Louisville and Nashville Railroad Company (L&N) "to build a line railroad between Louisville and the Tennessee state line in the direction of Nashville."

Over a year later, on December 4, 1851, the Tennessee General Assembly issued a similar proclamation allowing L&N to construct the Tennessee portion of the line. Completion of the railroad's charter came on October 27, 1859 when the line opened in Nashville, fulfilling over nine years of promise and hard labor, and launching one of the most successful railroads in US history. Its impact was so profound, in fact, as to lead railroad scholar T.D. Clark to declare: "What the railroad has done for the United States as a whole the Louisville and Nashville Railroad has done for the South."

Working with nearly every other railroad company east of the Mississippi, the L&N Railroad would eventually link passengers from the East Coast to the Gulf Coast, from Pennsylvania to Florida and Cincinnati to New Orleans. At the height of its operations, the L&N Railroad covered 6,574 miles across 13 states.

However, by the beginning of the Amtrak era in 1971, many of the passenger trains that utilized the L&N route—like the Dixie Flyer (Chicago–St. Louis–Florida) and the Pan-American (Cincinnati–New Orleans)—had been discontinued, and the railroad's business focus turned solely to freight transportation.

Freight trains have been and still are used to carry commodities as diverse as corn, wheat and other grains; perishable agricultural products like vegetables and dairy; construction materials such as lumber and steel; airplane parts as well as entire automobiles; fuel such as coal and petroleum; and hazardous chemicals compressed into liquids that can be contained in specialized tank cars. Trains carrying freight often have so many different boxcars, gondolas, flat cars, and tankers that they seem to extend for miles, and the 96-car train that came through Waverly the night of February 22, 1978 was no exception.

The primary aim of one of the L&N's greatest expansions, in the early 1900s, was to provide transport for one of the most important freight materials of the time: coal. The railroad sought to connect the landlocked coal fields of eastern Kentucky with distribution sites, and eventually L&N access arrived in western Kentucky, Tennessee, and Alabama. Later years would find the freight trains along L&N's iron roads carrying other forms of fuel, such as petroleum and liquid propane, to power both the industrial and consumer needs of a rapidly growing nation.

The amount of freight moved by L&N trains soared during World War II, as all the nation's railroads were called upon to transport unprecedented numbers of passengers and supplies. According to the Louisville & Nashville Railroad Historical Society, more than 90% of the United States' military equipment and supplies, and 97% of all its troops, relied upon rail as a means of transport to military bases and ports of embarkation. The L&N Railroad in particular saw freight traffic increase by 80% during the war.

By the 1970s, however, competition from trucks and barges, coupled with a change in shipping patterns, had left most major freight railroads in the Northeast and several in the Midwest in a state of bankruptcy. According to the Association of American Railroads (AAR), by 1978, the rail share of intercity freight had plummeted to 35%, and bankrupt railroads accounted for more than 21% of the rail mileage in the United States during the 1970s.

As a result, railroad companies lacked the funds for proper maintenance of their tracks. By 1976, more than 47,000 miles of track were under operation at reduced speeds due to unsafe track conditions. Billions of dollars in deferred maintenance accumulated, and remarkably, the term "standing derailment"—used to describe how otherwise stationary rail cars would simply fall off tracks that were so poorly maintained the cars could no longer stand upright on them—became commonplace.

FOLLOWING FRANK CRAVER'S arrival at the scene of the derailment, more men from the fire department began to show up, along with others from the police department. At that time, the fire department operated on a weekly rotation, with a couple of officers and a few regulars assuming duty for an entire week, then rotating off to be relieved by another crew of similar make-up the following week. Frank had gone on duty that past Sunday.

The duty fireman was expected to answer all minor calls, like auto fires and grass fires, but when there was a major fire or other major incident, the entire department was called out. Well, Frank reckoned, this train wreck was as major as it got. And, sure enough, soon the entire fire department was on the scene.

Frank noticed that other people were beginning to arrive, too, people unrelated to the fire or police departments or their operations. They were spectators, milling about, all gawking at the mass of twisted boxcars before them. Waverly was a small town of approximately 4,700 people, 65 miles west of Nashville, which itself had a population of just over 500,000. Although it was busy enough during the day, at night the streets of Waverly were usually deserted, except for a police patrol and the occasional doctor or nurse called to the small county hospital for a middle-of-the-night emergency. Needless to say, a train wreck of any sort, much less one of this magnitude, was bound to attract spectatorship from the entire town. Frank felt that setting up a perimeter was going to be needed to ensure public safety.

He joined the rest of the fire department and train crew personnel who were now crawling around and on top of the wrecked train cars, trying to assess the damage. In addition to the Frazier brothers, the Deputy Sheriff, Frank Taber, was there. A discussion ensued regarding what on earth to do with this mess, whom to call, and what could be in the two tank cars that were now known to have fallen off the tracks with the rest. The train crew was there, of course, and Frank could overhear others speaking to them. He heard someone say that a wheel on one of the gondola cars had slipped its axle and caused the derailment. He couldn't make out what they all thought was contained in those tankers that had derailed. He did know, however, that tank cars like that were designed specifically to transport liquid and gaseous chemicals. He became all the more concerned about the need for a perimeter.

When a gasoline truck, of all things, tried to get into the area, members of both the police and fire departments began talking about setting up roadblocks. But the City of Waverly owned no barricades.

It was Frank's friend Buddy Frazier, along with his fellow officers, who succeeded in getting a very wide perimeter set up around the derailment site. Assistant Fire Chief Gisenhoffer had asked for a 1,200-foot perimeter, and Buddy had recalled that there was a contractor in town who was burying cable for the phone service, and there were multiple barricades with flashing lights on them as part of that project. So he and other officers took it upon themselves to commandeer all of those barricades, everywhere they could find them throughout town, and use them to set up the perimeter around the train wreck. They were finally able to complete an evacuation of the derailment site, clearing out spectators and redirecting traffic.

Included in this initial evacuation were the eight or nine residents of the James Cerebral Palsy Center, also known as the James Adult Group Home, which was just yards from the tracks and the site of the derailment. Frank had told the police on the scene, "If you've got anywhere to take those folks, get 'em out of here. Just in case something were to happen. If whatever's in these tanks were to explode, it would level the whole area."

———

FRANK WALKED UP to one of the tankers, flashlight still in hand, and with other members of the fire department, Bob Wessels and Charlie Garmon, began circling it, surveying as much of the damage as they could in the dark. Without any special detection equipment, they had to rely on their own senses of sight and smell to try to determine if there were any leaks or other obvious sources of danger. Although the moon was nearly full that night, it was hidden behind heavy cloud cover, and the darkness limited their vision, even with the aid of flashlights.

One of the tank cars lay on its side with the dome running parallel to the ground. Frank didn't smell a gas leak. He figured that if gas were leaking out, there would be a smell he could detect, some odor, something, like the rotten-egg smell from natural gas. But there was nothing. The long white tank simply lay there, silently, ominously, refusing to relinquish its inner secrets to Frank or anyone else.

BY THE TIME Cooter got done with the floor, it was nearly 1:00 A.M., the dead of night—there was that reference again; he couldn't seem to shake it—and the cold air cut through him as he exited the furniture building. The air had that heavy feeling like snow was coming. He decided he would go down to the railroad crossing and finally have that look, to see what was going on.

As he made his way down to Commerce Street and the railroad crossing, the darkness was broken only by the crisscrossing of thin flashlight beams and the gleam of headlights. Even so, he could begin to make out the behemoths piled on top of one another. They reminded him of dominoes, but not that neat. Not neat at all. This was one big, convoluted mess. Railroad cars jammed one into the other. Giant train wheels that had come loose and mammoth pieces of metal that were bent and twisted. Boxcars with their ends pointing toward the dark sky.

As the others showed him around, he took particular notice of the two tank cars that were lying on their sides like wounded beasts on the ground beside the tracks, with boxcars leaning precariously on top of them. He didn't know what was in them, but he knew as well as anyone that tankers like that were used to haul hazardous and volatile materials. One of them had a dent in it so large and deep, you could lay a person down in it. When he let himself consider that, he said to no one in particular: "I've seen about all I need to see. I need to go." And that he did; he went home and called it a night.

AROUND 2:00 A.M., a WSM-TV news van arrived from Nashville. *My goodness! The word is out now*, thought Frank. He knew then that the derailment would be all over the morning news. And no wonder, given the magnitude of the wreck.

Frank's fellow fire department volunteers, Riley Turner and Charlie Garmon, stayed with him until about 4:00 A.M. Shortly before they were to be relieved by the next shift, a white car pulled up, not far from the fire truck. Frank walked up to the man who was getting out of the car, ready to ask him to turn back; as they had already established, this was no place for spectators. But it wasn't anyone that Frank recognized, and he thought he knew everybody in town.

The man seemed to ignore Frank and walked around to the trunk of his car. He was in the process of opening his trunk when Frank asked him who he was. He told Frank that he was with the L&N Railroad, and from the trunk of his car he produced a hard hat. *Ah, well now, the hard hats are here*, Frank thought. *Won't be long now before we get some real help.*

The hard hat didn't deign to speak to Frank any further, so just a couple of hours before dawn on Thursday, February 23— finding no fire, no leaks, and no injuries, and realizing that nothing more could be done until higher authorities, including the Fire Chief, could be called in later that morning—Frank, Buddy, and most of the others finally went home. Frank would later remember that it had begun to snow, and he happened to notice, in the glare of his headlights through the snowflakes, that one of the derailed tank cars was labeled with three words, high-lighted in yellow: "Anhydrous Ammonia Only."

Morning Rounds

FEBRUARY 23, 1978
THURSDAY
7:00 A.M.

TENNESSEE IS A LAND OF RIVERS. The once-wild and still-mighty
Tennessee River divides the state into its three Grand Divisions:
East, Middle, and West Tennessee. There in the westernmost part
of Middle Tennessee, just ten miles from where the river forms
the division between Middle and West, lies the City of Waverly,
the county seat of Humphreys County, which in 1978 had one
practicing surgeon.

Three hours after Frank Craver left the derailment site, this
one surgeon, Subhi D. Ali, MD, was speeding down Powers Boulevard on his way to make rounds at Humphreys County's sole
hospital, Nautilus Memorial. The 34-year-old general surgeon
was always speeding in those days, and as the only active surgeon
for the entire county (and, at times, for the surrounding counties
as well), his days were always full, beginning early in the morning
and ending well past midnight. Even so, he had become quite
fond of Waverly, enjoying his work and quickly getting to know
the town and its people, and had long since learned to introduce

himself to patients in a way that was pronounceable to them, as "Doctor Soo-bee Ah-lee."

On this particular morning, Dr. Ali planned to take his usual shortcut down East Railroad Street, vernacularly known as Thunder Road—precisely because people would speed down it. On any other day, it would have been his surest bet for a fast route to the hospital. As he neared the main crossing at Richland Avenue, however, he encountered a barricade of sorts with a police officer redirecting traffic. It seemed there had been a train wreck, of all things, during the night, and the crossing was closed until further notice.

"Oh, good grief," Dr. Ali groaned to himself. His specialty was general surgery, patching together human bodies, not train wrecks of the literal sort, and his focus at that moment was on getting to the hospital as fast as possible so he could get on with his day, get through his rounds, and be on time for his first surgical case, which was scheduled for 08:00 sharp. As an officer in the US Army Reserve Medical Corps, he was a no-nonsense type who came across as stern and reserved, and he had a hard time relating to the laid-back pace of Tennessee. He was a seasoned trauma surgeon from his training and first days in practice in the 1960s and early 1970s at DC General Hospital, located in one of the most poverty-stricken sections of Washington, DC. And his modus operandi now was simply, "Get it done."

To him, this train wreck was a minor inconvenience.

DR. ALI HAD been born in Palestine in 1943, in the West Bank village of Deir Debwan, less than five miles from Ramallah. He was the first person from his hometown to become a physician, and he was not a stranger to the ways of small towns. His experiences over the years had honed his need and talent for efficiency, competence, and immaculate organization in all aspects of his life.

He had spent most of the past two decades in Washington, DC, attending medical school at Howard University College of Medicine from 1964 to 1968 and then completing five years of surgical training, followed by what amounted to two chief residencies and an ensuing faculty appointment as an assistant professor at Howard. It was not uncommon for him to fill in as de facto acting chief of surgery at that time, providing much-needed coverage when higher-ups were required elsewhere.

Throughout his tenure in DC, he saw firsthand the medical ravages of inner-city life, regularly treating gunshot wounds, stabbings, multiple trauma due to vehicle accidents, and burn injuries, among many others. His senior year at Howard found him delivering babies during the 1968 riots that followed the assassination of the Reverend Dr. Martin Luther King Jr.

He had become a US citizen in 1966, and was drafted during the Vietnam War and assigned to the Army under the Berry Plan, which allowed physicians in needed specialties to complete their residency training. He sought out and received extra training in chest and trauma surgery. One of his mentors at Howard, Dr. LaSalle D. Leffall, Jr., Chair of the Department of Surgery, continuously—and famously—urged "equanimity under duress," and Dr. Ali strove to master that concept in practice. By the time he and his wife moved to Waverly in July 1976, he was well equipped to stabilize any patient who came his way.

He had met Maysoon Shocair, MD, at DC General Hospital, and they married in November 1974. Dr. Maysoon, as she came to be known in Waverly, was the daughter of Dr. Abdel Rahman Shocair, a well-known Syrian physician, poet, and politician who had been a candidate in Jordanian parliamentary elections before the bitter politics of the region sent him into exile. Dr. Maysoon had studied medicine at Damascus University in Syria, one of the only medical schools in the world that taught all courses in Arabic. Graduating in 1971, she sought further training in the United States, and arrived in Cleveland, Ohio, to do her internal medicine internship at Huron Road Hospital.

Then, as now, those known as "foreign medical graduates," or FMGs, often found only smaller and lesser-known hospitals open to them for training, but in a justly ironic twist, these were the very places that provided the broadest training opportunities and the highest-value hands-on experiences. Not for the faint of heart, these hospitals were often where the nitty-gritty details of medicine were learned, with every-other-night call schedules that provided ample—and sometimes harrowing—patient care encounters.

Dr. Maysoon left Cleveland in 1972 to complete her internal medicine residency at DC General Hospital on the Howard University Medical Service. Family friends put her in touch with Dr. Subhi Ali, who, with his surgical colleagues at Howard, created Howard University's first fellowship program in gastroenterology. In 1974, Dr. Maysoon became the first gastroenterology fellow on Howard's service at DC General. The two fell in love in the interim, and the rest became their shared history.

Dr. Ali already had two children of his own from his previous marriage, and he and Dr. Maysoon knew that they wanted to have children together—and they also knew that they did not want to raise them in Washington, DC. Looking for other options that were within a day's driving distance of the Atlanta area, where Dr. Ali's first wife and children now resided, they scanned the classified ads in the *New England Journal of Medicine* and found a quite promising one requesting both an internist and a surgeon to join the medical staff at a place called Nautilus Memorial Hospital in Waverly, Tennessee.

Neither of them had ever been to the American South before, but when they visited in late 1975, they took an immediate liking to Waverly. With Dr. Maysoon due to deliver her first daughter in February of 1976, they felt they could build a home, a family, and a life in Waverly. The two made the final move from DC into their new home in Waverly's Rustling Oaks subdivision in July 1976, less than five months after their daughter was born, and Dr. Maysoon became a US citizen not long after their move to Waverly.

Nearly two years later, as Dr. Ali turned his car around at the Richland Avenue roadblock, his time in Washington could not have been farther from his mind. Now he was simply focused on making up lost time and getting to Nautilus Memorial as quickly as possible to take care of the patients who were waiting, always waiting, for him there. Arriving at the hospital just a few minutes after leaving the roadblock, he found his surgical scrub nurse, Ms. Carolyn Tucker, RN, ready to accompany him on rounds.

NURSE TUCKER, KNOWN to most by her nickname, "Sam," was unfailingly punctual, always ready for Dr. Ali when he arrived. Sam was a native of Waverly and had earned her registered nurse's (RN) degree in 1970, but had been on the Nautilus Memorial Hospital time sheet since 1962. She worked first as a nurse's aide and then as a licensed practical nurse (LPN), learning to scrub in with the operating team and becoming a top-notch scrub nurse—and the Operating Room (OR) Supervisor—along the way. She was 33 years old and one of only two scrub nurses in Humphreys County, the other being her good friend, cousin, sidekick, and "partner in crime," 29-year-old Nancy Daniel.

The duty of the scrub nurse, as the title implies, is to scrub in with the surgeon and serve as his first nursing assistant, preparing the surgical field and handing the surgeon his instruments. In Waverly, limited resources necessitated that the scrub nurses perform other advanced nursing duties as well, including accompanying the surgeon on rounds and following up with postoperative patients on such issues as wound care and discharge instructions. The best scrub nurses, like Sam and Nancy, could anticipate their surgeon's next move so well that they would often have the next surgical instrument in his hand before he even asked for it. A surgeon knew he'd struck gold if he had such a nurse by his side. Together, Sam and Nancy kept the OR and the surgical service in top-notch condition, and with their competence, extensive nursing capabilities, and unwavering commitment to delivering the best care possible, they were truly first-class nurses, and the doctors who worked with them knew this and were grateful for it.

Nancy and Sam took call 24/7 without complaint, and did so at a time when hospital personnel were not paid any extra for being on call. It was simply expected as part of the job. Not only were there no cell phones in those days; at first, the scrub nurses did not even have pagers (or "beepers," as they were often called then). When Nancy needed to run an errand, she would have to go by the hospital and let someone know, "I'm going to the grocery store; that's where you can find me if you need me." She often felt that the hospital staff knew more about her life than they needed to, and probably more than her own family did.

When the two scrub nurses did receive beepers, they were so excited—and yet the receiving range for the pager was only a 20-mile radius. It was a tiny device that did nothing more than beep. No message, no text, no phone number; just beep, beep. They simply knew that if the beeper went off, it was the hospital trying to reach them. If they were driving around town when the device started beeping, they had to make a call from a pay phone or stop in at a friend's house, or else drive straight to the hospital to find out how and why they were needed. Going farther than 20 miles out of town was simply unheard of, except in cases of emergency. Such was their dedication to their vocation that they thought nothing of these conditions; on the contrary, they considered themselves fortunate for their situations in life, proud of having achieved a coveted station in their careers and in their community.

———————

IN ADDITION TO the scrub nurses, the OR had a circulating nurse, whose job it was, as the title suggests, to circulate around the room and attend to all needs outside the sterile field. Thus, the circulating nurse did not scrub in, but rather handled specimens; accounted for all the instruments, sponges, and other equipment used during the operation; helped monitor the patient; and made preparations for the next operation, among other tasks. She had an overall view of everything that was happening in the room, and helped to instill a calm atmosphere—or as calm as possible, depending upon the case.

At the end of every operation, before closing the surgical field and suturing the incision, Dr. Ali did an instrument count and a sponge count—twice—to be sure that neither had been left inside the patient. The circulating nurse was a crucial part of ensuring the accuracy of this count.

At Nautilus Memorial Hospital, the circulating nurse was Barbara Horner. Barbara was born in Waverly and had grown up in Humphreys County, on her family's farm in Buffalo, and from the time she was around five years old, nursing was the only thing she ever wanted to do. In 1945, a couple of years before Barbara was born, her mother, Elizabeth Duncan, had been severely burned in a house fire, just prior to the end of World War II. Penicillin had come into use in clinical medicine in 1941, and by the end of the war, a sizeable supply was making its way into civilian hospitals. Barbara's mother became the first patient at St. Thomas Hospital in Nashville, Tennessee, to receive penicillin. Prior to that, patients with severe burns often died from infections before they could recover from their burns.

Barbara's mother was also one of the first patients at St. Thomas to receive skin grafts. At that time, skin grafting was being performed in postage-stamp fashion. Surgeons would take a small area of viable skin from her mother's leg, then graft it onto her burned arm, and if the graft took, they would do another. She was in the hospital for four months while they did her entire left arm that way. She was left handed, and eventually regained good use of her hand and her arm, in spite of the multiple scars.

As with many burn victims, Ms. Duncan's scars were more than physical. The fire had begun in an accident involving kerosene while she was in the process of lighting her family's wood cookstove. Both her children were in the kitchen—one an infant in a bed—when the minor explosion knocked her out. When she regained consciousness, her older little boy appeared to have been killed instantly, and she was so confused from the concussion she suffered that she kept trying to pull the infant's bed out the door with her instead of picking him up and running out with him. The rest of the tiny house became an inferno before she could get him out.

People who were there at the main house of the farm on which they lived said she had no clothes left on her when she finally stumbled her way over a distance equal to about two blocks to seek help. Her clothes had been blown and burned off. They wrapped her in sheets and got her to medical attention; she was lucky to be alive. For the rest of her life, though, she would struggle with severe depression due to the loss of her children. She was brave enough to have two more children after that, and Barbara was one of them.

At one point during her hospitalization at St. Thomas, Ms. Duncan shared a room with the grandmother of John Seigenthaler Sr., who was a young man at the very beginning of a career that would take him to great heights in American journalism and politics. Among Seigenthaler's many career highlights were his service as administrative assistant to Robert F. Kennedy in the US Department of Justice in 1961; his tenure as longtime editor and then publisher, chairman, and CEO of the *Tennessean* newspaper; his position as founding editor of the *USA Today* editorial pages; his legacy as an author, civil rights advocate, and staunch defender of the First Amendment; and his gift to the future, as creator of the First Amendment Center at Vanderbilt University in 1991.

In 1945, when Elizabeth Duncan met him, the young Seigenthaler was only 18 years of age, and would visit his grandmother regularly while she was in the hospital. Like so many others over the rest of his career, Elizabeth Duncan came to admire and respect him. In later years, she would always tell her daughter Barbara how interesting he was, and how much she "always liked that young man. He was really a nice man."

Growing up, seeing her mother's scarred arm every day and hearing her story, Barbara was drawn to nursing as a career. As she neared her high school graduation, the girls she knew were getting married, or planning on becoming teachers, or they were going to the Life & Casualty Insurance Company in Nashville to work as secretaries. Barbara wanted none of that. So she stuck with her dream of becoming a nurse, and matriculated into Methodist Hospital School of Nursing in Memphis. Since the age of 18, she knew more about nursing than she knew about anything else. And ever since she had trained with scrub nurses and circulating nurses in school, she had wanted to be a circulating nurse.

She didn't become a circulating nurse right away, however; first she went to Philadelphia with her new husband, Richard Horner, and worked in one of the first coronary care units (CCUs) at Albert Einstein Medical Center. There she learned the basics of cardiac monitoring and reading electrocardiograms (ECGs), which she really enjoyed, just as she always enjoyed the challenge of learning new things and expanding her horizons.

When she returned to Waverly in 1969 and went to work at Nautilus Memorial Hospital, she encountered another challenge: how to be a generalist. Registered nurses were scarce at community hospitals like Nautilus, so the four or five that would be on staff were expected to oversee all kinds of patients with a variety of needs and conditions, from obstetrics to emergency medicine to common ailments like influenza and digestive disorders, all while managing the LPNs and nursing assistants who worked under them. So rather than focusing only on cardiac patients, Barbara had to learn how to care for all conditions, some of which she had only previously read about in her textbooks or seen briefly as an observer while in school.

When the Drs. Ali arrived in 1976, Barbara was excited to learn about yet another field of medicine: endoscopy, which was then in its infancy. Working with Dr. Subhi Ali, she also got to see a wide range of cases in the OR, and could see that the new surgeon was truly dedicated to helping people—not just the patients in front of him, but the people he worked with, too. She could tell that he liked people who were interested in their work and wanted to learn, and who were not just there for the paycheck.

WHEN DR. ALI rounded on his patients every morning, it was Sam who routinely accompanied him and quickly became his right hand when it came to nursing assistance. She had a way of explaining details to patients in a manner that was, miraculously, both efficient and thorough, and she could make herself understood with ease, knowing how to speak to patients in language that was comprehensible and easy to remember. This was an undisguised blessing for Dr. Ali, whose intimidating professional demeanor and thick accent sometimes made communication difficult with his Tennessee patients. Six feet tall and thin as a rail, with black hair, dark eyes, black-rimmed glasses, and a black moustache to match, Dr. Ali cut a striking figure in the hallways of the small hospital. Add to that the Arabic accent of his booming bass voice, and hospital rounds could make for an interesting time indeed.

Most of Sam and Dr. Ali's patients eventually became familiar with the following amusing routine. Dr. Ali might advise a patient to use "warm soaks" for a swollen area or a wound-related issue. However, in his accent, the patient often heard the phrase "wool socks" instead of "warm soaks." Being too polite and perhaps too intimidated to ask Dr. Ali himself to clarify, the aforementioned patient would then turn to Sam once Dr. Ali walked out of the room, and ask her, "Did he say he wanted me to put wool socks on this??"

Sam, in her calm and utterly matter-of-fact way, would answer, "No, honey—warm soaks. That's just the way it sounds when he says it. He wants you to soak it in warm water or put a warm washcloth on it. Okay?"

Eventually, Dr. Ali became so perturbed by this routine that he had the words "Warm Soaks" stamped in ink all over the walls of the examination rooms in his clinic, and thereafter would simply point to the writing on the wall.

Sam had a great many practical skills as a highly experienced nurse, and one such skill grew naturally from a working life spent behind a surgical mask: the capacity to express nearly anything using only her eyes. This was an era that antedated face shields and protective goggles, and a demure glance downward from above the white mask could mean, "I think what you've just said is incredibly foolish, but it is not my place to tell you so." Eyes turned sharply upward from the OR table spoke volumes, the content of which varied with the circumstance, but always caught its recipient's attention immediately. A look toward a nursing assistant could at once bring said assistant hastily to her feet, and one of those quintessential "Sam glances" could, alternately and depending on the events and mood of the day, have the equivalent impact of a punch to the stomach, a pat on the back, or a squeeze of the arm, all accomplished with sterilely gloved hands glued to the operating field. The tiniest crinkling at the corners of the eyes was all that was needed to convey hilarity. And a wink? Well, that was the rare moment that all awaited and treasured.

Sam's perfect foil was Nancy Daniel, full of energy and enthusiasm and a voice that would be heard, a dynamo in every sense of the word. She was one of nine children and her mother had died when she was very young, so her older sisters raised her. When she was 15 years old, she fibbed about her age and said she was 16 so the hospital would hire her. Nancy had the rare capacity for taking every part of her job seriously while still keeping her infectious sense of humor and visibly enjoying every minute. She loved nursing. She felt it was a privilege to have the opportunity to care for patients; she loved helping them and seeing them get better. She looked for no reward other than a hug around the neck from a patient for whom she had cared; for her, that was better than anything. The job was its own reward.

Nancy and Sam were Nautilus Memorial's equivalents of *M*A*S*H*'s Hawkeye and B.J.—without the still—and the practical jokes that the two nurses would occasionally play on the surgeons who came their way became the stuff of legend, with Dr. Ali being one of their favorite targets. His seriousness in all matters marked him early and frequently with a bull's-eye for their pranks. It would not be unusual, for instance, for him to find that his most-liked cassette tape had gone missing, with no one avowing any knowledge as to its whereabouts. Unbeknownst to him, Nancy and Sam had endured all they could of the constant playing of his Arabic music in the OR, and behind the scenes, had conspired to put an end to it. What Dr. Ali would find in the tape player instead would be an album of the greatest hits of Conway Twitty or Johnny Cash. And he could find no one who knew how it got there.

These were the days before surgical needles came pre-threaded; each needle had to be threaded by hand by the scrub nurse before giving it to the surgeon. Dr. Ali was known to be a fast surgeon, especially with commonly performed procedures like hernia repairs, and he would sometimes get ahead of Nancy, asking for the next suture before she had it ready. He would become so impatient that Nancy, not to be outdone, would put an empty needle between his gloved fingers. Once he realized it, upon moving his hand back into his field of view, the time he spent cursing gave her the extra moments she needed to catch up and hand him the next, fully threaded, needle. She would chuckle to herself, knowing that she had also handed him and the rest of the room some much needed levity in an otherwise grueling schedule.

In spite of the stress-busting antics, when it came to nurses with straight-up surgical skills and acumen, there were none better than Sam and Nancy, and Dr. Ali always wanted one or both of them to scrub with him on all his operations. They knew his techniques, and they respected his skill, his knowledge, and his example as a leader when it mattered most. They knew that there were times when he could blow a fuse over the color of their lab coats, or whether they were wearing their name tags correctly, or how close the surgical tray was to his elbow ... but when the blood and guts were rolling, he was fine. He got it. When the chips were down, he could step in there. He kept everybody in control, steered the ship where it needed to go. And they had seen him handle enough gunshot wounds, stabbings, and motor vehicle accidents to know that he would do what he had to do, and with good outcomes.

Early one foggy morning after his arrival in Waverly, Dr. Ali was called to a hospital in a neighboring county to operate on a patient who had been in a terrible motor vehicle accident. He was told there were multiple fractures and internal bleeding, likely with multiple organs involved.

Dr. Ali went right away. In the ER, he met the 80-year-old doctor who was admitting the patient. "Okay, I'll see you in the OR," he said to the elder physician.

The doctor smiled at him and shook his head. "Oh, no, Doctor. I don't scrub."

So in an unfamiliar OR, Dr. Ali found himself the sole physician on the case, accompanied by Sam, who had also come from Waverly; their nurse anesthetist, John Bryant; and a circulating nurse.

Dr. Ali opened with a single thoracoabdominal incision, from the patient's left shoulder to just above the right hip, splitting the diaphragm as he went so he could visualize and repair the injured organs underneath it: liver, pancreas, spleen. There was blood in the chest (thorax) and blood in the abdominal cavity, and he had to find the sources of the bleeding and repair them if possible.

Some of the sources were obvious, but there was still an unseen artery dumping large amounts of blood into the abdomen. Dr. Ali knew that, as soon as he went hunting for the torn hepatic vessels that supplied the liver, the mortality rate for this operation jumped to 90%. But there it was, the injured hepatic artery deep in the abdomen, and it had to be fixed to have even that 10% chance of survival.

He clamped the artery in order to repair it, stopping the bleeding—but also cutting off blood flow to the liver. He told Sam to watch the clock.

Every five minutes, she would lean over and whisper the time to him.

"Five minutes, Dr. Ali."

"Ten minutes."

"Fifteen minutes."

He worked quickly but carefully to repair the artery and the other damaged hepatic vessels, while trying to minimize the amount of time the liver's main blood supply was cut off by his clamp.

He achieved the needed repairs and released the clamp. He then asked his nurse anesthetist the question he would continue to ask throughout the operation: "How're we doin', John?"

"Oh, we're all right," came John Bryant's typically nonchalant response.

Dr. Ali could see that they were not all right. He could see how weak his patient's circulation was because he was literally looking at it, literally had his finger on the pulse. Could see the weak beating of the heart and the significantly diminished pulsing of the aorta, which ordinarily would be the strongest artery in the entire body.

"Could probably do better with a little blood, though," John's voice came again.

"That's what I thought."

This conversation repeated itself throughout the operation, and they went through every unit of blood that hospital had, and then some. It was the most difficult operation of his entire life, largely because he had no surgical assistance. He was doing the work of at least three surgeons. He kept having the circulator call around to surrounding hospitals in other counties, anywhere there might be a surgeon or a physician with surgical experience to scrub in and assist him. But nobody was answering the call.

He knew he was doing his very best, though, and saw with his own eyes that it was paying off as the operation progressed and he repaired organ after organ.

It wasn't until Dr. Ali was wrapping up the operation and closing the diaphragm that a surgeon finally showed up from 40 miles away, and helped him close the rest of the thoracoabdominal incision.

When they had finally finished, Dr. Ali had a good feeling about the outcome. Yes, it had been the most difficult operation of his life; and yes, this kind of surgery had a 90% mortality rate, but he knew the quality of the work he had done in there. He believed he had beaten the odds this time.

He was right.

The patient not only survived, but thrived, and went on to live a normal life.

CHAPTER THREE

Nautilus Memorial Hospital

FEBRUARY 23, 1978
THURSDAY
8:00 A.M.

AROUND THE SAME TIME THAT Dr. Ali and Sam were scrubbing in to their first case, Dr. Maysoon was nearing completion of her medical rounds on the floor above them. One of her patients that morning was the mother of Mrs. Jennie Lee Monroe, a woman whose family had lived in Humphreys County for generations.

Mrs. Monroe's grandfather had fought as a Confederate infantry soldier throughout the Civil War, from beginning to end, and lived to tell the tales. His family homestead in the neighboring town of McEwen was now Walnut Hill Farm, the verdant and serene property of Jennie Lee and her husband, Sam.

At first Mrs. Monroe had not known what to make of this new female doctor with the foreign accent, but so many in Waverly, McEwen, and the surrounding areas were beginning to talk of her excellent clinical skills and caring bedside manner. So Mrs. Monroe figured she would take her mother to Dr. Maysoon and see how things went. After all, this was the first time there had ever been a fellowship-trained, practicing gastroenterologist in Humphreys County, and that was something—and, well, her mother

31

had been needing to see a gastroenterologist, so it made sense to try this one so close to home.

So on this morning at the hospital, Dr. Maysoon was getting ready to perform a colonoscopy on Mrs. Monroe's mother. At that time, colonoscopies were done in the hospital and patients were admitted for the prep a day or two in advance. Dr. Maysoon had scheduled the colonoscopy for Friday morning, and she was checking on her patient as part of her morning rounds prior to doing the procedure.

Dr. Maysoon had heard the talk around the hospital that morning about a train derailing, but was so busy that she paid it little mind, dismissing it as another event to generate small-town gossip. She hadn't gone that route on her way in to the hospital, and she wasn't planning on going down to see the derailment, as some others said they were. The train wasn't in danger of exploding, as some melodramatics were saying; there were people in the railroad industry, experts in these things, who were taking care of it, and that would be that. She was sure of it. Time to get on with her day.

ON AUGUST 3, 1958, the USS *Nautilus*, the world's first nuclear-powered vessel, also became the first submarine to pass beneath the North Pole. At its helm as commanding officer was a Humphreys County native and US Naval Academy graduate, Captain William Robert Anderson. His voyage, at a depth of 400 feet below the Polar ice cap, became the first in history to be made from the Pacific to the Atlantic Ocean by way of the North Pole. In honor of their fellow Humphreys Countian and in memory of this historic voyage of the *Nautilus*, a group of local physician founders named their newly built hospital Nautilus Memorial, and opened its doors for service in 1961. The new hospital was located on Tennessee Highway 13, farther up the same hillside as Fort Hill (Fort Waverly).

Dr. Wallace Joe McClure, who was also making his rounds that Thursday morning, had joined his half-brother, Dr. Doris Sanders, in this new venture soon after its founding, adding his name to the medical staff around the same time as fellow general practitioner Arthur Winfrey Walker, MD. Dr. McClure had graduated from medical school just a few years before the hospital opened, and had always hoped to return to Waverly. He had grown up in Humphreys County, in the unincorporated community of Hustburg, which was known as a "country town" south of New Johnsonville. It had a couple of grocery stores, and a barber shop, and an old high school, Tribble School, which closed in 1955. The school's decline had left only four people in what would have been Dr. McClure's graduating class, so he transferred to Waverly High School for his last two years.

Joe McClure had no trouble deciding to become a doctor. His maternal grandfather, James Joseph Shannon, was a country doctor who saw patients in their homes and in an old office across the road from the house on his farm in Humphreys County. Although his granddaddy died before he was born, Dr. McClure grew up hearing his mother talk about him all the time. And of course there was his half-brother, Doris, his elder by ten years, who was also a doctor.

Dr. McClure earned his medical degree at the University of Tennessee (UT) at Memphis. He had held on to some of his granddaddy's medical books, including a first edition of *Gray's Anatomy*. The first six quarters of medical school then consisted of the basic courses: anatomy, bacteriology, biochemistry, physiology, pathology. The last six quarters were all clinical experience, and medical students could apply for a medical license upon graduation, even before doing an internship, if they passed the state boards. Newly graduated MDs could go right out and practice. But that didn't seem enough to Dr. McClure; he chose to pursue extra training before entering independent practice.

There were no straight, specialized internships in those days; all internships were rotating, meaning that the physicians in training would spend a set number of months on each service, then rotate to the next one. Thus, a rotating intern would gain experience in surgery, pediatrics, obstetrics and gynecology, internal medicine, and more. During his rotating internship at Nashville General Hospital, Dr. McClure learned to set fractures, do hernia operations and tonsillectomies, treat hemorrhoids, deliver babies, and treat all the usual and common maladies, from strep throat to diabetes. He even went beyond most in his day, seeking out extra training in surgery after his internship, to have a bit more confidence before entering practice.

When he did enter practice, it was in Huntingdon, Tennessee, with an older physician named Dr. Wilson. He was with Dr. Wilson for only a year before returning to Waverly, but it was the best year he had ever spent. Dr. Wilson was a master at the art of medicine, knew how to deal with people, and taught Dr. McClure a lot of what he knew.

When Joe McClure was growing up in Hustburg, everyone would come to town—to Waverly—on Saturdays. And on Saturday, as he remembered it, you could hardly walk up and down the sidewalk, there were so many people in town. Waverly was a bustling little town back then, in the 1940s and '50s. There were a number of stores and shops providing all you could need. There were two dry-goods stores; you could buy a suit of clothes, pick up a set of furniture, get some groceries and sundries. You could even take in a newly released movie at the Mi-De-Ga theater that was owned by the Flexer family. By the early 1960s, you could hardly find an open parking spot on West Main Street. Kuhn's 5-10-25 cents Variety Store took up most of a block; Rex's Fine Foods was just a few steps down the street; and Luff-Bowen's general store was a few blocks down on the corner, with several more stores and smaller shops in between. Everybody knew everybody; people waved and stopped to talk to you, asked you how you were and how your family was doing. It was a town to which he felt he would be glad to return and where he would be proud to raise his children. So when his brother asked him to join them at the newly opened Nautilus Memorial Hospital, he was happy to oblige.

THE HOSPITAL THAT Drs. Walker and McClure helped get off the ground was, by 1978, a busy and fully functioning enterprise, with 52 beds, a four-bed intensive care unit (ICU) complete with mechanical ventilators, two operating rooms, an obstetrics room, on-site lab, radiology, and an ER.

Dr. Ali, as a general surgeon and trauma surgeon—and the only one in the county—did almost every surgical case that came his way, everything from hernia repairs to vascular surgery. He performed multiple kinds of abdominal surgery, including gallbladder, stomach, and colon. During his first year in Waverly, he performed 12 gastrectomies (stomach removals). He did skin surgeries, including grafts and burn treatments; neck surgeries (usually involving the thyroid); and surgeries for breast cancer, colorectal cancer, stomach cancer, ovarian cancer, and more. He even performed Cesarean sections and hysterectomies, as there was not then nor has there ever been an ob/gyn specialist in Waverly.

The night before his elective procedures, he would pull out one of his atlases or textbooks of surgery and review the anatomy and techniques for the next day's operations. He did this without fail, even if he was doing that operation for the two-thousandth time. And after he had operated on a patient, in addition to his daily morning rounds, he would check on that patient three more times throughout the day: shortly after the operation, again during his afternoon or early evening rounds, and then once more late at night, before returning home to sleep—unless he was on night call, when he often slept in the hospital.

He and Dr. Maysoon set up an endoscopy suite, first at Nautilus Memorial and later at their own Waverly Clinic, and began performing upper and lower endoscopies and instituting colon cancer screenings on all their eligible patients. For Waverly, Humphreys County, and several of the surrounding counties, it was the first time these screenings had been made locally available, and there was much excitement among the nursing staff as well as the general community regarding this new technology. When the first endoscope (then known as a "panendoscope") was purchased, the county newspaper, the *News-Democrat*—which labeled itself "A Growing Paper for a Growing Area"—hailed the new diagnostic tool as "a medical wonder!" and reported that it was the "only machine of its type between Nashville and Memphis."

THERE WERE OFTEN so many patients admitted to the hospital that there would even be some on stretchers in the hallways, waiting on rooms to open up. In an era before managed care, what are now outpatient procedures, like colonoscopies, would frequently be done on an inpatient basis in the hospital—and sometimes patients would be admitted for four or five days. Even with a simple hernia repair, a patient could be kept until the stitches came out.

Nautilus Memorial opened in the same year that the first CCU was introduced, and the concept of intensive cardiac care was still in its infancy. There were no cardiologists at small community hospitals like Nautilus. As Dr. McClure recalled, if a patient had a heart attack, they stayed in the hospital for three weeks, spending the first week lying flat in bed. The second week, their doctor would let them start sitting up for a few days. Then they'd be allowed to sit in a chair, and then the chair would be moved out a little bit from the bed so they could walk to the chair.

And then in three weeks the patient would go home and throw a pulmonary embolus due to the long period of inactivity, have a sudden death, and the doctors would say, "He had a bad heart attack come back on him."

Having a heart attack then was akin to a death sentence. Guidelines for the use of aspirin and other life-saving cardiac medications were not yet established. Warfarin (under the brand name Coumadin), initially approved in the United States as a rat poison in 1952 and as a blood thinner for humans in 1954, was used for heart attack patients, and would eventually become the most widely used blood thinner in the world. By the late 1950s, the clot-busting drug streptokinase also came into use for patients with acute heart attacks. Well into the 1970s, however, there were no widely accepted, standardized protocols for using these medications, and no established practice guidelines. In the 1970s, in-hospital mortality rates for patients with acute heart attack ranged from 10% to 45% (compared to 15% at the high end of the range in 2015).

In the late 1970s, Dr. McClure and his colleagues knew streptokinase existed; they knew it could dissolve clots, but no one really knew how to use it. In general practice, it was known that there was within the body a clotting cascade and a mechanism for dissolving clots like the ones that formed in the coronary arteries to cause a heart attack. But the fine details had yet to be worked out, and using streptokinase on patients who came into the ER with a heart attack was fraught with peril. In theory, it worked, but because the standardized dosing and protocols had not been established, in practice it caused serious bleeding complications like brain hemorrhages and massive gastrointestinal bleeds.

It was not until 1977 that a German-born cardiologist by the name of Andreas Gruentzig successfully performed the first coronary angioplasty, using a catheter to open a balloon within a blocked coronary artery, thus reopening the artery and restoring blood flow to the heart muscle. This procedure revolutionized cardiac care and ushered in a new era in cardiovascular medicine. But as fate would have it, it would never be performed in Waverly.

AT NAUTILUS MEMORIAL, the ER consisted of two rooms, about seven feet by ten feet for the smaller room, and eight or nine by ten feet for the larger room. The entire ER thus consisted of 160 square feet at most. There was no front desk, and patients entered the ER through what would be considered the hospital's back door. By opening that door, a patient would be standing in the waiting room, and would need to walk no more than five yards up a small, sloped, low-ceilinged corridor to reach either of the two ER rooms. There was a third, slightly larger room at the top of that corridor, and it was reserved for obstetrical procedures like Cesarean sections.

In 1973, after the state issued new requirements regarding medical certification for ambulances and their attendants, Luff-Bowen chose not to renew its ambulance contract with the county, effectively quitting the ambulance service in order to focus on the company's other businesses, including the funeral home, general store, and furniture store. Another funeral home, directed by Wayne Lambdin, still had two ambulances, and the county subsidized him to continue running the ambulance service.

There was no air-evac or hospital-affiliated emergency helicopter service anywhere in Middle Tennessee in 1978; the first air medical transport service for the region was Vanderbilt University Medical Center's LifeFlight program, which initiated operations in 1984. Until then, when an emergency air transport was needed from Nautilus Memorial to a larger, tertiary-care center (usually in Nashville), a medical helicopter from Fort Campbell, the US Army base and home to the 101st Airborne Division in nearby Clarksville, Tennessee, would do the job.

There were five on-staff doctors who rotated call, covering the ER for 24 hours at a time. If a patient came into the ER during the day, the doctor on call was paged or called at their clinic, and they had to put their clinic patients on hold to go see the ER patient. Dr. Ali covered Tuesdays, and Dr. Maysoon covered Fridays; however, to allow Dr. Maysoon to be at home at night with their two baby daughters, Dr. Ali covered Friday nights as well. Weekends were usually rotated among the five physicians.

Some weekends, a resident physician would moonlight in the emergency room; these young physicians spanned a variety of specialties, and many came from the residency programs at UT Memphis. One weekend night, around 1:00 A.M., a radiology resident who was covering the ER at Nautilus Memorial phoned Dr. Ali and told him, "I have somebody here with a slashed throat. They tried to sever his carotid and his jugular, and they nearly succeeded. It's way beyond my expertise. I need you here as fast as possible."

Dr. Ali responded, "Well, first of all, get the nurse to call my OR team. And second, put pressure on it 'til I get there! You're in Waverly, Tennessee, and you've got a neck that's turned into a fire hydrant. No time to send him anywhere else. Just hold pressure and I'll be there!"

When Dr. Ali arrived, he went straight to the OR. He had already scrubbed in when one of the nurses alerted him that the people who had slit his patient's throat had entered the first floor of the hospital and were on their way to the OR to finish the job. The nurses were in a panic. Dr. Ali said, "No problem." He scrubbed out, put on his white coat, and headed them off by the medical records department in the middle of the corridor leading up to the OR.

He didn't know what weapons they might still be carrying with them, but knew that he had to confront them.

"I understand you're here to finish the job you guys started," he said.

They seemed taken aback that he knew who they were and what they were there for. He decided to put it to them as plainly as possible. "This operating room is my domain. You're not going through that door. You try to go through that door and we're gonna have a real problem. You understand me?"

He saw that they were hesitating, and leaned in. "You go in and interfere with that patient who is in my custody, and you're gonna regret it. I'm here out of my bed in the middle of the night because of you guys, and if you think I'm happy about that, you're wrong. You go in there, and there'll be hell to pay. My nurses are calling the police right now, as we speak."

This seemed to make up their minds for them. They turned around and left. Dr. Ali turned around and went back to the operating theater, where he conducted a successful operation, saving his patient's life twice over.

AT NAUTILUS MEMORIAL that Thursday morning, the banter in the operating theater, at the nurses' station, and even in the examination rooms was all about the derailed train. No one was sure why it had derailed, but they knew it was a major inconvenience and a major mess, and the discussion centered on when and how it would be cleaned up and cleared out. There was talk of two tank cars being part of the derailment, but what that meant was beyond the knowledge of anyone in the hospital at that moment.

Several times over the preceding year, all hospital personnel had taken part in drills and mock disasters to prepare for potential large-scale emergencies. In fact, they had just had a mock disaster drill the week before. "Code Blue" was the name already given to resuscitation emergencies, a situation within the hospital in which a patient had suffered respiratory or cardiac arrest and required the immediate efforts of the code team to perform CPR and advanced cardiac life support (ACLS). For a potential disaster, the code name decided upon was "Operation Black." Calling Operation Black would mobilize all available medical personnel and other employees across the county to come to the hospital. To send out the call, a courier would be sent from the hospital to the local radio station, WPHC-WVRY, to ask them to broadcast the emergency alert code message.

In the operating theater that morning, Dr. Ali and his nurses discussed their hopes that they wouldn't have to use it.

CHAPTER FOUR

The Man Called Toad

FEBRUARY 23, 1978
THURSDAY
9:30 A.M.

AT THE EDGE OF THE 1,200-foot perimeter he had been instructed to hold, Waverly Police Sergeant Elton "Toad" Smith stood and surveyed the wreckage as a crew of L&N and Steel City personnel began the arduous process of restoring the tracks and rebuilding the damaged train cars so they could be pulled down the rails again. Until they could do that, all of L&N's freight rail traffic going west through Tennessee would remain at a standstill.

There was a light layer of snow on the ground, but not enough to stick to the pavement or to impair the cleanup operation. Standing there in uniform at his full height of six feet, two and a half inches, Toad cut an imposing figure against the overcast sky, and he had no trouble controlling traffic and maintaining the advised perimeter. He couldn't really blame people in town for wanting to come see the train wreck; in all his 44 years on earth, he had never seen—or imagined—anything like it.

When Chief Barnett had called him the night before to inform him of the derailment and to request that he report early for duty on Thursday, nothing the Chief could have said over the

phone that night would have prepared him for what he was looking at now. Even during his time in the military, Toad had not
seen anything to rival the scale of this. And he couldn't shake the
ominous feeling he had about it, the leaden feeling that sat in the
pit of his stomach every time he glanced at the mangled train cars
and the derailed tankers.

Over toward the west, well outside the perimeter, he saw T.O.
Perkins shooting photographs for the *News-Democrat*, and he could
just imagine the headlines the county paper would be sure to run
in its next issue. Toad knew he wouldn't have to worry about T.O.;
it was the growing crowd of onlookers coming around to lollygag
that would have to be chased away time and again. This site was
fraught with danger, and who knew what potential hazards rested
in those damaged tankers. The Assistant Fire Chief, Mr. Gisenhoffer, had given orders the night before to cordone off a perimeter
of 1,200 feet around the wreck, and Toad's job was to keep any non-
essential traffic and spectators at least that far away from the scene,
and that was exactly what he was determined to do.

He scanned the perimeter again, looking across to the intersection at Richland Avenue where one of the oblong tank cars
had come to a rest on the north side of the tracks. The tanker was
lying there in the street, right across the intersection. The wreck
had inverted one end of that tank, causing it to cave in and leaving a big indentation; of the two tank cars that had derailed, this
damaged one was causing the most immediate concern. The
water hoses of Waverly's fire trucks were trained on it. Toad didn't
know yet what was being stored in it, but it was a hazardous material of some sort, and there wasn't a body in the whole town
that wanted it to blow up.

As TOAD PATROLLED the area on foot, he walked along the snow-
covered banks of the small, shallow creek bed that ran out of

Trace Creek, not many yards from the Richland crossing. The temperature had really dropped overnight, and he knew the snow would not melt that day. Looking down into the mostly dry creek bed, he was reminded of how he got his nickname.

When he was around two or three years old, his father and a couple of his brothers would go frog hunting in the countryside where they lived, where there was no shortage of ponds and creeks and riverbeds full of bullfrogs. They would catch them and eat the frog legs, and little Elton would hear his dad talking about how good those frog legs were, and how he'd like to have some more of them. Elton had seen all kinds of little frogs and tadpoles out at the pond near their house, and, not knowing the difference between these and the large bullfrogs, he thought, *Well, I'll get Daddy some frogs so he can have more frog legs.*

He found a small bucket and went down to the pond to catch the little frogs, not telling anyone where he was going. Of course, it was not long before his mother and father missed him, and came out the door hollering for him. When their little boy answered from the pond down the road, they came running down there, worried, both asking him what on earth he was doing all the way down the road and reminding him that he was not supposed to be there on his own.

Elton would always remember how tall his daddy looked then, tall as a tree, towering over him. His father asked him again, "What are you doin' down here?"

Elton picked up his bucket and held it up to his dad, saying, "I got itty toads for you, Daddy."

His father's concerned face broke into a smile and he answered, "You're *my* itty toad. But I don't want you to come back down here no more by yourself."

Forever after, Elton Smith would be known as Toad.

LIKE MANY IN his generation, Toad grew up without electricity. What they couldn't find in Waverly, his family mail-ordered from Sears Roebuck and Montgomery Ward. In many cases, they ate what they raised, and he would later reflect that his formative years were part of an era in which people were used to figuring out how to do things themselves, no matter what that might entail—and if they didn't, they suffered. He saw firsthand how necessity was the mother of invention.

Toad enlisted in the Marines when he was old enough, and was part of the battalion that went to Beirut, Lebanon, in 1958 on a peacekeeping mission. Not long after he returned home, in 1960, he started working as a police officer in McEwen. He was a police officer for no longer than six months that year. He was 26 years old, and was cutting hair as a barber during his off-duty hours. One afternoon on a holiday weekend, he and his partner were called out to apprehend a suspect. Toad's partner was shot and badly wounded, and the situation left Toad wondering if law enforcement was the right line of work for him.

In 1972, Toad was still working as a barber in McEwen when Guy Barnett became Waverly's Chief of Police. Barnett had been a US Army officer during the Korean War and was an officer on the Tennessee Highway Patrol for seven years before taking leadership of Waverly's police department. Toad heard that he was hiring, and figured he would throw his hat in the ring once more.

CHAPTER FIVE

From the River to the Rail

FEBRUARY 25, 1862
TUESDAY

THERE HAD NOT ALWAYS BEEN an iron road running through Waverly.

One hundred sixteen years before the L&N train derailment, when Union forces under Don Carlos Buell first captured the city of Nashville during the Civil War, Waverly was a highly utilized stop on the main road of the Nashville & Memphis Stage Line, regularly hosting horse-drawn stagecoaches and their passengers. Having been established for this purpose in the early nineteenth century by a local lawyer, Steven Pavatt, the community had eventually become the county seat of Humphreys County, with a courthouse built in 1836, and official city incorporation to follow in 1838.

A fan of the Scottish author and historian Sir Walter Scott, Mr. Pavatt had named the community he established after Scott's popular Waverley Novels—many of which, like *Rob Roy* and *Ivanhoe*, would become well-known classics. The town of Waverly bore little resemblance to the settings of Scott's novels, but had its fans nonetheless, and with its proximity to three major rivers—the Tennessee River, the Buffalo River, and the Duck River—the area attracted numerous farmers as well as business owners.

By 1860, Humphreys County had grown to a population of 10,573; 1,463 of whom were enslaved and 14 of whom were free Blacks. Unsurprisingly, then, as in most of the towns and cities across the South at the time, Waverly voters were pro-Confederacy, with Humphreys County voting unanimously in favor of secession from the Union in 1861.

It was less than a year later—on February 25, 1862—when, 65 miles east of Waverly, the Army of the Ohio, under the command of General Buell, seized Nashville, making it the first Confederate state capital occupied by the Federal Army. This, in combination with the Union's capture of Fort Henry and Fort Heiman on the Tennessee River in early February 1862, followed by General Ulysses S. Grant's capture of Fort Donelson on the Cumberland River two weeks later, gave the Northern Army nearly unfettered access to the Tennessee River. Use of the river by the military, in turn, changed Waverly's neighboring community of Lucas Landing from a small, quiet landing spot along the river to a busy inland port and supply depot. And that change in status would turn out to have important implications for Waverly.

NASHVILLE'S POSITION SITUATED the Union Army in the heart of the Confederacy, and the Army soon realized it would need protected, steady supply lines to maintain its hold and expand its reach. The Cumberland River that ran through Nashville was unreliable as a supply route due to low water levels in the summer, and by the middle of 1862, the Federal Army was forced to search for a water route that was navigable year-round. The captures of Ft. Henry, Ft. Heiman, and Ft. Donelson earlier that February had given the Union carte blanche from the Ohio River to the Tennessee River in Kentucky's southwest corner, but bringing those supplies a little farther south would require a port and loading station to get them from the river to Nashville.

The Union found its answer in the broad, deep waters of the Tennessee River itself, which, in the mid-nineteenth century, was navigable from the Ohio River to the Great Bend at Muscle Shoals in northern Alabama. Union generals identified Lucas Landing, ten miles west of Waverly, as an ideal location for a supply terminus. Steamships and barges could easily reach it from the northern part of the river, and there they would establish a large depot to provide all the many provisions an army would need to fight and win a war. However, in order to execute their plan to bring supplies from the river to Nashville, a second mode of efficient transportation was needed: a railroad.

Fortunately for the Union, 28 miles of the Nashville and Northwestern Railroad already existed, as far as Kingston Springs to the west of Nashville. The railroad was originally chartered in 1852, but construction had been interrupted by the outbreak of the Civil War. Workers from all over the country as well as from across the Atlantic—mainly from Ireland, where the Great Famine had led to a mass exodus—had labored in Middle Tennessee to build the railroad.

A number of these workers settled in the area and built communities all along the rail line, including the towns of Erin and McEwen (Waverly's neighbors to the north and to the east, respectively). The church and school built by the immigrant Irish railroad workers in McEwen and named after the patron saint of Ireland, St. Patrick, remain in existence to this day, having provided solace, spiritual growth, and invaluable education to countless parishioners and students for over a century and a half. Among those parishioners and students were Nurse Nancy Daniel and her family, as well as Drs. Subhi and Maysoon Ali's daughters.

IN AUGUST 1863, Andrew Johnson, then Military Governor of Tennessee, urged Union General William S. Rosecrans to capitalize on the existence of the unfinished single-track Nashville and Northwestern Railroad, and in October 1863 Rosecrans ordered its extension from Kingston Springs to Lucas Landing. Designed by the First Michigan Engineers, the tracks would end at the Tennessee River. The Union Army conscripted several thousand Blacks, recently freed by President Abraham Lincoln's Emancipation Proclamation of January 1, 1863, and forced them into labor to expedite the completion of the railroad.

By May 1864, in just eight months, these Black laborers had laid the 50 miles of track from Kingston Springs through Waverly and on to Lucas Landing, which had by that time been transformed into 90 acres of hectic, teeming activity in its new role as a major Union supply depot. The landing now existed as a full military supply operation, replete with wharves and docks, offices and warehouses, a sawmill, housing for 2,500 soldiers, and horse corrals large enough for at least 1,000 horses and mules. On May 10, 1864, Andrew Johnson rode the first train from Nashville to Lucas Landing in order to officially open the supply depot. With no small bit of pomp, Johnson broke a bottle of wine over the railroad tracks and named the location after himself. The depot and surrounding community would forever after be known as Johnsonville.

Completion of the Nashville and Northwestern Military Railroad in so short a time frame has been deemed "one of the greatest engineering feats of the Civil War" (Wooten 2019). The time frame is even more impressive when the constant threats to the rail line are considered. Even as the railroad was under construction, it was a target of regular attacks by Confederate guerillas. To guard and protect the new military railroad, the Union Army constructed Fort Waverly high on a hillside with an unfettered view of the rail line and the surrounding area. Many of the Black laborers who had completed the railroad became part of the 12th and 13th infantry regiments of the United States

Colored Troops (USCT) stationed at Fort Waverly, along with troops from the 8th Iowa Cavalry and the 1st Kansas Battery. The soldiers of the USCT were thus guarding the very tracks they themselves had laid.

Troops were marshaled from all over the Union to protect what was now known as the Northwestern Military Railroad from Confederate attacks. In fact, over a hundred years later, both of Dr. Subhi Ali's scrub nurses could trace their ancestry back to one Union infantryman, Keno Mitchell, who had marched from Pennsylvania in order to join the forces guarding the railroad. Mitchell was Carolyn Tucker's great-great-grandfather, and his daughter was Nancy Daniel's great-great-grandmother. And had his ghost been watching from the superior vantage point at Fort Waverly—what his descendants came to know as Fort Hill—on the cold night of February 24, 1978, his angle of view would have been such that he would have seen 23 train cars go careening off the tracks of the railroad he had come hundreds of miles to protect.

THE TRANSFORMATION OF Johnsonville into an essential military supply depot had sealed Waverly's fate as a railroad town, and the coming decades would see passenger as well as freight trains travel regularly through Waverly, contributing to the town's economic growth. However, Johnsonville's status as a vital supply terminal during the Civil War had other far-reaching implications as well.

With the completion of the military railroad and the official opening of Johnsonville in May 1864 assuring him a robust, protected supply line, Union General William Tecumseh Sherman began his campaign to take Atlanta, a key part of his strategy to force an end to the entire war. The campaign would also have important implications for President Lincoln's embattled reelection bid, as Northern morale was ebbing and even Lincoln himself feared he would lose that November.

Sherman led three Federal armies totaling approximately 100,000 men: the Army of the Ohio, the Army of the Tennessee, and the Army of the Cumberland. On July 22, 1864, Sherman's armies engaged with the forces of Confederate General John Bell Hood, commencing the Battle of Atlanta. The battle raged for over five weeks, culminating finally in Confederate surrender on September 2, 1864.

The fall of Atlanta reverberated throughout the Confederacy, and Confederate generals wasted no time strategizing ways to re-take the city and to dislodge Sherman from Georgia. Sherman himself later acknowledged the critical importance of the region's railroads in making his campaign possible. Indeed, his supply line to Atlanta ran from the Tennessee River at Johnsonville, to the railroad through Waverly and on to Nashville, down through Chattanooga, and then onward another hundred miles through the North Georgia Mountains. It was tenuous at best. And by the following month, one of the Confederacy's most widely known generals, Nathan Bedford Forrest, had set his sights on the origin of this supply line: Johnsonville.

Forrest was a skilled cavalryman known for successfully using guerilla tactics to defeat Union forces that often outnumbered his. He was also skilled in the terror tactics of psychological warfare— experience he would draw upon with nefarious effect after the war, as the first Grand Wizard of the Ku Klux Klan.

On October 29, 1864, Forrest began his raid on Johnsonville, re-leasing the first barrage of cannon fire in the Johnsonville campaign in a calculated attack on a Federal steamship that was towing a barge toward the railroad terminus on the Tennessee River. For-rest's soldiers then appropriated the barge's cargo, which had been intended for the Union garrison stationed at Johnsonville.

The next day, Union gunboats appeared, but they were tin-clads rather than ironclads, and thus vulnerable to artillery. Forrest's men disabled several and commandeered others, which they moved toward Johnsonville before being forced to abandon them to Union forces once again. By November 3, 1864, however, Forrest's chief of artillery, Confederate Captain John W. Morton, had uncovered a serious shortcoming in Johnsonville's defenses. He positioned artillery on the river's west bank in such a manner as to be untouchable by Union fire from the river (as the gunboats could not shoot low enough) or from the land (as the guns at Johnsonville could not be depressed enough to hit cannons behind the levee on the river's opposite side). At 2:00 P.M. on November 4, Forrest's forces launched their bombardment. The Battle of Johnsonville had begun.

The Confederate attack was fierce, and so convincing that the Union commander at Johnsonville, Colonel Charles R. Thompson, feared the Confederates would capture the naval vessels and supplies docked along the riverfront. Thompson thus ordered the burning of the naval transports, and while Union soldiers set about burning gunboats and barges, Forrest's men continued their artillery attack. Panic ensued at the depot, with mules and horses stampeding and Union soldiers failing to return fire against the Confederate onslaught.

The early November winds began to pick up, and the flames from the boats and transports spread 600 yards across the entire wharf. Soon structures on land were burning, and the fire spread rapidly through the depot, destroying 60% of the warehouses and supplies, and causing more than $6.7 million in damages. Looting by both civilian employees and Union soldiers became uncontrollable. Forrest's psychological tactics had worked. He and his troops withdrew that night by the light of the burning depot.

ON MONDAY, NOVEMBER 7, 1864, General Sherman, who was then operating around Kingston, Georgia, telegrammed General Grant, "that devil Forrest was down about Johnsonville and was making havoc among the gun-boats and transports." The next day, November 8, 1864, President Lincoln was reelected to a second term, this time with Andrew Johnson as Vice President.

In Johnsonville, Union forces worked feverishly to reinforce the depot against additional Confederate attacks, but it was not until mid-November that it became clear to Union commanders that there would be no further immediate threat from Forrest. By that time, with the origin of his supply line decimated, and with Lincoln's reelection—and continued support—secured, Sherman had made the decision to leave Atlanta and "march to the sea," ordering the destruction of anything that might be of value to the Confederates. By most accounts, when Sherman's forces departed Atlanta on November 15, they burned the entire industrial district and left nearly half the city in ruin. These scorched-earth tactics were to be repeated throughout Georgia, proving that Forrest was not the only Civil War general skilled in the art of psychological warfare.

There are conflicting reports regarding how much influence Forrest's raid on Johnsonville ultimately had on Sherman's plans to divide his forces and march out of Atlanta, but the proximity in timing of the loss of his supply line at Johnsonville and his decision to abandon that supply line and quit Atlanta 11 days later would seem not to be a coincidence. If that was the case, it would not be the last time an inferno at the bed of the Nashville and Northwestern Railroad would sway the course of American history.

CHAPTER SIX

Minding the Perimeter

FEBRUARY 23, 1978
THURSDAY
12:00 P.M.

STATE ROUTE 1, ALSO KNOWN as the Memphis to Bristol Highway, spans the length of Tennessee, rising from the flat banks of the Mississippi River in the state's southwest corner to the ear-popping heights of the Appalachians in its northeast corner. It is over 500 miles long, and is a beautifully scenic route for most of its length. It becomes the main street of many of the towns and cities through which it travels—and in 1978, Waverly was one of these. Approximately two-thirds of SR 1 through Tennessee runs concomitantly with US Highway 70, and alongside the highway, visible for much of its length, runs the railroad.

Standing beside that railroad, Buddy Frazier held his position on the perimeter, and Thursday gave him a lot of time to think. He'd joined the military straight out of high school, when he was 18, and served in the Army Military Police. Before he went into the Service, he was like a lot of others who grew up in Waverly—and, for that matter, in small towns across the nation: all he could think was, *I want to get away from here. This is the most screwed-up place on the planet.* But when he got out there on the planet, he discovered it's not Waverly, Tennessee, that's screwed up. It's everywhere. And he decided, *It's what you make of it.*

When he returned home after his service, he did what most people in Humphreys County seemed to do at that time, and got a job at the DuPont plant in New Johnsonville. He was working in production, helping to produce the titanium dioxide pigment that was the primary output of that plant. It took very little time for him to discover that that wasn't what he wanted to do, hold down a job where every day was the same, where his ticket was punched, where there was no challenge. He knew he needed a career that presented him with a variety of challenges, something that was different every day.

When Mayor James Powers recruited Guy Barnett to become Waverly's Chief of Police, Buddy Frazier took notice. Barnett had been a highway patrolman in the area, and, as far as Buddy could tell, was the first police chief in Waverly with a law enforcement education and formal law enforcement training. He began to professionalize the police department. He had even become president of the International Association of Chiefs of Police. Buddy could see what was going on, and wanted to be a part of it. He knew his heart was in law enforcement, so at the age of 22, he went to see Chief Barnett, who took a chance on him by making him the youngest police officer the city had ever hired.

He started out with Sergeant Toad Smith, and they rode together for several months until Buddy went to the police academy. He went to the academy to try to learn how to keep somebody from shooting him or sticking a knife in him, to learn how to write a search warrant, and all the rest. But never in the academy did they tell him, "Buddy Frazier, there's a strong likelihood you're gonna end up on a train derailment with two tank cars of hazardous chemicals." That wasn't part of it. *But maybe they oughta have that kind of training*, he thought, *because when you have an instance like this, the first people that's gonna ever be there is the police.* Well, he had done the best he could the night before, and it had been good enough, and he would just keep on doing the best he could with the knowledge he had.

FRANK CRAVER, HAVING left the derailment site at 4:00 A.M., had slept in until nearly noon, at which point he hastily got up and went right back to the wreck, in spite of there being no schedule set up for how the fire department personnel were to handle their shifts or duty roster. There was simply no precedent for an incident of this magnitude.

Frank felt drawn to duty, however, and so he returned to see how things were going. After parking in the vicinity of Bradford's Grocery Store, close to the Viaduct, Frank got out and took in the scene before him. The wreckage looked even worse in the light of day. There were now two large boom cranes on the tracks, one from L&N and one from Steel City, along with a railroad salvage crew and a couple of bulldozers. The two derailed tanker cars were still lying on the ground, but some of the boxcars and wheels that had surrounded them had been moved to clear more space around the tankers. He could see now that the two tank cars were owned by Union Tank Car Company and labeled UTLX 83013 and UTLX 81467.

The cleanup crews had set up more fire hoses, running from a plug beside the Spann Building all the way out to where one boxcar was lying on top of another beside the tracks. An L&N wrecker truck was also there, and Frank saw it pick up the end of a boxcar and try to set it back on the tracks. It wasn't an easy job, and, in Frank's mind, it didn't seem to be going particularly well. He also saw the bulldozers going back and forth across the tracks, spreading gravel and hooking on to other boxcars, which they would then drag away from the rest of the wreckage, down toward the northern part of the Viaduct.

Several people that Frank recognized were already at the scene: Fire Chief Wilbur York, Assistant Fire Chief Dutch Gisenhoffer, Deputy Assistant Fire Chief Billy McMurtry, and volunteer firemen Melvin Matlock, David Dillingham, Almond Adams, and a young man Frank knew only as Milligan. Frank also noted Sergeant Toad Smith and a few other officers patrolling the perimeter.

Frank put on his fire boots and his gear and walked over to where Billy McMurtry was standing. "So, what's going on now?" Frank asked him.

"Oh, they're just cleaning up, tryin' to get 'em all straightened out, you know."

Frank asked about the duty roster, and was told that somebody from the fire department was wanted on the scene at all times if possible. Dutch Gisenhoffer came over to him and asked if Frank could stick around for a couple of hours, long enough for Dutch to go home and eat lunch.

"They're just cleaning up here, Frank; just keep your eyes on 'em and on our equipment."

Frank was happy to provide the relief, to have something to contribute, and he walked around monitoring the cleanup as requested. He got within 150 to 200 yards of the tank cars during that time, and as he was walking around he overheard someone saying they contained liquid propane, not anhydrous ammonia as their exterior labels indicated. The anhydrous ammonia tankers were apparently used for various purposes when it came to transporting chemicals, and these two were, in fact, carrying liquefied petroleum gas (LPG)—thought of simply as propane in the United States—when they derailed the night before. Frank would not discover until much later, too much later, that improper labeling was one of the more minor concerns when it came to these two tanks.

One of his fellow firemen mentioned to Frank that the L&N crew was going to try either to move the tanks or unload the propane into another, undamaged tank, but it was unclear when this was scheduled to happen. Around 1:00 P.M., the mayor of Waverly, James M. Powers Sr., DDS, showed up at the site, and Frank saw him join a huddled group of personnel from the Tennessee Office of Civil Defense.

Also in this group were representatives of the Emergency Medical Services office, the Public Service Commission, the L&N Railroad, and, of course, Waverly Police Chief Guy Barnett. Frank took note of all of them, standing there in a big group having a discussion, but was not privy to any of the plans that were agreed upon when the meeting concluded.

He did notice that a few members of the Civil Defense service were fanning out with their sniffer dogs, weaving in and out amongst the wreckage, particularly in the area of the two tank cars, trying to detect any leaks. Buddy and Toad and the other police officers were doing a good job maintaining the perimeter while the detection and cleanup were ongoing, and Frank was glad to see that no civilians or unnecessary personnel were able to approach anywhere within 1,200 feet of the propane-filled tankers.

By 2:30 P.M., Frank checked in with Gisenhoffer and McMurtry, telling them he was leaving, as he had some things to do and there seemed to be sufficient personnel at that time. He asked them to be sure to call him if he was needed.

CHAPTER SEVEN

A Two-Ton Barbell

FEBRUARY 24, 1978
FRIDAY
9:00 A.M.

FRANK CAME BY THE FOLLOWING morning to see Billy McMurtry, to tell him that he and his wife, Sue Craver, were thinking of leaving town, going down to Georgia to pick up Sue's mother, and would be out of town the rest of the weekend. Sue worked for the Tennessee Department of Human Services, and was in Nashville that day. If they did go, they would be leaving right after Sue got home that afternoon, around 4:30 or 5:00 P.M., and then he wouldn't be back before Monday morning.

"All right," said Billy. "When you know something for sure, come back over here and tell me so I'll know that you are going to be here or you're not going to be here. Just come back over here and tell me." He needed to be able to make a schedule for the weekend to maintain a fire department presence onsite, because no one knew how long the cleanup was going to take.

"Okay," Frank nodded. "I will."

TOAD SMITH WAS just pulling in as Frank was leaving. Chief Barnett had asked Toad to come back early on Friday, this time to focus his efforts on keeping people out of the immediate area where the crews were working. Train personnel were still rebuilding the rail cars, but local authorities had been told that all the tests on the tank cars had shown no leaks and therefore no danger. It was felt that, because the tanks had been sitting there that long without incident, there was unlikely to be any. The police had been told that, if they wanted, they could relax the perimeter and let some of the spectators in, just as long as they stayed out of the workers' way. So some of the businesses along Commerce Street had started reopening.

A member of the train crew informed Toad that they wanted the electricity cut off around the tracks, so he put in a call to Meriwether Lewis Electric Cooperative to have the current cut. The crew also wanted the gas cut off in the area, because they planned on beginning the gas transfer later from the damaged propane tank. Toad contacted the gas company and asked for the line to be cut off, but was told, "Well, we can cut it off at the houses immediately around where the wreck's at, but that trunk line feeds on into Houston County; therefore, we can't cut the line off."

The gas company did manage to cut off the gas all the way up most of Richland Avenue, and Toad confirmed that at least the houses within the 1,200-foot perimeter of the day before were within the cutoff zone. It seemed to him to be a safer distance to maintain, regardless of what the train people were saying.

By 11:00 A.M., everything seemed to be going all right. Toad watched with interest as the two cranes, one from Steel City and one from L&N, picked up rail cars one by one and set them down on the tracks. It looked as though they were just pushing them down onto the rails. Toad knew he was not the only one fascinated by this entire operation; the big-city reporters were down from Nashville, not to mention the local crowd that had by now surrounded the much smaller perimeter he was holding.

All was going smoothly until one of the cranes picked up an open rail car that had been lying on the other side of the tankers. The tanker, UTLX 83013, which had fallen to the northwestern side of the tracks, was lying closer to Richland Avenue, and it was the one that the railway personnel seemed to be most concerned about because of the damage it had sustained during the derailment. At that moment, it also happened to be underneath the rail car held aloft by the crane. When the crane picked up the rail car and swung it over the tank car, Toad noticed that a stray set of wheels had gotten caught up with the rail car. Not a minute later, he saw that set of wheels fall and dive into the egg-shaped end of the tanker, hitting it with a gigantic popping noise.

Everybody jumped, and Toad waited for the dreaded explosion to occur, but nothing happened. So the crew went on with their work, continuing to pick up cars with the cranes. Toad turned to a crew member and asked, "How much does that set of wheels weigh?"

"Oh, about two tons. But, you know, the walls of these tankers are made of steel three-quarters of an inch thick. And it's still got that water hose on it, so it looks all right."

Still, Toad thought, *that was a pretty good whack from a 4,000-pound barbell.*

Mr. Dorsey Yates, the county health and food inspector who had been at the site investigating the possible contamination of the well in that area, was standing beside Toad for this exchange, and said, "You know, I believe I need to be back over at the office!"

"Well, yeah, I think a lot of us feel that way, Mr. Yates!" Toad responded.

But of course Toad and the crew couldn't leave their posts, and, unbelievably, he saw bystanders starting to get closer and closer to the tankers. Although the police department had been assured by railroad authorities that there was no danger in relaxing the perimeter, Toad still felt uneasy about the proximity of civilians to what seemed like a touch-and-go situation.

By the time the morning drew to a close, most of the cars were back on the rails, and the cleanup crew had cleared a great deal of the wreckage and rebuilt several cars. The tracks were effectively cleared. To Toad's astonishment, they actually brought a train through there, easing along at about four or five miles per hour, going right beside the two tankers that still lay on the ground beside the tracks. That was a violation of the regulations, Toad knew, and he wondered at the brazenness of it. He guessed the railroad industry was in a big hurry to get freight moving again.

IN THE OR that morning, the nurses were discussing the train wreck again. "You know, Dr. Ali, everybody's been running down there to see the train wreck. I hear it's quite a sight," Sam said.

"Yes, I'm sure the whole town is over there," he muttered.

"Well now, Dr. Ali, you know everybody's wanting to see it. It's not every day folks get to see a train wreck in person."

Barbara Horner, who was in her usual position as the circulating nurse, spoke up. "You know, people really don't need to be over there. Not with those propane tanks the way they are."

"I see enough train wrecks on a daily basis," Dr. Ali grumbled. "The last thing I need is to see a literal one."

"Well, they're sayin' it's all right, but I don't know," Sam replied as she handed Dr. Ali another surgical instrument.

"Everything is all right until it's not," Dr. Ali said.

CHAPTER EIGHT

The End of the World

FEBRUARY 24, 1978
FRIDAY
2:30 P.M.

BUDDY FRAZIER WAS NOT SCHEDULED to report for duty until 3:00 P.M. on Friday, but at that time, Friday was a very important day if you were a city employee, because it was pay day. Every city employee got paid on Friday, and everyone wanted to get to the bank to deposit their paycheck. Buddy got paid $80 a week. So he came into town early that day and took care of his banking.

Next he got his patrol car and went down to the derailment site to see Chief Barnett, to find out where the Chief wanted him assigned. Everyone in the police department was very close, and the officers often commented that Guy Barnett was more of a daddy to their tight-knit working family than an intimidating or unapproachable police chief. The Chief was a personable man, the kind of man who never told anyone what to do; rather, he asked. And that afternoon Chief Barnett asked Officer Frazier to go back to town and pick up a fellow officer, Ted Tarpley.

Three of the department's four patrol cars, including Buddy's, were at the derailment site. That morning, in fact, had heralded the arrival of two brand-new cars, and the Chief was in one of

65

them by that afternoon; the other was just coming off transport at Sloan Ford in Waverly that day. So Chief Barnett asked Buddy to pick up Ted Tarpley at Ted's house and take him to the Chief's house to get the remaining patrol car that Ted would be needing.

Buddy headed to Ted's house off Main Street and collected him, then took him to the Chief's house near the westernmost edge of town a few miles away. Ted got into the remaining patrol car, and the two police cars both headed back toward the train site, Buddy in the lead.

AT THE CHIEF'S house, his youngest son, 12-year-old Tim Barnett, was home alone when he saw a patrol car pull up. He had just been dropped off from junior high basketball practice. His oldest brother, Aaron, was on active duty in the US Navy, and his second-oldest brother, Guy Oakley Barnett Jr., whom they called Oak, was working at the Cee Bee Food Store. His mother was also out, so Tim was by himself. When he saw the patrol car, he figured it was his dad. He had been hoping to see his dad that day, and almost ran out to say hello to him, but he saw Ted Tarpley get out and head toward the other patrol car. It looked as though they were in a hurry, and Tim didn't want to bother them.

2:40 P.M.

Humphreys County schools had let out early that day, at 1:00 P.M., due to a county-wide teacher planning session, and so Frank had gone by Waverly Elementary School to pick up his six-year-old daughter, Susan, before returning to the derailment site to let them know his plans for the weekend. They had stopped by their house first, where Frank wrapped a couple of packages he was going to mail to his nephew, made some long-distance phone calls, and got things ready for their trip. Not wanting to leave his six-year-old at home by herself, he brought her with him to the derailment site. As they drove back through town and down to the site, he did not notice any roadblocks this time. *They must have released the perimeter.* He pulled his car up and got out with his daughter; they walked together to the tracks where several firemen were standing.

He saw Richard Wheeler and Melvin Matlock fiddling with what the fire department called a Gatling gun—a big, long nozzle that swiveled up and down or left and right, and the fire line's hose could be hooked into it. They had it sitting atop a boxcar in front of the Spann Building, and they were trying to get it aimed correctly, so that if needed they could put water over there on that damaged tank car, or in its general vicinity. Billy McMurtry was yelling instructions to them, but he couldn't seem to make them hear what he was trying to say.

McMurtry saw Frank and said, "Here, Frank, hold this walkie-talkie for me a minute."

Frank held it while McMurtry walked closer to the tracks and over to the boxcar to give them instructions on how and where to aim the "gun." When he returned, Frank handed the walkie-talkie back to him and said, "Bill, my daughter and my wife and I are fixing to leave town soon. My wife gets off work and we're going to Georgia to get my mother-in-law. We'll be gone the rest of the weekend."

"Okay," McMurtry said. "Go over and let Chief Barnett know, too."

Frank squatted down and fastened his little girl's coat up, pulled the hood of her coat over her head and tied it under her chin. "Come on, we've got to go," he told her.

2:43 P.M.

It had been an exceptionally cold week, but relief from the cold finally came that Friday, when the sun made its reappearance and warmer air crept into Middle Tennessee. It had, in fact, been a beautiful day, full of the promise of spring. By that afternoon, just as Toad was getting ready to go off duty, the temperature had warmed up to the mid-fifties.

Chief Barnett was standing beside Toad across from Slayden Lumber, surveying what was left of the wreck. Many of the train cars had been rebuilt and cleared, but the white tankers still lay beside the tracks. The gas transfer had yet to begin on the tanker, and they were both looking, for perhaps the hundredth time, at the bullet-shaped tank, with the myriad scuff marks that covered it from top to bottom and the punched-in, inverted end from the original wreck nearly two days before. Finally, the Chief turned to Toad and said, "Toad, it's gettin' about time for you to be relieved, ain't it?"

Toad, knowing that Buddy was on his way with Ted Tarpley, replied, "Well, yeah, but I may just stay over here until they relieve the pressure in that tank. Looks like they're gettin' ready to unload it."

Toad had watched and listened for two days while the different so-called experts had argued about what to do with those tankers, how to unload them safely, how to get them back on the tracks. By now everyone in town knew there was liquid propane in them, not anhydrous ammonia as there was supposed to be, as it said right there on the side of the tanks, the writing on the wall as plain as day for anyone who could read.

So L&N had called Liquid Transport in there to do the propane transfer, and Steel City was there to add their crane to the effort of lifting and moving the train cars, but no one could seem to agree on how best to proceed with the propane tanks.

Toad gathered from their discussions that the safest way to do the transfer was to remove the propane from the tanks and fill them with water before lifting and mounting them back on the tracks again.

But there had to be something to transfer the propane *to*, and apparently L&N had called all over the place, and the nearest rail tank cars they could find that were empty were down in Alabama somewhere. It would be three or four days before they could get them to Waverly. Liquid Transport, however, said that they could get some highway tank trucks to Waverly. So by Friday morning they had brought in a fuel truck from Jackson, Tennessee, and set it up on North Railroad Street. It looked to Toad like a semi-trailer truck, and he wasn't sure how safe that was going to be to drive out of there, but nobody asked him, so he kept his mouth shut.

The L&N folks who were clearing the wreckage had apparently decided it would be best to move the tank cars from where they had fallen in order to facilitate the gas transfer. Once the derailed freight cars that had been lying on top of the tankers were removed, they could move the tank cars into a position alongside the tracks, and the fuel truck was then able to come up beside them. The cleanup crew placed a cable sling around the damaged tank car labeled UTLX 83013, and dragged it 12 feet.

Toad had watched as the crew loosened the hoses from one of the trucks in order to connect with the rail tankers, but then there was the problem of adapting the fittings to match those on the rail tankers in order to release the propane, since the truck was obviously of a different size and make than the tank cars. It had taken them just about all morning to finally get it all hooked up, and now here it was, middle of the afternoon, and they still hadn't started the offloading process.

Toad was also taking note of the chaos that was beginning to ensue as the three o'clock hour approached and everyone, including the volunteer firemen as well as the train and crane crews, were preparing to change shifts. With everybody going every which way, it looked to Toad to be about as organized as a bunch of squirrels running from a dog. There was even, unbelievably, a Steel City employee, Rex Gaut, sitting on top of a bulldozer, smoking a cigarette. He was telling a reporter from the *Nashville Banner* how everything was just fine and it would be no problem to get it all cleaned up.

With all this disorganization going on, Toad just didn't feel comfortable leaving. So he and Chief Barnett walked together to the Chief's patrol car, which was sitting in front of the tavern, the Starlite Inn, facing the tracks. Seeing the Chief into his vehicle, Toad then proceeded east up the street to his own patrol car, which was near Tate Building Supply and Lumber Company. Along with that of the railroad claims adjustor, Mr. Melvin Holcombe, whose vehicle was pointing eastward, Toad's vehicle, pointing west, effectively blocked off the small bridge that allowed entry from South Railroad Street. Toad had the intention of waiting in his patrol car until Buddy and Ted arrived.

As Toad passed Tate Lumber, he noticed young Terry Hamm, known to his friends as "T Boy," working with his dad and another young man by the name of Van Johnson. The three of them were out there with a big delivery truck that had arrived that morning, and they were unloading giant sheets of insulated board. They had been working at it all day.

As Toad came by, he yelled, "T Boy, what are y'all doin' over here today?"

T Boy answered, "Well, I asked the boss if he was gonna work today, and he said, 'Well, yeah, if we closed today we might as well be closed every day.'"

Toad listened with little patience as T Boy proceeded to tell him that everything was all right, that the train situation was clear and under control, and this, that, and the other, until Toad finally said, "You know, T Boy, I don't believe in premonitions, but I never have felt good about that thing."

"Well, I hadn't, either."

Toad knew that T Boy, of all people, would catch his drift. T Boy had worked as a deputy sheriff for a while, and the two of them had attended a hazardous materials training seminar about a month before, where they had learned about dealing with propane, ammonium nitrate, toluene, all of that. Hazardous, flammable, very explosive materials. They had learned about how it was ammonium nitrate down in Galveston Bay that sank that ship and blew away half the harbor of Texas City, and that was years ago, in 1947. And there were two small airplanes flying over at the time, and it knocked them out of the sky. Hundreds of people were killed. It might've been the worst industrial accident in US history. That was ammonium nitrate.

And here, just yards from where they were standing, was a damaged tank car full of liquid propane. They had also learned in that class about what's called a BLEVE, or boiling liquid expanding vapor explosion, which had happened with a railroad tank car less than five years earlier in Kingman, Arizona, and killed nearly a dozen people. Learned about how propane is a refined and liquefied petroleum gas, and how it can be almost like an atomic blast when liquid propane hits the air, because its low boiling point at -44 degrees Fahrenheit makes it vaporize as soon as it escapes from any pressurized container. How they called it "flammable steam," because just one gallon of liquid propane can vaporize, all at once, to more than 250 gallons of flammable gas. And they learned about how propane is denser than air, so if a tank carrying propane leaks, the propane will sink into any surrounding enclosed area, just waiting to explode or catch fire. Any spark, even the smallest one, could ignite it.

They had learned all this, and yet here were all these people standing around watching or going about their business as usual, like it was nothing. Everybody wanted to watch the action, and since the schools had let out early, there were teenagers, high school students, having to be chased away from the Viaduct. The authorities never should have eased up on those roadblocks and that wider perimeter, as far as Toad was concerned.

All this weighed on him as he studied T Boy one more time, trying to think of what he could possibly say that would persuade him to leave. From his days in the military, Toad recognized that little voice in the back of your mind that tries to give you a head's up, tries to warn you, and he knew you'd better listen to it. This was what he tried to convey to 20-year-old Terry Hamm, one last time.

But T Boy finally just held his hands up, shrugged his shoulders, and said, "Well, the boss said to come in and it would be all right and everything."

"Okay, T Boy, I'll see ya later."

2:52 P.M.

Sam was driving south over the Viaduct on her way back to the hospital after dropping off John Bryant, their nurse anesthetist, at Humphreys County Airport in Waverly. He had a small plane that allowed him to get to multiple small hospitals in the region, and that afternoon he was headed to Erin. Sam and Dr. Ali had an outpatient case under local anesthesia scheduled for 4:00 that afternoon at the hospital, and she intended to be there by change of shift at 3:00 P.M.

Coming back over the Viaduct, she looked down at the train wreck, and at the white propane tanks still lying on their sides. It was an interesting sight, and there was so much of a mob down there, so many spectators milling about and taking it in. She slowed down as she went, thinking what a mess it was, and wondering why it was so hard to tear one's eyes away from a train wreck.

TOAD CONTINUED WALKING up the street to his patrol car, passing the small vacant lot behind Bateman's Bait Shop before arriving at his parked car. He opened the car door and started to get in, then thought to himself, *Well, if I'm gonna stay over here, I may as well get my jacket.*

He had left his jacket in the back seat of his patrol car when the weather had warmed up earlier. He estimated it had warmed to about 55 degrees that day, and the snow on the ground was melting. But now, if he was going to be sitting still for a while, he might get chilly, so he got back out and opened the back door of the car, grabbed his jacket, and slipped it on. He also had a walkie-talkie, which he took and laid on the dash, then caught hold of the top of the car with his left hand, and slid back in to the driver's seat and sat down. He happened to glance down at his watch. It was 2:55 P.M.

ON THE WAY back to their car, Frank and his daughter Susan stopped by Guy Barnett's vehicle in front of the Starlite Inn, about 100 feet from the tracks. Chief Barnett was sitting in the driver's seat, scooted down in it like he always did, and he had that cap on his head, the one he liked to wear. "Have you had any sleep since the derailment?" Frank asked him.

"No, not much. I was just thinking about going to the house and laying down for a while."

Frank stood there for a few moments, conversing with the Chief and letting him know he would be out of town for the weekend. He stood with his back toward the tracks and the tank cars. His right hand was on his six-year-old daughter's right shoulder as she stood in front of him; his left hand was resting on the ledge just inside the open window of the Chief's vehicle. Glancing down at the Timex watch on his left wrist, the wrist that rested beside Chief Barnett's left shoulder, he noted the time. It was five minutes before three o'clock. And that was the last thing he saw and the last thought he had before the world exploded.

CHAPTER NINE

Inferno

FEBRUARY 24, 1978
FRIDAY
2:55 P.M.

DRIVING IN FROM THE BARNETT house on the west side of town with Ted Tarpley behind him, Buddy was on Highway 70, headed back to Chief Barnett's position, when he saw a fireball go skyward from the northeast horizon and roll outward in slow motion. It was a mushroom cloud, just like the images of an atomic blast he had seen on television. And as soon as he saw it, he knew what had happened.

Forgetting completely about Ted being behind him, Buddy cut lights and sirens on, and barreled at top speed toward the derailment site.

ON THE HIGHWAY 13 hillside at Nautilus Memorial Hospital, Cheryl Allen, RN, Director of Nurses, had just finished an inservice training with some of the other nurses, which had been led by a visiting nurse from Nashville. They were all getting ready for the change of shift at 3:00 P.M. when they felt the whole hospital shake. Cheryl knew exactly what it was. The sudden boom that rose from the north was like the sky breaking apart, and it was unmistakable. The train had exploded.

Cheryl immediately told the hospital operator to overhead-page Dr. Maysoon, who was the doctor on call that day for the ER. She and the other nurses began running down to the ER, with the exception of the visiting nurse, who left the building and took off in the other direction down Highway 13 South, headed back to Nashville.

IN THE HOSPITAL room where Jennie Lee Monroe had been staying with her mother, Dr. Maysoon was just finishing up with her mother's discharge instructions and was getting ready to leave the room, smiling at them and wishing them a wonderful weekend. Mrs. Monroe and her mother hadn't had a newspaper for a couple of days and hadn't turned the television on while they had been at the hospital. They had heard there had been a train wreck at the Richland Avenue crossing, but hadn't seen it and didn't know anything about the extent of it. Mrs. Monroe said goodbye to Dr. Maysoon, and before her mother's doctor got down the hallway, the hospital operator was paging her to come to the emergency room.

FIFTEEN MILES AWAY, Barbara Horner, RN, could see the mushroom cloud from her home in Buffalo. She got dressed and was heading out the door when her phone rang; it was the hospital secretary calling her in for Operation Black. As soon as she heard the secretary's voice, she answered, "I'm on my way out the door." As Barbara sped north toward the smoke and the fire, she would have passed the visiting nurse who was fleeing south.

SAM HAD JUST walked into the hospital building from the side entrance, and as she walked in, she heard the page: "Dr. Maysoon to the ER. Dr. Maysoon to the ER, stat." She wondered what on earth could be going on, and figured she would just have a look. Then she heard, "Carolyn Tucker to the ER. Carolyn Tucker to the ER, stat."

Sam ran into Nancy coming down the hallway, also headed to the ER. "Nancy, whaddaya suppose is goin' on?"

"Let's find out."

By the time they reached the ER less than two minutes later, all hell had broken loose.

As HE WAS looking out the windshield of his patrol car facing west, Toad heard what sounded like a low-pitched, heavy clap of thunder that made the buildings shake. He would remember later that it wasn't a particularly loud sound, just a low rumble that shook everything. And yet he knew what it was. He knew exactly what it was. The tank had blown.

He saw the smoke starting to roll across Railroad Street. Clouds upon clouds of white smoke. And then there were streaks of white that shot ahead through the clouds, and then the smoke clouds caught up with them. Toad knew that the white streaks were the liquid propane spurting out of the ruptured tank and then vaporizing. The propane came out in sheets, and then the smoke would catch up. In that surreal fraction of a second, he thought about what an awesome sight it was, something that you capture in your mind like an instant take before it disappears.

But the time for thought had gone. Toad moved fast. He reached out and grabbed his walkie-talkie in his left hand and got out of the vehicle. Just as he was standing up to exit the patrol car, though, something hit him in the forehead.

He looked up to see what was going on and what had hit him, and saw rocks the size of golf balls flying through the air. He realized later that it was the crushed rock from the railbed. It looked as though some tremendous shovel had filled the air full of those rocks. Then he looked back up the street, and took note of the three rail cars sitting diagonally across the tracks; they were all that stood between him and where the explosion was. Past that, all he could see was the smoke and vapor coming up around the sides of the rail cars.

Glancing upward again, he saw more debris flying in a whirlwind through the air, and noticed a hard hat or two floating around up there in the air, too. He figured those must've come off somebody's head, and he said to himself, "You know, Self, we better get outta here!"

So he turned, and got about three or four good running steps from the vehicle. And then all of a sudden, he looked down and there was this blue flame. For a long moment, he was waist-deep in nothing but blue flame, and then it had gone past him, out to Commerce Street, in front of Slayden Lumber Company. It went out as quickly as it came, and he thought and hoped, *Well, maybe that's the end of it.*

His next thought was a repeat of his first and most urgent one, which was to get himself out of there ASAP. He kept talking to himself to make his feet move. "Now, Self, we gotta get outta here! Move! We gotta get behind a building, anyway."

But then, just as he thought he had seen the worst of it, a split second after the blue flame went out, he heard something. It sounded like a piece of raw meat being put into hot oil, a searing noise that seemed incredibly close but that he couldn't place. He turned his head to the left, in the direction it seemed to be coming from, and looked around, but saw nothing that could account for it. Only much later would he realize that it was he himself that was literally boiling: his hair, his hat, and the backs of his ears.

The police jacket he had thought to put on at the last minute had an artificial fur collar on it, and that had been singed, too.

He started running again, parallel to the front wall of Slayden Lumber, and hearing another noise behind him, glanced back. The far end of the wall spontaneously combusted. Toad watched with his heart in his throat as it went up in one big fireball. He heard people screaming. Those flames rolled on out between the buildings behind him and hit the concrete plant, then rolled back over themselves, just like a wave of water.

Oh, those poor souls.

Toad had nearly reached the other end of the wall. *You know, if I can get behind it, if I can just get behind this building, maybe I could stay out of it.*

But he was out of time. When he got to that front corner of the building, the fireball had caught up with him.

Toad shut his eyes and gave himself to the fire, running in it and with it. At first, when he got to the other side of the fireball, he thought he was dead. But then he felt his hands, and his hands felt funny. He could feel them, they were his hands, they belonged to him; but somehow, they felt different. He had gotten out of the fire, he didn't know how, and he had run around the building, and now he was looking down at his hands. The top layer of skin on both hands had turned into a large blister, and little flames popped up and went out, bursting the blister and taking the skin with them. Underneath what had been the skin of his hands, all that was left was a whiteness, as white as a sheet of paper.

His hands were burned white but dotted with yellow flames all the way up to where the sleeves of his jacket ended. He shook his hands and the flames went out. Shaking his hands like that, he realized that he was still holding the walkie-talkie in the palm of his left hand. He keyed the mike. Surreally to him, he found that he could still work his fingers, and it didn't hurt. Because the nerves in the skin had been destroyed, it didn't hurt.

He keyed the mike and got the police dispatcher on. He couldn't believe how calmly the dispatcher answered. *They don't know.* "Ten-four, 339," the dispatcher said, calling Toad by his car number. "339, go ahead."

Toad spoke frantically into the mike. "Get all the help over here you can, because this thing just ruptured!"

The dispatcher yelled, "TEN-FOUR!"

Toad caught his breath and glanced over to his right. Over at Carman Oil Company, Exxon's bulk oil plant and gas distributor behind Slayden Lumber, they had, against everybody's wishes, brought a truck in that morning and unloaded 6,000 gallons of gasoline. The old upright tanks holding that gas were there just to Toad's right, and when he saw them then, his heart nearly stopped. The tanks were smoking and the paint was trying to catch fire, and there was dirty oil all around there, and that was trying to catch fire, and the little old Carman Oil building itself was trying to catch fire, and Toad thought, *Lord, I'm out of the fryin' pan and into the fire!*

So he ran on again, and got about halfway around the Carman Oil building when four people he knew came out the back door of Slayden Lumber. They had a pickup truck parked right there beside the door. As they jumped into their truck, Toad yelled to them, "Can I ride with y'all? Can you drive me up to the hospital?"

They yelled back, "Yeah, jump in."

WHEN FRANK CAME to, everything was on fire. He himself was on fire. He was no longer standing beside the Chief's car, and he didn't know what had happened. There was so much debris in the air, flying around and hitting him as he tried to move. Railroad cross ties, gravel and dirt, pieces of metal, all blowing around. It seemed as though, all of a sudden, he and everything else were in orbit. Everything was gone, thrown up from the ground and into the air.

He saw a piece of the tank car come sailing through the air, and following its trajectory, realized it was headed his way. He saw his daughter standing there, and threw himself over her to shield her body with his. He told her to stay on the ground. He got back up, whirling around like a dervish, trying to get his clothes off and put himself out, as everything on him was on fire.

His daughter stood up again, and he fell on her again, trying to keep her safe as more debris came flying their way. Her clothes had caught fire too. He rolled away from her, still trying to put out his own fire, and for a third time, as debris blew past him and moved him farther away, he saw her stand up. She was standing over there, looking at him. He hollered and told her to get down and stay down. And then he lost sight of her as he rolled under Guy Barnett's car. He found himself looking at the gas tank, and told himself, "Frank, get out from under here. This thing could blow." He rolled back out from under it. And then the world went black again.

BUDDY PULLED UP on the Commerce Street bridge parallel to the Highway 13 Viaduct. All the surrounding buildings were on fire, and he could get no farther, so he stopped his patrol car there. The first person he saw was his police chief, walking toward him. He was burned severely; his clothes were gone. Buddy got him into the back seat of the car.

Then, to his left, he saw someone crawling up the bank of the street that went down to Trace Creek. It was Officer Nancy Bell. She was wearing a rain jacket that was not fire retardant, and it had basically melted into her. He ran to her and helped her into the back seat beside Chief Barnett.

He got behind the wheel and was ready to turn the car around to drive the mile up the hill to the hospital when another man came to the car. It was an employee of the state Civil Defense. He was around Buddy's age, and his hands were burned. Buddy put him in the front seat.

When he got to the hospital, he helped the trio into the emergency room, and then caught sight of the hospital comptroller, Margaret Brown, in the hallway. He sprinted over to her and said, "Ms. Brown, the tank's blew up. Activate your disaster plan."

His next thoughts turned toward his wife. Buddy had been married about two years at that time, and his wife worked in the hospital, downstairs in the business office. He thought, *I've got to see her. I've got to let her know that I'm okay, because her world's fixin' to change, what's fixin' to happen to this hospital. Plus, I've gotta get back.*

He flew down the stairway, just to put eyes on her and tell her, "I'm all right." That way, he knew she could do her job at the hospital, and he could go back and do his.

THE NEXT THING Frank knew, he had ended up somewhere in the street behind Chief Barnett's car, and fireman David Dillingham was throwing his fire coat around him. He told Frank to get in his car. By the time Frank got in, David was already backing out the car.

"What happened?" Frank asked.

"The tank blew," David answered. He sped up to Nautilus Hospital, where he ushered Frank into the ER. On the way there, Frank realized that his clothes were gone. He had been wearing jeans, a long-sleeved flannel shirt, and a heavy corduroy coat, and the tank rupture had blown or burned all of these off him. He also became aware that he was in his stocking feet. The explosion had blown him out of his shoes.

CHAPTER TEN

Triage in a Two-Room ER

FEBRUARY 24, 1978
FRIDAY
2:58 P.M.

WHEN DR. MAYSOON ARRIVED IN the ER, the staff informed her
they had been notified that one of the two propane tanks had exploded, and to expect casualties. Mass trauma was certainly not
her specialty, but she did happen to know a good trauma surgeon.
She immediately picked up the phone and dialed the main
number for Waverly Clinic. She told their executive secretary,
Glenda Phelan, to get Dr. Ali and tell him to come to the ER right
away. By the time she hung up the phone, the first casualties were
pouring in.

What she would later remember seeing was a crowd of people
who all seemed to be on fire. Many were jumping up and down,
screaming in pain. She could not tell who any of them were, such
was the extent of their burns. There was smoke rising from their
skin, with the epidermis visibly sloughing off. And there was an
overpowering smell that filled the ER and the hospital corridors.
It was the stench of burning flesh.

She felt the panic rising in her throat, and willed herself to
focus. There were lives to be saved now. There would be time for

emotions later. But to whom should she attend first? There were so many patients, and all of them wanted, needed, to be treated. All were asking for help, all at once. "I need help" and "I need water" were pleas she heard over and over. They were calling out to the nurses by their first names, but the nurses didn't recognize them either. People they had worked with and been around all their lives, and they couldn't recognize them. So many patients were asking for something to drink, because they were dehydrated. Fluids had been sucked from their body along with the burned skin they were actively losing.

She sent one of the ER nurses to get Dr. Walker; Dr. McClure was already there, having seen the explosion from his office. She asked the available doctors to help the nurses start IVs for fluid resuscitation. She, too, started peripheral IVs in the hands or arms if a suitable vein could be found; she had had so much experience starting IVs in her time at DC General Hospital, especially on the patients with severe gastrointestinal (GI) bleeding who needed fluids immediately, that she was quite adept at finding and sticking a vein even when the nurses could not.

Within minutes, Dr. Ali arrived and took over triage, and she set about doing what she could as an internist and gastroenterologist. She checked vital signs and breathing status, making sure everyone had oxygen who needed it. She ordered electrocardiograms (ECGs) to check for arrhythmias and signs of heart attack. When it was possible to draw blood, she asked the nurses to send specimens to the lab to check complete blood counts and electrolyte levels. She focused on getting patients ready for transfer, knowing that time was of the essence, and realizing that the longer they stayed, the more organ damage would begin to show, and she was keenly aware of the lack of specialty facilities at 52-bed Nautilus Memorial. They didn't have a dialysis unit. There was no cardiac unit. There was no cardiologist. There was no pulmonologist. And she was the only internist.

When she began examining the patients, she still could not tell who they were. It was not until she looked at the soles of their feet that she could even identify their race. Someone told her that one of the patients was the Chief of Police, Guy Barnett. She was stunned. She knew him, and yet she could not recognize him that day. He had had to identify himself to the nurses too, apparently, because they had not been able to recognize him either. From the extent of his injuries, she knew that he needed to be one of the first to be transferred, either by ambulance or by helicopter, whatever they could get and as soon as they could get it.

Other people were still screaming; their cries of pain seemed endless, as did the number of victims. She had never seen a disaster like this, on a scale like this, and certainly never expected to see it in a small town like Waverly. She had worked on GI bleeders day and night at DC General Hospital, patients who were vomiting blood and bleeding out and knocking on death's door, but never, ever, had she had to deal with that number of people, all shouting at one time, all screaming with pain, still smoking hot and with their skin coming off. It was the worst possible situation.

DR. ALI HAD been in surgery until noon, and had returned to Waverly Clinic to see more patients as part of his Friday afternoon schedule. Until a knock on the door to the exam room changed all his plans for that afternoon, and for many more afternoons to follow.

Dr. Ali opened the door to find none other than his executive secretary, Glenda Phelan, standing there. The picture of calm, she said in a quiet, even tone, "Dr. Maysoon just called from the Emergency Room. The train has exploded. She wants you to come to the ER as soon as you can."

He threw his stethoscope around his neck and left. The drive from the clinic to the hospital took less than ten minutes, and from his car he could see the smoke from the explosion. It looked like an atomic bomb had gone off in the middle of Waverly. Arriving in the hospital parking lot, he was met with a sight that confirmed his worst fears. There were so many vehicles parked in front of the ER, he had to park farther back. All around him, people were getting out of cars and truck beds with their clothes still smoking, white plumes rising from their bodies as they headed toward the back door to the ER. And he thought then, *We have a disaster on our hands.*

Rushing to the ER, he opened the door, and the scene that greeted him was straight out of hell. There were so many patients. So many nurses, running around not knowing what to do. Doctors, all the doctors, trying to help. But none of them were surgeons. None of them were trauma specialists. And the train had just exploded minutes ago, it had just happened, and nobody had had time to think or process. On top of that, the power was out, and the generator had yet to kick in, so the nurses and doctors were trying to examine patients with only the aid of handheld flashlights.

And then there was everybody else. It seemed as though the rest of the town was there too, crowding through the back door that was less than five feet wide and thronging the corridor. Everybody seemed to be looking for somebody. For a member of their family, he supposed, or a friend. Or even just being busybodies. He didn't know. He'd been there only a year and a half; he didn't know who was who.

Dr. Leffall's words echoed in his mind: "And above all, equanimity under duress."

He took a deep breath and straightened his spine.

As luck would have it, 3:00 P.M. was also the time of the nurses' shift change, as it was and still is at most US hospitals. That meant there were two shifts of nurses on hand, already in the building. That was something positive. That was a great start. He saw his scrub nurses, Sam and Nancy, already there. The Director of

Nurses, Cheryl Allen, was there. And there were many others from the nursing and medical staff arriving to help, including Dr. Mark Hartley and one of the hospital's founders, Dr. Doris Sanders.

One of the nurses, Vicki Stoops, came up to him and asked, "Dr. Ali, what should we hang up? We don't have enough lactated Ringer's, or normal saline, or anything."

"Hang whatever you can find," he told her. "First, you hang D5 in lactated Ringer's or D5 in normal saline. If you don't find D5, you just hang plain normal saline or plain lactated Ringer's. You don't find that, you hang D5W. But you gotta have an IV."

Another nurse came up behind Vicki and told him, "Dr. Ali, we don't know what to do. We're not getting any guidance. We don't know what to do about narcotics. And we don't have enough."

He instructed, "You give either 100 mg of Demerol with 50 mg of Phenergan, or give morphine and Phenergan, and just don't worry about an order. You have my order."

He turned to another nurse. "And call Operation Black," he told her.

He began trying to push forward into one of the small rooms with Vicki, who, frustrated, told him, "We can't move around; people are everywhere."

At that point, Dr. Ali got up on a gurney in the hallway between the two rooms and announced in his loudest controlled voice, "I am Dr. Subhi Ali. I am a trauma surgeon, and I am a Major in the US Army. And I AM IN CHARGE.

"We have asked Fort Campbell to send helicopters, but right now, we cannot do our job with everybody in the corridor. We appreciate your concern, but if we're gonna be able to do this job, we need people to clear out. If you are a patient, please stay. If you are a nurse, please stay. If you are a doctor, please stay. If you are an EMT or with the police or the ambulance service, please stay. If you are not any of those, please get out of here. NOW. So that we can deal with this."

Most people did clear out then, and he turned to Dr. Walker and asked him to call the hospitals in Nashville. One of the ambulance personnel informed them both that he had already put out a mayday call. The call had gone out on ambulance radio dispatch: "Mayday, mayday, mayday. If you have any ambulances you can spare, we need them in Waverly, Tennessee."

Dr. Ali noticed then that there was a lot of activity around the obstetrics room, so he headed that way. There he found Dr. McClure asking for instruments to do a venous cutdown, and in the room were two stretchers. On the stretchers were a man and a little girl. The girl wasn't as critical as the man, who was so badly burned that Dr. Ali didn't recognize him.

The man apparently knew him, however, and called out, "Dr. Ali!"

"Yes!"

"Dr. Ali, it's Frank Craver. Please help my daughter."

SAM AND NANCY did what they could, starting IVs and giving morphine. They couldn't believe how badly the patients were burned. So much so as to be unrecognizable. Sam passed by someone, and he hollered, "Sam! Please help me!" She had no idea who it was. He said, "It's Riley. I'm Riley." It was Riley Turner. She had worked with him in the hospital, where he was an orderly; he was also one of the volunteer firemen. And she didn't recognize him now.

Because of the shortage of ambulances, patients were brought up in personal vehicles, in cars and even lying in the beds of pickup trucks. But some literally walked in by themselves. Their clothes were burned off, everything but their leather belts and shoes. Their hair was gone. But they were walking in, like the living dead.

And many didn't want to be touched. Everywhere was painful. Those who were sitting up sat in a stiffened and unnatural posture, not wanting to move because of the pain. Some were already beginning to swell, and fluid was seeping from their deep, full-thickness burns.

Sam looked around at all these patients and thought, *What am I doing? What can I possibly do?*

She wanted to scream. The patients, they were just . . . everywhere. There seemed to be no end to them. Within 18 minutes, the Humphreys County Ambulance Service had delivered 39 additional patients, most of whom had severe second- and third-degree burns. And they kept calling her name, and Nancy's name, and the names of the other nurses, and she didn't know them. She and Nancy were in scrubs, and as they walked through the rooms and the corridor, with patients on the floor and sitting leaning against the walls, some of the patients would pull on the legs of their scrub pants, asking, "Can you please give me some pain medicine?"

From her mock-disaster training the week before, Nancy remembered the tags. The ID tags that would help them keep up with all these patients. She ran to get them, and told her fellow nurses to put one on the wrist of every patient. The tag would become that patient's chart while they were in triage. The nurses would ask each patient his or her name and write it on the tag, ask if they were allergic to anything if they were conscious enough to answer, and then, as Nancy instructed, they would record on the tag who had gotten morphine or Demerol, how much, and what time it was given. She had recognized the very real risk of overdose in that chaos.

Nancy put her head down and worked as if in a trance, not thinking, not feeling, just trying to be on autopilot to help the patients who were all around her now. Dr. Ali was calm, and he was keeping everybody else calm. There was no reason to panic. If she had seen him panicking, she couldn't have done it, because she would have known then they were in deep trouble. But they had a good leader and a good medical staff, and she knew they could handle it.

The patients who could speak clearly kept telling her about how the tank had exploded, how the fires were everywhere in New Town, how badly so many were injured, but she couldn't believe what they were telling her. She kept thinking, *That couldn't happen*. But she knew the train had derailed. She knew there was propane in those tankers. She knew all this, and still she thought, *Nah, it can't be this bad. I don't believe it*. Even though she was seeing all these patients, the severity of their burns, with her own eyes, and how they kept coming in, she still could not believe. This sort of thing only happened in mock drills. This sort of thing couldn't happen in Waverly.

COOTER BOWEN HAD been behind the funeral home helping to unload a delivery truck when he heard a tremendous boom. He felt the ground beneath him vibrate, and saw the vibration go through the stores on Main Street. He knew immediately what it must be, and looking down the hill toward the railroad, his suspicion was confirmed by the giant fireball going up from the derailment site. It was a great big ball of red flames with black smoke that kept expanding and expanding, and in just a few minutes, the two ambulances from the county ambulance service, which was by that time located by the nursing home beside the hospital, came off the hill behind him and sped down toward the railroad crossing.

He knew that those were the only two certified ambulances for the entire county, and thought to himself, *They're not gonna have enough help*. He watched one and then the other of them come back through, back up the hill to the hospital, and seeing no more ambulances coming from anywhere else, he made the decision to go down to the explosion site himself. It was his father's voice in his head saying, "You get who you get. When the call comes in, you get going. You don't hesitate. If you're doing something, you just drop it where you are and go."

Luff-Bowen still had one of the combination vehicles, and it still had emergency equipment on it, so Cooter turned to the delivery truck driver and said, "Y'all finish unloading this truck. I got to go. I'll take an ambulance over there and see if I can help."

When he arrived at the site, it was bedlam. There were people standing around, people with their clothes on fire, people yelling for help, men from the fire and police departments running back and forth trying to help victims and trying to get hoses on the fire. There were people rolling in what snow was left on the ground, people running down to Trace Creek to throw themselves into the cold water. Part of the propane tank had blown clear over a building and landed on a car by the garment factory. He learned later that another part of the tank landed in somebody's front lawn over 100 yards away. And then there was that cloud of black smoke, which could be seen for miles.

Cooter loaded one burn victim on the stretcher, and found four others who were mobile and told them to pile into the combination vehicle with him. As he came back through town on his way to the hospital, he saw his uncle, Fred Hutchison, who was manager of the furniture store, standing in the middle of the intersection of Highway 13 and Main Street, directing traffic. Cooter could not process, at first, why his uncle was standing there in the middle of Main Street. Then he realized how congested the streets were becoming, with people trying to get down to their loved ones who might or might not have been at the derailment site, and with others who had just been going about their Friday afternoon at the moment the tanker blew. But that intersection had to be kept clear for emergency vehicles to get to the hospital, and the fact that it was his uncle, a civilian, taking charge of traffic must mean there was no one else to do it. As Cooter sped past his uncle, a sobering thought took hold: all of Waverly's existing police force must either be helping at the explosion site or among the injured themselves.

When he got to the hospital, it looked like a madhouse. He couldn't believe the number of people trying to get into the emergency room. As he helped unload the five people from his ambulance, he saw Dr. Ali directing triage. Of course they were lucky to have a trauma surgeon on hand; still, he didn't know if that little hospital was equipped to handle a disaster of this magnitude. With the way things were looking, he just didn't see how they could do it. But he would keep doing his best to help, and he knew the folks at the hospital would too. He left and went back to the explosion to get more people out.

3:05 P.M.

A man, a young man, came into the second-floor hospital room that was still occupied by Mrs. Monroe and her mother. "Do you have a towel I can wet?" he asked.

"No, but I've got this gown," Mrs. Monroe replied. "You wanna wet it?"

"Well, that'll do." He took the used gown from her and left.

Mrs. Monroe and her mother knew there was some sort of emergency going on, because they had heard Dr. Maysoon paged to the ER just minutes before, but they did not know the nature or extent of the crisis. They made their way to the top of the stairs leading down to the first floor of the hospital, and waited there on the landing for some help. The electricity had gone out for several minutes. Their nurse came running up to them and told Mrs. Monroe, "Get your mother downstairs best way you can." Then she ran off again. *Well, how strange,* Mrs. Monroe thought.

She waited until the lights came back on and got her mother down the stairs on her own.

When they got to where the cafeteria was on the first floor, they saw people in there frantically getting ice and throwing it all on their backs. Other people were hollering for towels and clean sheets. It was pandemonium down there, and they still didn't know why.

THE PICKUP TRUCK carrying Sergeant Toad Smith pulled up at the back door to the Nautilus Hospital Emergency Room. As Toad stretched one leg out to descend from the truck, he realized that the pair of double-knit trousers he had been wearing were now welded onto the backs of his legs. He had not known before that his legs were burned. And the jacket he had reached for and put on as a second thought the moment before the explosion, the back of it had burned too, but thankfully, there was fiberglass insulation inside the lining, which in the end helped to save his back, limiting the percentage of his body affected by full-thickness burns. He had a wool shirt on underneath his jacket, and when they got that wool shirt off in the ER later, Toad saw that it had gotten hot enough through that jacket that it looked as though someone had taken a very hot iron to an ironing board and scorched the shirt. If he hadn't put his jacket on, he might not have survived.

Toad was also wearing an old police cap made of plastic, and it had melted and run down into his hair. Although his hair was singed, the cap had served to protect most of his head, which had been another unexpected bit of good fortune.

Outside the entrance to the ER, David Dillingham was helping to transport other casualties, and when Toad saw him, he gave him his walkie-talkie, which had by now burned a permanent imprint into the palm of Toad's left hand. "David," he said, "I'm not gonna need it. And y'all will probably need it down at the site."

Toad walked into the ER of his own volition, and saw how busy it was. All the doctors in there were so busy, and the nurses were running around helping out; he wasn't sure whom to ask for help. Finally Dr. Ali saw him, and told a nurse to take him back to the ward. As he walked back there, he could see there were people, burn victims, all over the ER. One person was stuck down in a bed like they were doing a push-up, with all the flesh on their arms hanging off like shreds of cloth. Toad thought it was a man, but couldn't be sure. He couldn't identify the person's race, sex, or anything else, but he knew the image would remain with him for the rest of his days.

The nurse who took him back helped him get out of his burned clothes and into a hospital bed. Pulling the melted trousers off the backs of his legs was agony, and he was certain some fibers must still be stuck in his burned legs. He helped the nurse remove his gun belt, and was still stunned that he could use his hands as well as he could. Once the belt was off, she gave him a shot of Demerol, and the world faded.

3:10 P.M.

When Buddy returned to the site of the explosion, he found a boy who had been burned quite badly. He didn't know who he was, but he got him into the car as soon as he found him, and rushed him to the emergency room. As he was helping him into the ER, the boy said, "I can't see." It was then that Buddy recognized the voice. It was one of his friends. He had his arm around him, helping him navigate that narrow doorway, and until that moment he hadn't even known who he was.

Buddy was in the ER that second time for just a minute, but during that minute, he recognized Frank Craver, lying on a stretcher. He didn't know how he knew him; maybe it was the shape of his head or the look of his eyes. But he knew it was Frank, just as he had known it was Chief Barnett when he had picked him up earlier. When Buddy saw Frank, he thought, *You can't live. There's no way you could live.* The only parts that weren't charred on Frank's body were the whites of his eyes and his teeth. *There's no way you can survive this, my friend. There's no way you're going to survive this at all.*

DR. MCCLURE SPOKE in Dr. Ali's ear, "This is my friend, Frank Craver, and his daughter Susan. I can't find anywhere to get an IV started on him."

"Try his ankle," Dr. Ali advised. "The nurses are bringing more IV kits."

Dr. Ali walked back down the corridor and in and out of the two rooms, taking stock of the scene. The helicopters were not there yet. Ambulances were not there yet. Auxiliary power had not come online yet, so they were still in the dark. And the hospital was already near full bed capacity with the doctors' regular patients. But the most pressing issue would be deciding which of the burn victims would go first on the helicopters that would soon be arriving from Fort Campbell, and he wasn't going to send a patient on a chopper without an IV. And they had to have something for pain.

He asked Vicki, who was still by his side, to bring enough central venous catheters and gloves to start central venous lines on everyone. It was impossible to start the usual peripheral IV lines in most of the patients, since so many had burns on their extremities, and there really was no time for him alone to attempt venous cutdowns on the lower extremities of all these patients—and too often, many of them had full-thickness, third-degree burns on their legs that would have made that a daunting and time-consuming task in the best of circumstances.

He was prepared to insert the central lines by flashlight, but after what felt like hours, and just as Vicki had finished gathering the necessary equipment, the auxiliary power unit was started and the lights came on. So he and Vicki went from patient to patient to begin central lines, via the subclavian vein beneath the clavicle. Vicki handed him the equipment, and he located and stuck the veins, establishing crucial intravenous access for fluids and medications.

They did this on one patient after another. With Vicki as his assistant, Dr. Ali cleaned the puncture site, performed the procedure to insert the catheter into the central vein, confirmed access, changed gloves, and moved on to the next patient and the next central line. And on to the next. And to the next. Until everyone had IV access. The subclavian vein can be hard to find, especially in burn patients, but Dr. Ali would remember later, with some astonishment, that he didn't miss a single stick. Amidst the chaos, he hit every vein on the first try.

As he was inserting central lines, he was also assessing which patients were most in need of emergent transfer, and after all IVs had been established, he was able to tell the nurses which patients would go first on the helicopters. He labeled them by number in order of priority, and pointed them out to the nurses: "This is Number One, Two, Three . . ."

He had told Drs. Walker and McClure earlier that he would take responsibility for the prioritization of patients for helicopter transfer. His status as a newcomer had suddenly become an advantage. "You can't do this; you're from town," he told them. "You know these people well and they know you. I'll do it."

3:15 P.M.

Buddy returned to the explosion site again, where it was mass chaos. He came upon a lady who told him her name was Florence Matlock and that she was a nurse. "If you can get me to the hospital, I can help people," she said.

"All right, get in and I'll get you up there."

As he was trying to work his way through the traffic that had now clogged all of downtown, trying to find a path to the hospital, Buddy wrestled with whether or not to tell Ms. Matlock what he suspected. Although he didn't know the Matlocks well, he did know that her husband, Melvin Matlock, was a volunteer fireman for the Waverly Fire Department, and he had a strong suspicion he'd been killed instantly when the tank blew, because he remembered where Melvin had been standing when he left the site to pick up Ted.

So here I am, Melvin's wife in the car with me, taking her up to the hospital so she can help other people. And her not knowing that her husband may have been killed. But he did not know it beyond a shadow of a doubt; he had not yet had it confirmed, so he kept silent.

3:55 P.M.

Nancy stood up from the floor, from the patient beside whom she had been kneeling, when she heard the unmistakable sound. Choppers. They were finally there. It had been less than an hour, but seemed like many more. She went to the back door of the ER and opened it, and was overjoyed to see the straight, dark line of whirring metal birds in the sky. It looked like Fort Campbell had sent all their medevac helicopters. One would land and pick up patients while the others hovered above, then the next would take its turn.

Nancy and the other nurses helped transfer the patients onto the choppers in the order Dr. Ali had designated, running alongside their stretchers and holding their IV bottles, just like a scene out of *M*A*S*H*.

Forty patients were triaged, treated or stabilized, and given dispositions in the Nautilus ER—all within an hour's time. Ninety-eight of Nautilus Memorial's 105 employees had responded to the call of Operation Black. Even receptionists and clerks helped out in the ER, fetching equipment and supplies.

After the helicopters, ambulances from surrounding counties began streaming in, around 4:30 or 5:00 P.M., with more supplies. Thirty counties responded to Waverly's mayday calls with 49 ambulances. Patients who were not triaged as severe enough for helicopter transport, but who still needed transfer to burn centers in Nashville, were loaded into the ambulances. By the time the first out-of-county surgeon arrived by ambulance, Dr. Ali and his team had already completed triage, transferred the worst cases by helicopter, and were prepping to operate. The outside surgeon told Dr. Ali, "Well, I came to help, but it looks like you've already taken care of everything! I'll go back with my ambulance."

5:00 P.M.

Nancy had a child at home, and couldn't get to him due to her duties at the hospital as well as the blockade of the town that had been set up by law enforcement agencies, to allow firefighters to deal with the existing fires and to keep the area clear in case the second propane tank should blow. Her brother-in-law had been burned; he was working in the lumber yard at the time of the explosion, and a part of the burning wall had fallen over on him.

Sam also had a child who had been at home since school had let out earlier that day. Both she and Nancy were concerned for their children's safety, and for the safety of their other family members and friends—those who had not already come through the ER as their patients.

Once patient transfers had been completed and dispositions determined, in the briefest lull between the madness of triage and prepping for surgery, they found an open landline, and each of them took turns calling home and calling family members. Once they knew their children were safe and could spend the night with family, they were relieved enough to refocus their attention on the operations to come.

AFTER ALL PATIENTS had been given dispositions (readied for transfer or admitted to Nautilus Memorial), Dr. Ali began rounding on the admitted patients. Dr. McClure had already admitted Toad Smith to the ward, and asked Dr. Ali to consult on him. When Dr. Ali examined Toad's burns, he was particularly concerned by the extent of the damage to both of his hands. "You need to go, Mr. Smith," he told him. "You need to be transferred."

"Nope," Toad replied. "There are people more sick than me. I'll stay here and let you operate."

Five others had also sustained burns that would require surgery, and Dr. Ali offered all of them the chance to be transferred to one of the major burn centers in Nashville or elsewhere in the region, but each wanted to stay at Nautilus Memorial.

6:00 P.M.

Nurse anesthetist John Bryant had returned immediately when news of the train explosion reached him, and Dr. Ali and his team began operating on the first of the six patients scheduled for surgery that night, a volunteer fireman whose burns were the most severe.

Surgical treatment of burn patients involves debridement (removal) of burned and nonviable tissue as well as thorough cleaning to aid with wound healing. The fireman's face was burned so badly that Dr. Ali had to debride skin from his neck all the way up to his scalp.

For Toad Smith, whose hands were completely burned from the wrists down, Dr. Ali surgically degloved his hands, removing all the skin from the wrists to the fingertips. Failing to do so would have meant leaving necrotic tissue that would become infected, leading to a range of possible complications that could include finger or limb loss due to gangrene, sepsis due to systemic infection, and even death. Having a surgeon on hand who could complete the necessary operations before much time had elapsed gave the Nautilus burn patients the best possible advantage when it came to avoiding complications.

To prepare each patient for surgery, Nancy, Sam, Barbara, and a fourth nurse, Mary Frank Williams, had to clean them from head to toe as best they could, focusing especially on the burned areas to be debrided. It was a near-impossible task, given the amount of debris that had covered and settled on everyone in the vicinity when the explosion occurred, and how any remaining clothing stuck to the burned flesh, but they did the best they could. Barbara saw firsthand what her mother must have gone through. The smell of iodine filled the room as they then washed the areas to be surgically treated with Betadine, the golden-brown, povidone-iodine antiseptic solution used to disinfect skin before operating.

After each debridement, the nurses applied Furacin (nitrofurazone) dressings to the burn wounds. Furacin—still in use to this day—is a medication used on burns and certain other wounds, such as skin grafts, to prevent and treat infections. The nurses had to make the dressings themselves by mixing the Furacin with Vaseline and smearing it over layer after layer of gauze.

To make multiple dressings, they started with a white, porcelain tray. They took a roll of Kerlix gauze and unrolled it, then cut it into strips. Then they took another Kerlix roll and did the same, and another and another. The nurses smeared a layer of the medicinal mixture over the gauze, and laid some more gauze down on top of that. And when that was done, they put a lid on the porcelain tray and put it in the autoclave to sterilize the dressings. Each time they dressed a wound or changed a dressing, they would take the tray out of the autoclave, take a strip of the specially prepared gauze, now heavy and greasy with the medicinal mixture, and lay it across the wound, one strip at a time.

If, when preparing the dressings, they happened to put too much Furacin on the gauze, it would bubble out in the autoclave, and then they had that greasy mess to clean up.

Conveniently prepackaged, single-use, disposable latex gloves were not yet widely available or standard of care. Instead, the nurses sterilized the surgical gloves by washing, drying, and powdering them, turning them inside out, laying them in a package on top of each other, and putting them in the autoclave.

The nurses repeated this sequence of events throughout the night, with each surgical patient. Bring the patient down to the OR, clean them, prep them, assist Dr. Ali during the operation, apply the Furacin dressings, move supplies to the next OR, clean up the room just vacated, and sterilize gloves and more dressings. They were exhausted, but they had to keep moving. The patients were depending on them. And on their minds was that second propane tank. They didn't know what they were going to do if it also blew. There would be no end to the destruction.

7:00 P.M.

Dr. Maysoon had stayed late at the hospital, until all the patients had dispositions and had either been transferred or settled for the night, then went home to relieve her daughters' teenage babysitter. As she left the hospital, she was grateful, not for the first time, for her training at DC General Hospital on the Howard University Medical Service. The residents and fellows there had been expected to start IVs, draw blood, do nearly everything, especially overnight when the day nurses and phlebotomists were gone. She and Dr. Ali had had grueling but excellent training there, and she felt Waverly had benefited from that on that day.

She had taken extra time writing her patient notes before leaving for the night; she wanted every burn victim she had treated to have careful documentation in case it was needed later, because she couldn't shake the feeling that there would be lawsuits to follow. Surely the railroad would have to do something to compensate all these people.

As she drove back down the hill from the hospital on her way home, she could not believe what she saw: all the debris, the devastation, the fires still smoldering against the horizon. The entire New Town section of Waverly was gone.

IN THE OPERATING ROOM, Dr. Ali had a Polaroid camera and a tissue camera, which had a string that could be placed 16 inches from a piece of tissue for the picture to be taken and sent with the specimen to pathology. That night, he used the Polaroid to take pictures of all the injuries he treated. He felt certain there would be litigation to follow, lawsuits that would be brought by the victims against L&N, and he documented as much as he could so that his patients and their attorneys could use the photos in court later.

At one point that night when Dr. Ali was between operations, the Fort Campbell helicopter pilots returned with two of the Nautilus nurses who had gone with them. The captain in charge approached Dr. Ali and told him, "You know, things seem to be quiet now, so we'll be going back to Fort Campbell."

He responded, "Like hell. You are not leaving yet. We have another tank, a second tank, that may blow at any time. They're calling it the 'time bomb tank.' That's what the police have told us. They've evacuated that entire area because the second tank could blow, the same way the first one did. And I've got a hospital full of patients. I don't have a single bed left."

"Well..."

"So, you understand? What we've got is a hospital that is at its max and a second tank in the middle of town that is literally in the middle of the fire, that could explode at any minute, and the whole town is on edge. And we've finally got your three helicopters here and you want to leave? No! You're gonna stay until I tell you that you can go. I'm a Major and I outrank you, Captain. I'll give you a place to rest, and sleep, and we'll feed you. We need you to stay."

Dr. Ali made good on his word, giving the helicopter crews room and board in the doctors' lounge, which had a few couches and a table, and was down the hall from the cafeteria, and offered them use of the shower in the doctors' locker room. They rested overnight while he operated.

Dr. Ali and his team operated through the night, moving back and forth between the two ORs. He wanted to get to all the patients that night who needed surgery; he did not want any waiting until the next day, due to the risk of infection taking hold in burned and necrotic skin.

Dr. Ali had had many years of experience treating burn patients at DC General Hospital, first as a surgical resident, then as chief resident, and then for three more years as an instructor and finally as assistant professor of surgery. The surgery department at DC General cared for all the burn patients who came to the city hospital, which was the only place they could go if they didn't have insurance. DC General did not have a dedicated burn unit, so the surgical intensive care unit (SICU) was used for all burn patients, and they stayed busy.

But nothing he had encountered in the past compared with a disaster of this magnitude. Reflecting on it later, he found he had gone into autopilot, exactly as he had been trained to do in the Army for a theater of war, where there would be a lot of casualties, and you do the best you can with what you have. He and the other doctors did the best they could, and the nurses did the best they could, with the training and the IVs and the narcotics they had on hand. And nobody died on their watch. Not a single living patient who entered Nautilus Memorial Hospital that day died while in their care. That was a triumph unto itself.

Between 3:00 and 3:30 A.M., Dr. Ali and his team finished the sixth operation. Dr. Ali's head hit his pillow at home about 20 minutes later. Around 4:30 A.M., after he had been asleep for barely half an hour, his bedside telephone rang. It was his father calling from Deir Debwan, his hometown in Palestine.

"People are telling me they saw on TV that there was a train explosion in Waverly, Tennessee. They saw it on the televisions in the cafes, and they called me. They've been calling me all morning here. But I guess if you are answering the phone, you're all right. Go back to sleep."

It was typical of his father to be so calm and matter-of-fact. Dr. Ali realized that by the time he had finished operating, international television news programs were already broadcasting the story of the explosion in Waverly. He hadn't even seen the news coverage himself, he had been so busy taking care of the patients, but people across the world were seeing it. Knowing there could be more to come, he went back to sleep.

COOTER SPENT ALL night in the warehouse at the back of the Humphreys County Gas Company building down on Church Street, next to Trace Creek. The warehouse had been turned into a makeshift morgue, and late that evening, a team of medical examiners had arrived from Memphis to help with the identification of the deceased. The state's chief medical examiner at the time was none other than Dr. Jerry Francisco, who, ten years earlier, had performed the Rev. Dr. Martin Luther King Jr.'s autopsy when Dr. King was assassinated in Memphis. And six months before he arrived in Waverly to provide his assistance in the wake of the disaster, he had overseen the autopsy on Elvis Presley (and unleashed years of controversy by refusing to make the autopsy report public). It was fair to say that Dr. Francisco had seen more dead bodies in his career than anyone else working in Waverly that night.

Five people had been killed immediately when the propane tanker blew open, and the bodies were charred and stiffened in grotesque positions. Identifying the bodies proved a difficult task due to the extent of the burns. Even race and ethnicity could not be discerned. If someone happened to have a leather wallet that was still attached and had a driver's license or some other form of identification that was still intact within it, that was a rare source of verifiable information for Cooter and the forensic pathology team. For most of the deceased, however, their clothing had been burned off them, as had much of their skin, so that the normal identifying characteristics, such as particular items of clothing, scars, tattoos, and the like, were absent.

One of the pathologists wanted to begin doing dental checks on those who could not otherwise be identified, but Dr. Francisco said, "No, take their shoes off." Like the leather wallets, if their shoes were made of leather, they did not burn. Nor did their leather belts. And once the shoes were off, the color of the skin beneath could be distinguished, and their shoe size, and that, coupled with accessories like their belts, at least gave Cooter enough information to begin calling families for verification.

Dr. Francisco's team left after all the deceased were identified, but Cooter continued working all night, making phone calls to families and different funeral homes when a family would indicate where they wanted their relative sent. A refrigerated trailer was brought in for cold storage of the bodies that couldn't immediately be sent out. For those whose services would be held at Luff-Bowen Funeral Home, he had to assess whether or not any accessible, uncharred vessels were left to make embalming possible. Whether or not an open-casket funeral was even an option.

FOR BUDDY FRAZIER, the rest of the evening and night remained chaotic. Outside resources started pouring in, from law enforcement and fire services across the state. There was more help than they could use; it was a good position to be in, especially with that other tank sitting there like a ticking time bomb. Mutual aid fire companies, including those from McEwen, New Johnsonville, Camden, and Dickson, had arrived early on and were pumping water from Trace Creek to hose down the multiple fires that were burning across New Town. They were also keeping the second propane tank, which was surrounded by fire, under a steady flow of water.

Within an hour of the blast, the mayor of Dickson, Tennessee, and Dickson's police chief, whom Buddy knew, were in Waverly; they had come from over 25 miles away and met Buddy in the street, where they asked him, "What can we do to help you all? What do you all need?"

I don't know what we need, Buddy thought. *I don't know. I'm not the chief and I'm not in charge. All I know is we got a mess.*

In addition to the Tennessee Highway Patrol and the Tennessee Bureau of Criminal Investigation, law enforcement relief units arrived from 14 county sheriff's offices and 17 city police departments. Thirty-eight fire and rescue departments from as far away as Memphis, as well as the Tennessee Association of Rescue Squads, sent personnel and equipment.

A staging area was set up at the National Guard armory on the west edge of town, with all the extra fire-fighting equipment staged there. A command post was set up in the police department, with representatives from multiple state agencies there. In City Hall, the politicians gathered. The Governor of Tennessee, Ray Blanton, came to Waverly. Major General Carl E. Wallace, the adjutant general of the Tennessee National Guard, who had previously lived and worked in Waverly, was there. The vice president of the L&N Railroad, Colonel Phil Hooper, was there. For lack of anywhere else to sleep, he wound up taking a bed in the Humphreys County jail for two nights.

Everyone was visibly shaken. As Buddy would always recall, the mayor of Waverly, Dr. James Powers, was a big man, a big statue of a man. He always seemed capable of handling anything, but Buddy could tell that this had taken everything out of him. The police chief was his personal friend, as he was to many. The fire chief was his good friend. In a small town, that's the way things were.

Although the police radio system still worked, the phone circuits were jammed, and nothing could be done by phone. Barbara Horner's husband, Richard, who worked as a lineman for South Central Bell, toiled all night as part of the large crew trying to restore the phone lines that had been destroyed in the explosion or burned in the ensuing fires.

There was, however, a dedicated Civil Defense telephone line that was connected to nearly every police department in the state and to every state Civil Defense department. The Governor's residence was connected, as were many state agencies. Soon after the explosion, state officials cleared that whole net of any phone traffic unless it was related to Waverly.

At some point on Friday night, while Buddy was back at the police department, a call came in from the White House. It was President Jimmy Carter on the line, and he wanted to speak to

Mayor Powers. Buddy went over to City Hall to get the mayor and bring him back to the police department so he could be on the call with the President.

They finally got the call set up, and heard the President's voice on the line. "Mayor, what do you need? What do you all need down there?"

Mayor Powers answered, "Mr. President, we need Air Force hospital planes. We've got all these patients, and our surgeon is telling me we need to move them around the country. Some have been sent to Nashville, but they need to go farther than that, to the burn centers in Louisville, Cincinnati, Birmingham, and so on."

LATE INTO THE night, someone in authority sent Buddy to the Elks Lodge, where Lodge members had prepared big pots of stew and soup and sandwiches. They filled the trunk of his patrol car with the food, and Buddy went down to the site, behind the fire lines, to serve the firemen who were putting out what was left of the fires and keeping the remaining tank cool. He made several trips like this, delivering food on into the night. He'd pull up behind the lines, open the trunk of his car, and the firemen would go and get anything they wanted to eat.

One of the worst parts about Friday afternoon and evening for those who had not been injured was not knowing where their loved ones were. Phone lines were down across town, and Buddy kept running into people trying to find their husbands or wives or children. Even his own parents did not know how or where he was. At one point someone told him, "Your daddy 'bout tore the door off that police department over there trying to get in to find where you and your brother were, and if you were okay."

At the radio station, WPHC-AM/WVRY-FM, station manager Dean Bush allowed listeners to call in and let their loved ones know, over the radio, that they were safe. Hour after hour, in between updates and announcements from city and state officials, the station aired messages from frantic mothers looking for their children, some of whom had been evacuated from day care centers nearby; from adult children letting their parents hear their voices and know not to worry; from all manner of friends and family letting their loved ones know they were safe and where their current location was.

Mr. Bush and his staff had been covering the derailment since Wednesday night, and Friday afternoon, their police monitor had picked up Toad Smith's frantic plea for emergency help. They had only to look out the window of the radio station—which was four miles from the blast—to see the black smoke and flames from the explosion. They ran their first bulletin regarding the explosion at 3:02 P.M. on Friday, and continued broadcasting updates throughout the evening and night. WVRY-FM stayed on the air, providing round-the-clock coverage, while WPHC-AM switched to emergency broadcast to air information on emergency requests and procedures from 5:30 P.M. to 9:00 P.M.

In their updates, Bush and his colleagues broadcast information as it was received on the extent of property damage and the condition of the injured, including their transfers to hospitals in other cities. In addition to their broadcast bulletins, they also served as a key means of communication from Waverly to the outside world. City officials had asked them to broadcast a request for surrounding cities and towns to send firefighters and equipment, given not only the magnitude of the fire, but also the fact that both of Waverly's own fire trucks had been damaged beyond use and several of the city's firefighters had been severely injured or possibly even killed.

The radio station also broadcast Mayor Powers's announcements regarding the need to evacuate the city and which buildings were available to the public as shelters, including the

National Guard Armory and local schools and churches. A call to action went out for volunteers to donate food and bedding both for the evacuees and for those whose homes had been destroyed in the blast.

Buddy's own home, where he had taken the L&N conductor to call his supervisors Wednesday night, was in the one-mile evacuation zone that had been established until the second tank could be unloaded and the area declared safe. He and his wife were working constantly throughout the night, but they had friends on the east side of town who offered their home if they needed a place to stay. At the very least, it was a place where they could get a shower. Buddy had always found that, after working all night, if he could just get a shower, it brought him back around and gave him the rejuvenation he needed to keep on going.

JUST ACROSS THE street from the northern edge of the evacuation zone was the home of 14-year-old Zach Clayton and his family. Zach, like all the other schoolchildren in Waverly, had been home early that day due to the countywide teacher planning session. His father, Bill Clayton, who was the county supervisor for the Farmers Home Administration, was working in his office at the courthouse. His mother was also out, so he was by himself at their house on Stewart Lane, barely more than a mile from the derailment site.

At 2:55 P.M., he heard the windows pop, like when the wind blows hard against them or a severe thunderstorm has come up. But it wasn't windy, and it wasn't storming. He looked out the front window of the sitting room and saw the black smoke. From right across the tree lines, straight as an arrow, he saw it coming up.

Soon after, Dottie Dodd, a neighbor and friend from the end of Stewart Lane, came and got him. Somehow Zach's mother had gotten in touch with Dottie. "Your mother wanted me to come get you," Dottie told him. "The tanker has exploded in downtown Waverly. There's no telling how many people have lost their lives because of this."

AT TIM BARNETT'S house, his father had never come home. He didn't know what had happened for a while, because his mother hadn't come home either. It probably wasn't more than an hour or two, but it seemed like forever until the phone finally rang. It was his mother, telling him that his daddy had been hurt, and they were going to take him to Nashville. She asked Tim if she needed to come get him or send someone for him.

"No, Mom, I'm fine," her 12-year-old son told her. "Just get with Dad."

CHAPTER ELEVEN

The Day After

FEBRUARY 25, 1978
SATURDAY
7:00 A.M.

AFTER TWO OR THREE HOURS of sleep, Dr. Ali was back at the hospital early to check on his patients. As always, Sam was there to meet him for rounds.

"Did you ever make it home last night?" he asked her.

"No, Dr. Ali, I spent the whole night here. So did Nancy. A lot of us did. Cheryl and Barbara, too. And I think Dr. McClure's house may be in the one-mile evacuation zone they set up yesterday. There's still that second tank, and we don't know if it's gonna blow too. And I don't know what we'll do if it does. There'll be no end to the destruction."

"That's exactly why I told those helicopters from Fort Campbell to stay. And they will be here until we get the all-clear on that second tank."

"Well, listen, Dr. Ali—things would not have gone well yesterday had you not been here. I'm sure of it."

They began their rounds with the fireman who had gone to surgery first the night before. Dr. Ali had admitted him to the first bed in the intensive care unit, and was concerned about his

113

condition. Extensive burn injuries cause swelling, and given that his neck and face were involved, and that he likely had lung injury from smoke inhalation, he was beginning to have trouble breathing. He had wanted to stay in Waverly with his family, but Dr. Ali had to tell his family: "The next thing I would have to do on your dad is a tracheostomy and hook him up to the ventilator. And that is beyond what I would like to do in this little hospital."

He explained that without a burn unit, he had done all he could surgically, and he recommended immediate transfer. The family agreed.

When he got to Mr. Toad Smith, he saw that Mr. Smith's face and eyes had swollen as well, but not nearly to the extent of the previous patient, and his airway was not in danger.

"Dr. Ali, I can hear you but I can't see you."

"That's because your face and eyes are swollen, Mr. Smith. That's to be expected from the burns you had all around your head. You have third-degree burns on your forehead and down the left side of your face. The swelling will go down, but I would feel more comfortable if you would agree to be transferred to Nashville today. And it would be good to get rehab on your hands."

"Well, all right. Whatever you think is best."

"Good. I'll let your family doctor, Dr. McClure, know, and we'll get you transferred."

TIM BARNETT'S BROTHER, Oak, had come to get him after he was finally able to make it home from work Friday evening, and took him to their cousin's house in Dickson, where Tim stayed Friday night and Saturday night. Nobody was telling him anything, and the 12-year-old was angry and confused. *Where is everybody? Where's my mom? What the heck is going on back home?* Standing outside at his cousin's house, staring at the full moon, he kept wondering, *Is my dad alive?*

Back in Waverly, Tim's friend Zach Clayton had been reunited with his parents on Friday at their house on the corner of Powers Boulevard and Stewart Lane. Several friends and neighbors whose homes were within the evacuation zone started coming over to stay and wait for the all-clear to be given on the second tank. They gathered together in the Clayton family's basement and waited. And waited. Zach got the eerie feeling that they were all just waiting for the other shoe to drop.

On the nightly news, they saw that Waverly was the lead story. Much of what they first saw and heard about what was happening just over a mile away from them was on that television screen, reported by the likes of Walter Cronkite and John Chancellor on the national news.

Once the phone lines were restored, Zach's parents started getting phone calls from out-of-town friends who had seen and heard the news of the disaster in Waverly. "Hey, are y'all okay?" they would ask. "We heard there's been an explosion and all of Waverly has been wiped out."

While the extent of the damage was not quite as sensational as what was being presented on the news, there was still the threat of the second tank, and how much more damage there would be if it, too, exploded.

WVRY kept everyone informed with their continued broadcast. At 3:15 P.M. on Saturday, listeners learned that a rail car full of paper products had reignited and burst into flames, which were quickly put out, but demonstrated how volatile the conditions remained at the scene. When the update came that the liquid propane from the second tank was about to be unloaded and transferred to a new, undamaged tanker, it was a nail-biting time for all who were listening, including those gathered not only in Zach's basement but in basements and shelters across the city that Saturday. *Is it going to happen again? Will that second tank explode?*

IT WASN'T UNTIL 10:30 P.M. Saturday night that WVRY broadcast the final announcement from General Carl Wallace that the second derailed tank car had been secured and the transfer of its liquid propane contents completed. Sam, Nancy, and Barbara finally left the hospital for the first time in two days. Cheryl Allen stayed until Sunday morning.

Patients kept coming into the hospital over the weekend; it seemed there was a second wave of injured, mostly those with smoke inhalation and more minor burns. Many of them had gone down to the site in the wake of the explosion either to look for loved ones or to see if they could render any aid. Several others were employees who had been working in the various New Town businesses at the time of the blast.

Dr. Joe McClure had spent Friday night at the hospital. The area around his home had been evacuated, and his wife and children had gone to stay with her mother in Dickson County. By the time he finally went home late Saturday night, he was exhausted, and he had had plenty of time to reflect on what he had seen and what they all had been through. He had never seen anything like it. Part of his medical practice was in occupational medicine, helping out at the factories and plants in the county, and sometimes he would be called upon to treat a chemical burn. But never anything like this. He didn't recall seeing anyone with minor burns from the propane explosion; everyone he saw was severely and seriously injured with third-degree burns. He had never before seen anyone burned to that extent.

He knew that propane causes a flash burn, with an intensity much greater than would be seen in the average house fire, and now he had seen the terrible results with his own eyes. It was a hot, igniting gas; it was there and then it was gone. But it was so intense, anyone who was close enough to get burned, got burned badly. He had seen many patients in the past 24 hours with burned backs; they had clearly been trying to escape the explosion. And so many of the people he had seen, the people burned so badly, were his friends. They were people he knew well. He went to church with them. He celebrated births and weddings with them. He had treated them and their families over the years as a family physician.

He had heard, he couldn't remember from whom, that one of his good friends and fellow member of the Waverly Church of Christ, Guy Barnett, had been pretty close to the blast, and he had been burned so severely that he was taken to the burn center in Birmingham, Alabama, where he was in critical condition. There had been a couple of people standing at the back door of one of the lumber companies when the tank exploded; he'd heard that they had died. The L&N employee who had been operating the crane—he was the one who had been moving those rail cars back onto the tracks. Dr. McClure had heard how he had been trapped up there in the cab of that crane for the longest time, where no one could get to him, no one could rescue him, and he was burned so extensively that he died too.

He remembered there had been a boy—or he seemed like just a boy—that he had cared for in the ER. He was a policeman; he must have been a policeman, because all Dr. McClure could remember was that he had been wearing a gun belt. He may have also had his shoes on. But nothing else. His clothes had been burned off. Dr. McClure had taken his gun off him, and gotten the nurses to cover him with clean sheets. Either he or Dr. Ali had put in an IV to get him ready for transfer.

And then there had been his friend and patient Frank Craver and his daughter Susan, who were now in Cincinnati. And his friend and patient Toad Smith, who was now in Nashville. And the fire chief, Wilbur York, who was pronounced dead at Vanderbilt the same day as the explosion, which had been just yesterday, but seemed like ten years ago now. And so many others. Some of them burned almost beyond recognition.

When he finally got home that night, Dr. McClure did something else he had never done before in his entire adult life. He sat down and cried.

CHAPTER TWELVE

The Greatest Sacrifice

FEBRUARY 26, 1978
SUNDAY

DR. ALI AND HIS SURGICAL team debrided again the five patients that remained on Sunday. Some of the burn patients stayed for weeks at Nautilus, undergoing wound care. Each time Nancy or Sam would change their dressings, it was agony for the patients, because they had to pull the old, greasy Furacin dressings off, which would inevitably pull away dead skin that was very slowly being replaced with new skin. This would also pull at the viable tissue underneath that had been exposed during the surgical debridement process, and the wounds were extremely tender.

Dressing changes were so painful, in fact, that patients were given morphine prior to their scheduled wound care. Sam and Nancy could tell from their faces, though, as they pulled their dressings off, that the pain was still agonizing for them. And yet every patient would say, "Oh, thank you, thank you," throughout their dressing change. It was amazing to the nurses how appreciative both the patients and their families were, even as they were going through the worst time of their lives.

Sam and Nancy used the bathtubs in the patients' rooms as whirlpools. The use of whirlpool therapy in the management of burns was used as a method of additional debridement; it was also useful for keeping the wounds free of debris and superficial bacteria, and for encouraging wound healing.

The nurses knew they didn't have to double-check one another's work. If Nancy told Sam she had already done something, Sam knew she didn't have to worry about it and could move on to her next task. She knew if Nancy said she had done it, then it had been done.

THE SKIN IS the body's largest organ, and its three layers—epidermis, dermis, and hypodermis—serve as the first line of defense against all manner of external insults, from ultraviolet radiation, dust, and chemicals, to mechanical injuries and burns. Keratinocytes, cells in the epidermis (outermost layer), are the body's primary source of Vitamin D. Merkel cells, also in the epidermis, are what make possible the sense of light touch, and thus they are found in greatest numbers in the tips of the fingers.

In the second layer of skin, the dermis, sweat glands help with cooling through perspiration and hair follicles produce hair. The dermis houses many of the skin's support structures, such as collagen and elastic tissue, blood vessels, and nerve endings. An intact and well-functioning dermal layer gives the skin its strength and flexibility.

The third and deepest layer of skin, the hypodermis, is also known as the subcutaneous fascia. It contains fat cells as well as deep hair follicles, nerve cells for sensation, and blood vessels.

Perhaps most importantly, the skin serves as a barrier against pathogens that would otherwise cause infection. When the skin is damaged, whether by cuts or burns, the opportunity for infection is literally opened up—and the deeper the wound, the greater the risk.

Burn injuries have generally been classified by degree, depending upon how many layers of the skin are involved.

Traditionally, and at the time of the explosion in Waverly, the burn classification system referred to three degrees of burns, from first to third degree, the most superficial to the deepest. Today, a more precise system is commonly used, one which diagnoses burn injuries by depth or thickness. The two systems are much the same in their classification, with one exception: full-thickness burns are now recognized as fourth-degree burns, whereas before they were included among third-degree burns.

Thus, first-degree burns are the most superficial, involving only the first layer of skin, the epidermis. They are accompanied by pain, redness, and sometimes mild swelling, depending upon the extent of the first-degree burn.

Second-degree burns affect both the epidermis and the upper region of the dermis; these burns cause pain and blistering, splotchy skin, and severe swelling.

Third-degree burns go even deeper, down to the lower region of the dermis, and because they damage nerve endings, are relatively painless. Third-degree burns appear white in color and leathery to the touch.

Full-thickness, or fourth-degree burns, injure all three layers of skin, and leave the burned area with a charred appearance. They obliterate all nerve endings and nerve cells within the affected skin, resulting in no sensation at all.

To lose all three layers of skin is to lose light touch, flexibility, perspiration, pain, circulation, and the first line of defense against external assaults. And it was these full-thickness burns that had covered the first patients to enter Nautilus Memorial Hospital that Friday afternoon.

As noted before, the deeper the wound, the greater the risk of infection, due to the loss of the body's protective barrier against pathogens. This includes burn wounds, which, as Dr. Deirdre Church and colleagues have so aptly described, "are one of the most common and devastating forms of trauma." Major burn injuries create a state of immunosuppression and predispose patients to serious infections. Thus, most deaths in patients who have survived the acute phase of the burns are either due to burn wound sepsis (overwhelming, systemic infection) or complications related to smoke inhalation.

Fluid resuscitation and cardiac monitoring are essential parts of burn injury management, because the body's immediate response to extensive burns causes massive fluid shifts that result, paradoxically, in both severe dehydration and in swelling around the burn wounds, which can close off the airway if the burns are around the neck or face. These altered fluid states also demand sudden, hard work from the heart, which may not always be up to the task.

TIM BARNETT'S BROTHER, Oak, came to Dickson to pick him up on Sunday, saying, "Hey, we're going to see Dad." *Gosh, finally!* thought Tim. *Some normalcy or something.*

When they got back to their house in Waverly, it was full of people. Tim's oldest brother, Aaron, was there, home from the Navy. There were no outgoing long distance lines Friday after the explosion, but apparently, J.C. Morrisett, of the Humphreys County chapter of the American Red Cross, had used ham radio communications to get in touch with a Red Cross official at the Tennessee Civil Defense Agency headquarters. He was able to ask Civil Defense personnel to have the Red Cross official call him by phone, since incoming lines were still operational. Morrisett asked the Red Cross official to find a way to reach Aaron Barnett in the US Navy.

The official sent a message from Nashville to Washington, DC, which was then relayed to the ship on which Aaron was stationed. The message he received was: "Dad hurt in explosion." The only thing he could think of was the big natural gas tanker they had just had installed at the house for heating purposes. What else could have exploded and hurt his dad?

Black smoke from the explosion could be seen for miles.
Courtesy of City of Waverly

View of the wreckage on Thursday, February 23, 1978.
The white tank car to the far left of the photo, UTLX 83013, would explode the next afternoon.
Courtesy of Waverly Exchange Club

Thursday morning, February 23, 1978.
The white tank car is in the center of the photo, buried beneath wrecked boxcars and wheels.
Courtesy of City of Waverly

Cleanup proceeded on Thursday as boxcars and wheels were lifted off white tanker UTLX 83013. The day remained cold, with snow on the ground from the night before.
Courtesy of City of Waverly

Waverly Police Chief Guy Barnett, far left, surveys the wreckage, minutes before the explosion.
Courtesy of Waverly Exchange Club

Members of the all-volunteer Waverly Fire Department (WFD) speak with L&N crew just moments before the explosion. WFD members, from left to right: Riley Turner, Melvin Matlock (center of photo), and Billy McMurtry (far right). Melvin Matlock was one of the five killed instantly moments later. Others in the photo were injured; Riley Turner's burns were severe.

Courtesy of Waverly Exchange Club

Cooter Bowen (back to camera) helps disaster victims into an emergency combination vehicle. The man entering the back of the vehicle is still on fire: flames can be seen on his shirt. In the far right of the photo, a severely burned man with most of his clothes burned off makes his way past a white car.
Courtesy of City of Waverly

Cooter Bowen running past Police Chief Guy Barnett's car, on which a fragment of the blown tank landed. Between Cooter and the car are Frank Craver's shoes. His burned clothes are in the debris behind the car (foreground).
Courtesy of City of Waverly and Frank Craver

Friday, February 24, 1978.
Tate Lumber Company engulfed
in flames (background)
while Bateman's Bait Shop
begins to burn (foreground).
Courtesy of Waverly Exchange Club

One of the many New Town buildings
on fire after the explosion.
Courtesy of Waverly Exchange Club

Waverly firefighter David Dillingham, who rescued Frank Craver.
Courtesy of City of Waverly

Fire Chief Wilbur York's car in flames.
Courtesy of City of Waverly

The short-end portion of the tank (#9 on the NTSB map)
cratered the front yard of the Trollinger home on Richland Avenue.
Courtesy of City of Waverly

A fragment of the ruptured tank severed the car of retired firefighter Lloyd Florow as well as the water main in the ground under it. Florow (not pictured) was among those killed instantly in the explosion.
Courtesy of City of Waverly

The cracked wheel of Car No. 17, the cause of the derailment.
Courtesy of City of Waverly

Gutted remains of Slayden Lumber Company, the building Toad Smith
had been trying to get behind to escape the explosion.
Courtesy of Waverly Exchange Club

Saturday morning: devastation of Waverly's New Town section (which extends to areas not pictured here) after fires were extinguished. Water cannons remain trained on second, "ticking time bomb" tank car. A new tanker has been moved onto the tracks for the offloading process.

Courtesy of City of Waverly

Subhi D. Ali, MD,
at Waverly Clinic, PC, circa 1980.
*Photo by T. O. Perkins,
courtesy of Subhi D. Ali, MD*

Dr. Maysoon Shocair Ali in her office at Waverly Clinic,
on the phone with her husband's oncologist, 1994.
Courtesy of the author

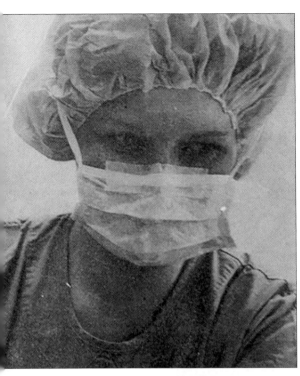

Carolyn "Sam" Tucker, RN,
Operating Room Supervisor at
Nautilus Memorial Hospital, late 1970s.
Courtesy of Subhi D. Ali, MD

Buddy Frazier as Waverly's
Chief of Police later in his career.
Courtesy of Buddy Frazier

Francis X. "Dutch" Gisenhoffer, Waverly Fire Department (left), and Waverly Police Sergeant Elton "Toad" Smith (right), at the newly unveiled monument in memory of the deceased, one year after the explosion. *Courtesy of Waverly Exchange Club*

Sue and Frank Craver, 2016. *Courtesy of Frank Craver*

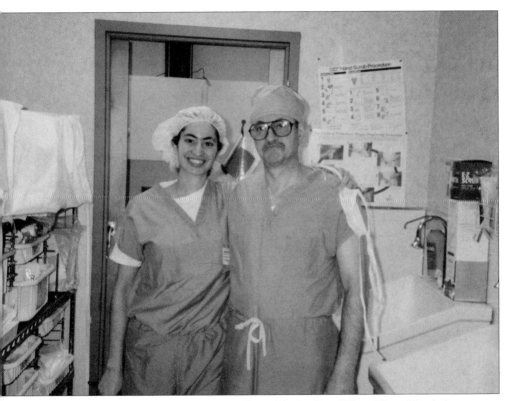

The author and her father, Dr. Subhi D. Ali, outside the OR of Three Rivers Hospital
(formerly Nautilus Memorial Hospital), following a hernia repair, circa 1999.
Courtesy of the author

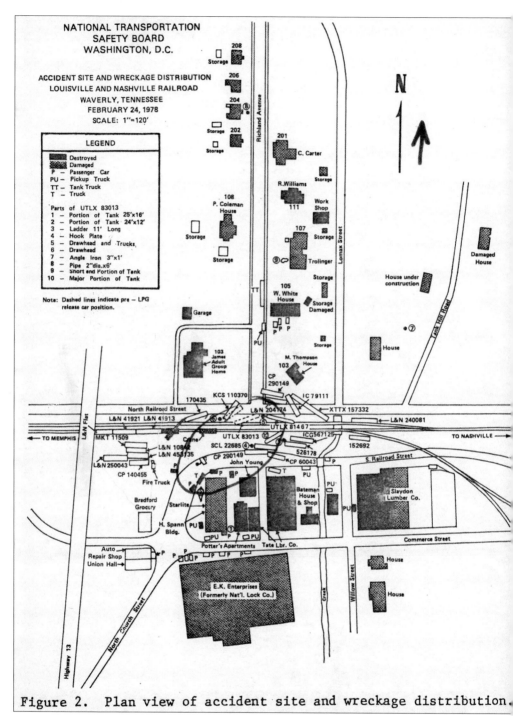

Figure 2. Plan view of accident site and wreckage distribution.

The original position of UTLX 83013, the tank car that exploded, is within the circle and outlined in dashed lines. Its ten fragments are identified by corresponding numbers throughout the map, as indicated in the map legend. (What was labeled on this map as "North Church Street" is known as the Commerce Street viaduct, or the Commerce Street bridge, in Waverly. The elevated portion of Highway 13 that crosses over the railroad tracks is known as the "Viaduct.") Map by National Transportation Safety Board

Courtesy of City of Waverly

When Aaron got to Nashville, the Metro Nashville Chief of Police, Joe Casey, picked him up and drove so fast to Waverly it seemed as if they were flying. "What's going on?" Aaron asked. Chief Casey told him then what had happened.

So when Tim returned to his house on Sunday, they were all ready to get on the Governor's plane that had been sent to fly them down to Birmingham, where his daddy was. Before they could leave the house, though, the phone rang. Somebody, one of the many men who was crowding Tim's living room, took the call, and Tim could tell it was his mother on the other end of the line. The man hung up the phone and said to Tim, "That was God calling. Your dad's gone."

BUDDY FRAZIER HAD heard the news Friday night that Fire Chief Wilbur York had died. Chief York was someone he had known all his life; Buddy grew up across the street from him. When Buddy was a little boy, there was an old, red box downtown that was the fire alarm box; it was connected to a big siren, and when there was a fire in Waverly, someone would activate that box, and the siren would blow all over town so the firemen would know there was a fire. And whenever Buddy would hear the fire alarm go off, he'd run to the window of his house, look out across the street at Wilbur York's house, and watch for him to get in his car and turn on his red flashing light.

So, yeah, he had known him all his life, and now he was gone.

Mayor Jimmy Powers had also known York all his life, and the loss was a shock to him as well, as he would later record:

> I had been Mayor for several years, and most of the
> people employed by the City of Waverly were people
> that I was fortunate enough to select and work with
> closely. When you see those people just drop right out

of the picture all of a sudden, it is a numbing loss; like
Fire Chief York, who started off with our original fire
department and whom I've known ever since I was
just a kid. (Exchange Club of Waverly 1982)

That Sunday afternoon, Buddy was back in the shop, trying
to get one of the patrol cars ready for service again, when he received more bad news. He didn't think he could take any more
bad news, but there it was.

"Chief Barnett didn't make it."

Buddy knew the Chief had been taken to the University of Alabama at Birmingham, which had one of the major burn centers
in the region. Thanks to Buddy, he had been the first patient to
arrive in the emergency room at Nautilus Hospital in Waverly,
and thanks to the efforts of the medical team there, he had been
the first patient on the first helicopter. Everyone had done all they
could to give him the best chance to survive, but the burns were
too much, evidently. He died in Birmingham that Sunday. He was
45 years old.

His wife, Shirley, had been with him when he passed. The
Tennessee Highway Patrol sent a car to Birmingham to bring her
back to Waverly, and the Governor's plane was sent to bring back
his body.

The plane made it to the Humphreys County Airport before
Shirley did, and a decision was made that Guy Barnett's body
would not be taken off the plane until she got there. So Buddy and
his fellow officers waited at the airport until she got there that
night. And then they themselves carried his body off the plane
and provided a full police escort to the Luff-Bowen Funeral Home.

CHAPTER THIRTEEN

For Whom the Bells Tolled

MARCH 1, 1978
WEDNESDAY

COOTER BOWEN ESTIMATED THE FUNERAL procession to be at least half a mile long, given the number of law enforcement vehicles as well as ordinary citizens who had come to pay their respects to the family and to the memory of their beloved Chief of Police, Guy Barnett, who would be laid to rest at Richlawn Cemetery in Waverly.

Sunday night, Cooter had been on the tarmac at Humphreys County Airport in Waverly, standing beside a hearse from Luff-Bowen Funeral Home, to meet the Governor's plane that was returning the Chief's body from Birmingham. Several law enforcement vehicles also lined the tarmac to receive the fallen hero, who had been one of their own for so much of his life. Cooter drove back to the funeral home with that full police escort.

In Mayor Powers's words, which were echoed by many others who knew the Chief:

> Guy Barnett was probably the best [Chief of Police] in Tennessee at the time ... recognized all over the state for his ability.... I was thinking, when they had

about 125 chiefs at his funeral, that if Guy Barnett had happened to walk in to that 125, he would stand out. That's what kind of man he was. (Exchange Club of Waverly 1982)

Cooter was grateful they were able to have an open casket funeral for Chief Barnett; they would not be able to do so for everyone. There were to be so many funerals, it seemed, and the ones who were from Waverly—well, Cooter knew them all. Guy Barnett and Wilbur York. Father and son, James E. and Terry Lynn Hamm. Earl Baker. Tommy Hornburger. Too many more. The funeral services stretched on for weeks, as some who were being treated in burn centers succumbed to their injuries. It seemed as though there was news of another death on a weekly basis until mid-April, when Daniel Lee Engle, an enforcement officer of the Tennessee Public Service Commission, became the 16th fatality of the explosion, dying in the burn unit at Cincinnati General Hospital at the age of 24. Of the 16, Luff-Bowen Funeral Home handled eight of the funerals.

It would never be an easy task to embalm one's friends, not ever—nor to see the funeral arrangements through from the embalming to the grave—and to do so many in a relatively short time span could take its toll. Cooter and the rest of the funeral home staff were grieving too, and found it difficult to keep their composure at times. But Cooter took the view that it was the last service that could possibly be provided to these victims, his own friends and neighbors, and he was privileged to have the capabilities to help them and their families in their most difficult time. As he saw it, what better compliment could there be than to be able to help somebody with your knowledge and expertise, and to provide a final memory that's a good memory, and actually let people be able to see and remember their loved ones and friends in the best light after an extreme tragedy like they had?

AT HIS FATHER'S funeral, Tim Barnett sat with his mother in the front pew of the Waverly Church of Christ. He couldn't believe how many people were there. His friend Zach Clayton was there too, and he saw that Zach also noticed the TV camera that was pointed at his family. Not just pointed at them, but stuck in his mom's face. During the funeral. It was driving Tim nuts. He directed his angry thoughts toward the camera crew. *First of all, man, you're not in this funeral. You shouldn't be here. And now you're taking pictures of my mother?*

That really got Tim bad; it really hurt. But he was just a kid and there wasn't much he could do about it. Just like there wasn't much he could do about all the people in his house, not giving him any space; wasn't much he could do about the lack of normalcy anywhere anymore. And there was nothing at all he could do about the train exploding in the first place and taking his dad with it.

Tim had not just loved his dad; he had really liked him. He thought his dad was a really good guy, the kind of guy he could actually talk to. He could tell his dad anything. Tim knew that some might think that with him being in law enforcement, it would sway how he thought about things, but Tim saw that he had a pretty open mind. And he had a comical side to him at home that not many people knew about. Every morning, he would come into the bedroom that Tim shared with his brother Oak and start singing. It was his way of getting them out of bed, and it worked! Tim thought his dad was the coolest alarm clock ever. And a really, really cool guy in a lot of other areas as well. He was very committed to his family, and especially to his mother, Tim's grandmother. They went over to her house in Dickson nearly every week, and all the family would gather over there, Tim's parents and uncles and cousins, and it was just great.

And now everything had changed. Everything.

FOR THE FOUR remaining officers in Waverly's police force, including Buddy Frazier, it seemed as though all they were doing for
several days was going to funerals. It was funeral after funeral
after funeral after funeral, a train of funerals, and Buddy started
to think he was never going to get through going to funerals. The
disaster had taken a tremendous personal toll, with the loss of
the police chief and the injury of three other officers: Toad Smith,
Nancy Bell, and Roy Douglas. Half the police department had
been lost in the snap of a finger. There were no counselors to help
them process and debrief and grieve; they ran on the fumes of
their adrenaline and handled it the best they could on their own.

For several weeks, the Metro Nashville Police Department
took over many of the law enforcement duties in Waverly in the
wake of the disaster and in light of the devastation to the local
police department. Two of Waverly's four police cars had been
lost in the blast. The Tennessee Valley Authority (TVA) plant sent
two Ford Mavericks to use as police cars; they also sent a fire
truck. Mayor Powers appointed Ted Tarpley as the new Chief of
Police, and the rebuilding process began.

Along with his many other duties, Buddy Frazier made hospital visits to those at Nautilus and in Nashville, and called others
he couldn't reach in person. When he went to visit Officer Nancy
Bell while she was in the hospital, she asked him, "Who was I in
the back seat of your car with?"

He didn't want her to know, not while she was recovering, so
he answered, "I'm not sure who that was. I think that man worked
for the railroad."

Months later, after she had returned to work, she looked
Buddy in the eye one day and said, "You lied to me when I was in
the hospital."

She went on, "I wanted to know who I was in that car with.
And I still want to know."

Buddy realized then that she probably knew all along, even when she was asking him at the hospital. He realized she just needed it confirmed. So he finally brought himself to tell her the truth, so she could hear it from his lips. He said, "That was the Chief."

CHAPTER FOURTEEN

The Misery of Hindsight

FEBRUARY 26, 1978
SUNDAY

TOAD SMITH DID NOT GET to attend the funeral of his fallen police chief, nor was Frank Craver able to attend the funeral of Fire Chief Wilbur York. Both were stuck in hospitals away from home.

On Saturday, the day after the explosion, Dr. McClure had transferred Toad to Parkview Hospital in Nashville, to the care of plastic surgeon Dr. John Frist. On Sunday morning, Dr. Frist examined Toad, and told him, "Mr. Smith, they did a great job for you down in Waverly, and now we're gonna have to do something with your hands."

Toad could see that his hands had swelled a great deal overnight, and the fingers looked like they were turning blue.

"That swelling is normal after being burned so badly, but we have to deal with it as soon as possible. We're going to have to restore the circulation to your fingers," Dr. Frist said. "If we don't, we may have to amputate them."

"Well, Doc, do what you gotta do."

Toad watched as Dr. Frist took a scalpel and started to make what looked to Toad like a grid on the backs of his hands, right down through the burned tissue. He could feel the pressure on his hands when the blade cut through, but it didn't feel like being cut. He had no sensation of pain. Every once in a while, Dr. Frist would hit a blood vessel, and it would bleed all over the place, and the bleeding was the only sign Toad had that an incision had been made. But the end effect was amazing: Toad could see the circulation in his hands opening up. It wasn't but a few minutes, and everything started to turn pink again.

"Well, I believe that took care of it," Dr. Frist announced.

The next day, Toad received skin grafts on his hands. Most of his fingernails had burned off, down to just above the cuticles, so his physical therapist made a contraption that looked like a heavy clothes hanger, to which he attached nylon strings, which were then attached to hooks that he had glued to Toad's remaining fingernails. Then he took a rubber band and stretched Toad's hand out so it held in a retracted position. He did the same to the other hand. Kept under tension, this would encourage the fingernails to grow up and out as they were supposed to, instead of growing back into the skin.

Due to the burns on the backs of his legs and head, Toad was kept on his stomach in a prone position with a pillow under each arm and his face resting on a donut made of gauze. He also had second-degree burns on his back and elsewhere, and those hurt a great deal, nearly all the time. It wasn't long before Toad felt himself to be one miserable person. When he woke up, everything about him, from his arms on down, felt like it had gone to sleep, just like all those body parts were dead. The only relief he had was when, every three hours, his nurses would come in and debride the backs of his legs. They'd pull the old gauze off, and all the pain would be focused in one location. It was actually a relief, to have something to focus on other than the more diffuse pain and misery he was in.

———

TOAD LAY ON his face in that hospital bed for as long as he could stand it. He lay that way until Friday morning, at which point he told everyone, "I don't want to talk to nobody; I don't want no more of this. I just want to lay here and die."

His wife wanted to see him that Friday morning too, but he told his nurse, "I don't wanna see my wife. I don't wanna see anybody. I just wanna lay here and die. Really."

His care team must have realized then that he needed some relief, because they got him up that day; they helped him sit up, keeping his hands propped up in the air. His physical therapists began the process of getting his fingers to move again, and that was encouraging.

Skin grafting for the backs of his legs was next, and then for part of his forehead. Forever after, he would joke with people who knew him, "I never know whether I'm comin' or goin' because my hands and part of my forehead came off my posterior. The front of the legs went to the back of the legs. So I've rightly got transferred around a little bit."

Toad spent eight weeks at Parkview. When the time neared for him to finally go home, though, he wasn't as excited as he thought he would be. He got to thinking about it, knowing that he would still need to have dressing changes for his legs, that he would not yet be able to work or do much of anything. And by that time he was on 40 mg of Valium—10 mg four times a day, a tremendous daily dose—and taking 100 mg of Demerol was like taking an aspirin. But it had all dulled the pain, numbed him, so he could tolerate it.

So as he ruminated over all this, he realized, *You know, everybody's gonna be comin' over to my house to visit, and my Chief, he's dead, and that young officer, my friend, he survived but he's badly injured, and T Boy and his dad are dead now, and the Fire Chief's died, and just about all the friends that I had there that got caught up in that thing got injured real bad or died.*

And the longer he thought about it, the crazier he felt. *I'm gonna go bananas; I know I am. I can't take this no more.*

When the next nurse came into his room and mentioned he was going home soon, Toad couldn't hold it back any longer. He started sobbing hysterically and repeating, "I don't wanna see anybody. I don't wanna talk to anybody. I don't wanna have to go home and deal with all that. I don't wanna do that. I don't wanna do that. I don't wanna do that."

Doctors and nurses came running into his room, such was the ruckus he was raising. Dr. Frist was paged to see him.

"Doc," Toad said, "I'm one of the type of people, I have to be doing something. I can't just sit still. I can't go home and just watch television. I can sit down and fiddle with somethin' for hours at a time, but put me where I just can't do anything, I get where...well, I'd just rather die."

"I certainly can understand that," Dr. Frist said.

"I was always like a frog hoppin' around, you know. That's not exactly how I got my nickname, Toad, but it turns out to be pretty accurate."

Dr. Frist asked, "Mr. Smith, would you like to talk to a psychiatrist?"

"If you think I need a psychiatrist, just bring 'em on."

The next morning, Dr. Frist told Toad, "There is a psychiatrist coming to see you today; he's one of the best in Nashville. He likes to fish, too. I think you all will get along."

Later that morning, a new doctor came into Toad's room. As a police sergeant, Toad was used to checking people out from head to toe, gleaning any information he could from first appearances. He noted that this man was not tall, and was wearing a motorcycle helmet. *So he not only likes to fish; he likes to ride motorcycles, too. This should be interestin'.* The doctor took the helmet off and sat down beside Toad's bed.

After introducing himself, he asked Toad, "Would you believe that I might be a heart doctor?"

Toad quipped, "Well, the Bible says, 'Out of the abundance of the heart the mouth speaketh.' So, yup, I understand you kindly wanna talk to my heart a little bit and everything, you know."

The psychiatrist asked the usual series of questions that Toad expected him to ask, and then: "What are you thinking?"

"Uh...well, I don't know, Doc. I feel kinda blank. I'm not really thinking about anything, really. Just sorta numb, I guess you would say."

"All right, I'll be back tomorrow, about the same time, and I'll talk to you again."

When he returned the next day, he asked Toad more of the usual questions, about his mother and his father, and the relationships he had with people, and this, that, and the other, and so forth, and so on. So Toad told him, "I had a real good lovin' family. Two good, lovin' parents, and everything. And I don't hold any grudges against L&N; it just was one of those things that happened. I hold no grudge against anybody, just hate that everything ended up like it did."

"Well, Mr. Smith, I tell you what—"

"Now, Doc," Toad interrupted, "if I got any short places in my head, any short circuits, you know, I wanna know about it. I'm a realist. If anything's wrong with me, I wanna know. That's the way I am. I don't wanna be whitewashed, or anything else. Just tell me like it is."

The doctor chuckled. "Don't worry—if you've got any short spots, Mr. Smith, we'll find them!"

"Good. And you know, Doc," Toad went on, "people say, 'Well, why'd it happen to me?' But I'm not like that. Well, am I any different than anybody else? I'm not. Why should it not happen to me? Really. I mean, that's life.

"That's just the way I am, really. Always been that way. My daddy was the same way. Mother too."

The psychiatrist smiled. "You know, Mr. Smith, I believe you'll see your way clear of this. How about I just see you in a month or so after you get out?"

"Okay. That's a deal, Doc."

FRANK CRAVER HAD been transported to Cincinnati on one of the Air Force jets that Mayor Powers had requested from President Carter. He had also been one of the first patients to get to Nashville from Nautilus Hospital in Waverly, because, as he would later recall, Cooter Bowen himself had rolled him and Susan out of the hospital and into his combination vehicle.

"Cooter, what are you doin'?" Frank had asked.

"We're going to the hospital up in Nashville."

"I want to go to Baptist," Frank said, referring to the hospital where he had taken his EMT training. Then he said to Cooter, "You don't have a siren on this hearse."

"No," Cooter answered, "but I got a big foot."

Frank had insisted that his daughter, Susan, be in the vehicle with him, but the hospital staff didn't want to put her in there with him, because—as he and his wife would later find out—they thought he might die within the hour it would take to get to Nashville, and they didn't want Susan to have to see that. But they did, finally, relent to Frank's demands, and loaded her in with him. They had to use somebody's belt to hold her stretcher in place so it wouldn't move around. One of the Nautilus nurses, Jean Cagle, had also been Susan's babysitter, so she rode in the ambulance/hearse with them.

On her way back to Waverly from her workday in Nashville, Frank's wife, Sue, encountered an inordinate amount of traffic on Highway 70, in both directions. She saw ambulance after ambulance, hearses, law enforcement vehicles, fire trucks, and passenger cars. Indeed, as she would later read from WNGE-TV reporter Tom Smith, "It was just an endless stream of ambulances going into Waverly, and coming out of Waverly, and I kept thinking to myself, 'This has gotta stop, there has gotta be an end, there can't be that much need.'"

Frank had installed a CB radio in the car Sue was driving, so she keyed the CB and asked what happened. "Well, a tank car has blown up, and Waverly's gone," was the response she got.

The reason Sue had been in Nashville that day was to accompany a foster mother and child to a doctor's appointment, and she turned to the mother now and said, "Frank and Susan have been in that."

"You don't know that."

"Yes, I know they are. I don't know why or how I know that, but I do."

When she and her passengers got within 20 miles of Waverly, they began to see the smoke.

Sue drove on to the foster home to drop off her passengers, and there, Janie Pace, one of the ladies with whom she worked, met her and drove her car back up to Nashville. Sue had no information as to where Frank and Susan had been sent or what condition they were in, so she and Janie went from hospital to hospital to hospital until they found them.

Sue went first to St. Thomas Hospital, then to Vanderbilt, and finally to Baptist. And when she walked into Baptist, she saw Susan, who looked up at her and said, "Mother, I'm okay. Go see about my daddy."

THE DAY AFTER the explosion, Frank and Susan were loaded, along with several other Waverly burn patients who had been transferred to Nashville, onto the US Air Force C-9 medevac plane, which flew first to Birmingham and Louisville, placing patients at those burn centers, and then on to Cincinnati for Frank and Susan.

At first, Frank and Susan's physicians at Baptist had planned to send them to different burn units across the country, but Sue Craver stepped in and told them, "Wherever they go, I want 'em both together."

They knew nearly everyone on the plane with them, including Guy Barnett and Terry Hamm ("T Boy"), and everyone was in bad shape. As the plane was getting ready to take off, one patient, a signalman for the L&N Railroad, had a heart attack, and the plane's departure was delayed while medical staff attended to him.

As soon as the plane was in the air, Sue got up and went to sit beside her daughter. Sue had learned that after Frank had lost sight of Susan during the explosion, she had gone over to some of the remaining New Town buildings to hide. Billy McMurtry found her and drove her up to Nautilus Hospital, where she was reunited with Frank.

After Sue found Susan at Baptist Hospital in Nashville, a doctor came into the room and took a look at Susan's left hand, the back of which was badly burned. "We're going to have to relieve this pressure," he said. On the spot, he took a scalpel and put a "Z" on her hand. Sue nearly fainted.

Later, when the doctor found out that Susan was to be transferred to Cincinnati, he was irate, and told Sue, "Well, *if* she keeps that hand, she'll never have use of it."

Sue couldn't understand why he was so upset with her, as she had nothing to do with the fact that her daughter was being transferred in the first place—she only wanted her husband and her daughter to go to the same city so she could visit both of them—but after that, she had to hope that the pediatricians in Cincinnati would find a way to let Susan both keep and use her hand.

Across from Sue and her daughter on the Air Force plane was a state employee who had also been injured in the explosion. Not long after the plane took off, he started gasping for breath. Sue watched as, finally, medical personnel on the plane did a tracheotomy on him so he could breathe.

Frank and Susan were the last patients off the plane. Susan was cared for at the Shriners Hospital for Children in Cincinnati, which had a specialized pediatric burn unit, while Frank was admitted to the burn unit at Cincinnati General Hospital. Susan was hospitalized for three to four weeks, and was discharged home from there. Frank was in the hospital in Cincinnati for five months.

In Cincinnati, Frank was told that he had second- and third-degree burns affecting 60% to 75% of his body. He was burned from his shoulders all the way down his back, from his left underarm down the left side of his trunk, on the inner part of his thighs on both legs, and through the entirety of his right leg, all the way down to his heel. The explosion had melted his fingernails and scarred the webbing between his fingers. Before the blast, he had had a full head of hair, and now just about all of it was burned off.

For his skin grafts, Frank's donor sites were from both of his arms, all the way up his shoulders; from the front of his trunk; and from nearly every bit of his left leg as well as across the tops of both feet. Doctors searched for and used whatever viable skin they could find. In the end, most of the skin on his body was either a burn site or a donor site.

He had to wear Jobst compression gloves and garments to hold down the swelling after all his procedures; the garments would also, he was told, help to manage scar tissue formation and keep it from becoming worse than it already was.

BUDDY FRAZIER KNEW that the mayor, Dr. Powers, loved Frank Craver like he was his own brother, so he was not too surprised when, one afternoon not long after the explosion, Dr. Powers said to him, "I want you to take time, just every few days, and call Frank Craver. Call him."

So every few days, Buddy did just that; he would call and talk to Frank while he was in the burn center in Cincinnati. And still at first, Buddy didn't think Frank could survive. He just didn't think he could. But each time he called him, Frank was a little bit better, until finally, Buddy was able to check on Frank in his own home rather than having to call him in a hospital room in a city far away.

Buddy found that he wondered, wondered for a long time, *how does a matter of a few minutes either put you in harm's way over there or keep you safe over here? And why? Why am I not hurt at all, and my friends are just scarred for life, or dead? Or dead. Either one.*

If Chief Barnett had not sent him to get Ted Tarpley when he did, Buddy would have been standing right there with him, alongside Frank Craver. And had he returned sooner, by just a few minutes, he also would have been on site when the tank blew. And then maybe someone would have been calling and checking on him in a burn center somewhere, or saying words over him while he was lowered six feet under. He would never, not as long as he lived, be able to make sense of it.

OVER THE DAYS immediately following the explosion, Dr. Maysoon searched her medical textbooks for anything and everything having to do with burn injuries and the care of burn patients. She had been second-guessing herself, but what she came to realize was that she had done nothing wrong. She had set the triage in motion in the right way, and she and all the physicians had done exactly what was needed, acted quickly in that first, most important hour. She also felt the entire team of hospital personnel had been saved by Dr. Ali's leadership, and that, in turn, had allowed them to save the lives and limbs of the patients in their care.

She feared the memories of that horrible day would stay with her forever. That weekend, she could not eat, she could not rest. She had nightmares. In them, everybody was coming at her all at once, jumping up and down and screaming in their blackened skin that was falling off. That scene in the ER had been very hard to handle emotionally, and whenever she looked back on it, she felt as though, in that moment, she had been transported to hell on earth.

She usually kept a journal, a diary, but this event, the biggest calamity she had ever had to face in her career . . . this she did not write down. She wanted to forget it. It was so hard to see how much suffering, in such a very short period of time, that so many people had to go through. She wanted to forget how she had had to control her emotions in the moment by separating herself from her feelings and focusing on the job that needed to be done. She wanted to erase the whole thing from her mind. But it stayed with her, and as much as she tried to block it, to cope through willed forgetfulness, she knew deep down that one does not, cannot, forget a catastrophe like that. It would haunt her for years.

FOR DAYS AFTERWARD, Nancy Daniel could not get the smell of burned flesh out of her nose or her mind. It seemed as though it was stuck to the hairs in her nostrils. And forever after, if she even thought about the disaster and the scene in the ER, she could still smell it. In later years, whenever she encountered a burn patient, the smell alone would take her back to that horrible day, that horrible time.

Nancy found out later that the visiting nurse who had left town as soon as the explosion happened eventually called Cheryl Allen to apologize, saying, "I should have stayed, but I had to leave. I couldn't stand it."

ZACH CLAYTON HEARD the sounds of sirens and helicopters for days. For him and all the other residents of Waverly, the day of the explosion would forever after be known as "Black Friday."

Zach's good friend, Tim Barnett, spent 43 years thinking it had been his dad who had pulled up to the house in the patrol car that Buddy Frazier was driving. All that time, he regretted not going out to speak to his father one last time. He did not know the exact time line of events; if he had, he would have realized that, had his father been in that patrol car at their house at that moment, he could not have been injured in the blast. It was not until Tim happened to be discussing the disaster with Buddy in March 2021 that they both realized what Tim had assumed all that time, and Buddy was able to give him the truth.

CHAPTER FIFTEEN

Recovery Road

MAY 1978

ONCE TOAD WAS AT HOME, things went more smoothly than he had anticipated. His wife learned how to dress his legs, and how to put the Jobst gloves on his hands. She helped him put his clothes on and attend to the usual activities of daily living. And after a month had passed, he did go back to see the psychiatrist, as promised.

They sat down and talked, and eventually the psychiatrist asked, "Well, how's your love life?"

"Just fine," Toad answered. "I have no hang-ups or anything there."

Toad told him that things had gone better than expected once he got home. "Well, how do you suppose that happened?" the psychiatrist asked.

"Well, Doc, you know, I found out a long time ago, and I try to practice this every day now, you know . . . well, it's kinda like the feller who's walked across the United States."

"Oh, really? Tell me about it."

"Well, there's a story about this fella who set out to walk across the United States, and he left New York and he walked all the way across the United States, and he got to California there, and the band was there to greet him, you know, and everybody was there, the news media, and the cameras, and the action, and all that thing, you know, and they said, 'Well, tell us about your trip.'

"And he said, 'Well, whaddaya wanna know about it?'

"They said, 'Well, how did the people treat you?'

"He answered, 'Great country. Great people. Everywhere.'

" 'But to cut right to the chase,' they said, 'what was the hardest part of your trip?'

"He said, 'Well, I guess it was going across the desert.'

"And the newsman who was asking him the question, he said, 'Well, yeah, I guess it would be hot and dry and everything, you know.'

"The fella said, 'That wasn't it.'

" 'Well, whaddaya mean?' the newsman asked.

"And the fella answered, 'It was those little grains of sand that kept getting in my shoes.'

"So, Doc, you just gotta keep that sand out of your shoes. You don't have to worry about the big rocks. 'Cause if you take care of the little things as you go along, the big things will just kinda take care of themselves."

The psychiatrist looked at Toad and said, "Well! I don't believe I need to see you anymore!"

WHILE HE WAS in the hospital in Cincinnati, Frank had all kinds of visitors, including celebrities. Baseball legends Pete Rose and Johnny Bench came by. A Church of Christ group came to pray for and with him every Sunday evening. The people he met in Cincinnati were so nice, he came to think that if he ever had to live anywhere other than Waverly, he would want to live in Cincinnati.

That didn't mean his time in Cincinnati was pain free, though; quite the opposite. Every day, following the protocol of the time, his nurses wrapped him in Furacin gauze, like a mummy. The next morning, they'd come in with scissors, cut the gauze wrapping, and peel it back, pulling the underlying skin with it. Frank reckoned then that they could hear him screaming all the way to Waverly. That agony happened every day.

Frank had no idea if he was going to make it, if he was going to survive. And, he was told, had he been ten years older, he probably would not have. And then when it looked like he was indeed going to survive, he was told that he'd never be able to bend his fingers again. Through it all, though, he held on to that zest for life that had always defined him. He kept a positive attitude and struck up a friendly conversation with everyone he met, and that kept his spirits up.

It was not always easy, especially as he continued to learn about the fatalities from the explosion, all these people who had been his friends and were now gone. He had plenty of time to think about it, there in the hospital, and as he thought about who had died and where they had been, he realized that those who died had been facing the tank car when it exploded, and had inhaled the flames, or the fumes. Their faces and throats and lungs must have been burned. While he and Toad Smith had had their backs to it. That was his theory, anyway.

After his five months in Cincinnati, he was sent to Vanderbilt University Medical Center in Nashville, where he underwent physical therapy. For seven months, he went once a week every week to work with the therapists there. They worked together on bending each joint of each finger and stretching his arms and legs, pushing them as far as they could bend and stretch each time, and then the next time going another bit farther.

In February 1979, Frank underwent further operations to release scar tissue in key areas of mobility, including under his arms and between the fingers of both hands. He spent 13 days in the hospital at that time. Five months later, he was still wearing a total suit of Jobst compression garments in the form of a pair of pants and a vest with full-length sleeves.

146 WALK THROUGH FIRE

He was able to drive again about two months after he returned home from Cincinnati, but was unable to work due to his injuries. He couldn't be out in the heat or the cold due to the sensitivity of his grafted and scarred skin, and the range of motion in his hands and arms was still limited. He also was no longer able to sweat, except through his scalp and face. Because of the heat, he couldn't mow his own yard or do much of anything outdoors, and in cold weather, he could become cold or get frostbite before he would even know it, due to the loss of sensation in all the areas where he'd been burned.

He was not able to do any embalming or funeral work due to the sensitivity of his skin and the potential of coming into contact with the embalming fluids, plus the concern for exposure to germs that could infect his skin grafts and other surgically treated areas of his hands and arms.

Frank's daughter Susan had also sustained multiple burn injuries. In addition to her left hand, her left wrist and lower forearm were burned. The fronts of both of her legs were burned, one from the knee down to the ankle and one from the knee halfway down the shin; a two-inch strip of skin around the back of her waist was also burned. She had a cut on her nose that left a small scar, and the bangs across her forehead were burned off. She received skin grafts in Cincinnati; the donor sites were her front thighs.

Like her father, Susan had to wear compression garments for a long time after her skin grafting. These included a glove on her left hand (which, to everyone's relief, she did keep—and regained 95% function of it)—and compression stockings on both legs. Both father and daughter also had to have a special cream rubbed into the burned areas regularly, and Susan had to have two baths a day. In spite of this, she was able to return to school in April, and completed the first grade at Waverly Elementary with the rest of her class.

CHAPTER SIXTEEN

A Force for Change

FEBRUARY 8, 1979
THURSDAY

A TRAGEDY OF THE SCOPE and magnitude of the Waverly Train Disaster is rarely, if ever, the result of a single error, suspended in time. It is nearly always the consequence of a sequence of errors, both immediate and long in the making. In this way it is not unlike the heart attack that follows from years of atherosclerosis, the chronic hardening of the arteries which, combined with multiple lapses in judgment that build up over time, leads finally to the sudden, cataclysmic event.

The National Transportation Safety Board (NTSB) wasted no time in launching an investigation following the derailment and explosion, a lengthy examination that took nearly a year to complete. In the final NTSB report of February 8, 1979, the following paragraph stands out for its succinct summary of conclusions:

> The National Transportation Safety Board determines
> that the probable cause of the loss of life and substan-
> tial property damage was the release and ignition of
> liquefied petroleum gas from a tank car rupture. The
> rupture resulted from stress propagation of a crack

147

which may have developed during movement of the
car for transfer of product or from increased pressure
within the tank. The original crack was caused by mechanical damage during a derailment, which resulted
from a broken high-carbon wheel on the 17th car
which had overheated.

The broken wheel that set the entire disaster in motion was
already cracked when the westbound L&N train was passing
Buddy and Joel Frazier on the east side of town that Wednesday
night of February 22, 1978. The resulting investigation revealed
that it had fractured in Dickson, Tennessee, at least 25 miles before the train reached the Richland Avenue crossing in Waverly.
At that crossing, there was a switch in the tracks, through which
only wheels that were properly aligned could pass. At 10:25 P.M.,
when the broken wheel hit that switch, it pulled its own car over
on its side, derailing it and the 22 cars behind it.

The wheel in question belonged to Car No. 17, a gondola
loaded with wooden crossties. This gondola car was not part of
the original train that departed Radnor Yard, near Nashville, at
6:32 P.M. on February 22, en route to Bruceton, Tennessee. Train
No. 584, when it first began its journey that evening, consisted of
three diesel-electric locomotive units, 92 cars, and a caboose. At
Colesburg, 39.5 miles north of Nashville, one car was taken out
of the train and five others were added. These five were connected behind 14 cars that remained coupled to the locomotive.
The gondola car thus became Car No. 17.

As the NTSB noted, "Train No. 584 departed Colesburg without its brakes being properly tested; a brake test is required by
Federal regulations." Because L&N had no requirements for a
brake test on cars that were added to a train at an intermediate
terminal, nor did they require a brake-pipe leakage test, the
NTSB stated that L&N's own air brake instructions "did not

comply with the requirements of the Federal Railroad Administration's (FRA) regulation."

This turned out to be a critical fault in L&N's method of operation, because, as the NTSB determined, it was the brake system on the wheel of the gondola car, Car No. 17, that created the conditions that caused the wheel to crack:

> Gondola car L&N 171228 was built in April 1961. This 57-foot-long car was mounted on 4-wheel trucks at each end; each truck was equipped with roller bearings and 33-inch wheels, and was designed for cast iron breakshoes [sic] ...
>
> The rear pair of wheels on the gondola car had been manufactured by the Southern Wheel Company with a higher carbon content than previously cast steel wheels, in order to improve the wearing quality of the wheel. However, when this high-carbon wheel was exposed to above-normal heat, such as that produced by dragging or sticking brakes, the wheel tends to crack, break, and derail.

The NTSB report went on to say that "this condition had become prevalent in the railroad industry, and the Association of American Railroads (AAR) initiated a program to remove these types of wheels." Remarkably, these were the very wheels that "had been mounted on tank cars hauling hazardous materials and on other types of cars which were often placed in trains that hauled hazardous materials."

The wheel in question cracked all the way through its rim, plate, and hub, which loosened the wheel from its axle and caused it to move inward. According to the NTSB, "this wheel and remaining wheels on the car showed signs of thermal abuse"—such as that caused by friction from improperly applied brakes or improper installation of the brake shoes. As it so happened, both were the case on Train No. 584 headed through Waverly: the NTSB concluded that the gondola car's handbrake had been left on and never released in Colesburg when the car was added to the train.

The NTSB's investigation also found that the composition brake shoe that had been at the position of the broken wheel had been "disintegrated by heat" at one end. As the report explained, composition brake shoes have a higher coefficient of friction than cast iron shoes, and thus, "railroad equipment designed to use the composition shoes provides less force for the same braking capabilities than for other brakeshoes [sic]."

Since there were no differences between the backing plates of the two types of brake shoes, nor differences in the methods used to attach the shoes to the brake head, it was possible for a composition brake shoe to be installed on a rail car that was, in the NTSB's words, "not designed for its use." As the NTSB further explained, "If a composition brakeshoe [sic] is so installed, excessive friction and heat are produced between the composition shoe and the wheel and can cause high heat inputs into the wheel."

In the NTSB's final analysis: "If the fractured wheel had been of lower carbon content, it probably would not have cracked."

The wrong shoe on the wrong wheel with no brake test on a car that was not part of the original train in the first place: these were the details at the origin of the tragedy in Waverly.

OF COURSE, THERE had been other errors as well, the accumulation of which contributed to the extent of the catastrophe. Everyone who witnessed the disaster in Waverly agreed that the 1,200-foot perimeter should never have been relaxed on Friday. All of the most serious injuries and fatalities occurred within that 1,200 feet of the derailment, as did most of the property damage.

Others point to a degree of complacency that had arisen by the second day of having a train wreck on the ground in the middle of town; no one had been hurt when the train initially derailed, and the longer the cars and tankers lay there, the more harmless they seemed, especially to spectators. A school bus had even come through the area earlier that Friday. Familiarity combined with the relaxation of the perimeter had delivered a false sense of security.

White tank cars are often used for carrying anhydrous materials, and it is still unclear why the tankers labeled specifically for "anhydrous ammonia only" were loaded with liquid propane. According to the NTSB, the tank car that did not explode was "properly placarded, but bore stenciling indicating that it was in anhydrous ammonia service, when in fact it was loaded with LPG."

The tanker that *did* explode, UTLX 83013, had been loaded with 27,871 gallons of LPG adjusted at 60 degrees Fahrenheit; product weight totaled 130, 994 pounds. Union Tank Car Company had built UTLX 83013 in 1961, and at the time of the derailment, it was being leased to AMOCO Oil company for LPG service. The tank had an external surface area of 2,119 square feet and an inside diameter of 97 3/8 inches. Its total internal capacity was 30,149 gallons.

The NTSB report stated that the last time the tank had been hydrostatically tested was in April 1971, at a pressure of 400 pounds per square inch gauge (psig)—a unit of pressure that is relative to the surrounding atmosphere. In March 1976, its safety relief valve (now known as the pressure relief valve) was tested for operation at 300 psig. The tank car did not have head shields or shelf couplers, nor was it insulated or provided with a jacket.

Regarding this tank car that exploded, the NTSB noted the same indentation that gave Cooter Bowen pause the night of the derailment:

> During derailment, this car received a gougelike scrape and indentation on the lower right side, which extended from the leading head to the center of the tank. The scrape had visibly altered the exterior bead of a weld between the second and third tank sheets. The fracture originated in and propagated in the axial direction of the tank from the damaged girth weld for about 5 feet in each direction along the gouge. The fractures then changed directions and resulted in circumferential fractures.

It is fair to say that no one in Waverly recognized the extent of the structural damage to this tank car before it exploded. The tank ruptured before its safety valve operated, which means that the tank's steel walls failed at a pressure below 300 psig, which was well below the "bursting pressure" of 1,000 psig. When it did rupture, the fractures described by the NTSB caused the tank to blow apart in four major segments.

The ambient air temperature was near freezing at the time of the derailment Wednesday night; by Friday, the skies had cleared, the snow was melting, and the temperature was rising rapidly from a morning low in the upper teens to a midday high in the mid-fifties. This led to expansion of the gas within the damaged tank, which in turn put increasing pressure on the fractured tank walls until they ruptured. According to the NTSB, someone (who has never been identified) on the scene did notice propane vapor leaking from the tank in the seconds before it exploded. The source of ignition—the match that lit the fire, so to speak—has never been determined, but given the extreme flammability of vaporized propane, it could have been any of a number of sources in the immediate area. Before anyone had time to react to the leak, the vapor had ignited.

Upon that ignition, the north-facing head of the tank, which had been lying across the outlet to Richland Avenue, shot 500 feet up the street and landed in the yard of the home of Mrs. Annie Trollinger's heirs (see #9, "short end portion of tank," on NTSB plan view map in photo insert). A second large piece (#2 on the map), 24 feet by 12 feet in size, landed beside the Starlite Inn, not more than 50 feet from where Chief Barnett's patrol car was parked—this was likely the part of the tank that Frank Craver saw flying through the air toward himself and his daughter Susan. This tank fragment came down on the Chevrolet of retired fireman Lloyd Florow, cut the car in two, and severed the water main in the ground underneath it. Mr. Florow, who had relocated from Pasadena, Texas, to Waverly with his wife for their retirement, was among those who were killed instantly in the explosion.

The third section of the tank (labeled #1 on the NTSB map), measuring 25 feet by 16 feet, sailed through the air and came to rest against the southeast corner of the wall of the Spann Building, approximately 250 feet to the south of the tank's original location. According to the NTSB report, "This section evidently was propelled with high trajectory, because the only damage noticed on a building was at the roof line over which the section passed."

The final major tank segment (#10) was also the largest, comprising about 60% of the tank; it blew outward 50 feet and rolled on its side beside the tracks.

These four main segments were not the only pieces of the tank to blow apart, however. Six other tank pieces (see "Parts of UTLX 83013" on map)—including the tank's ladder, hook plate, wheel truck, drawhead, angle iron, and pipe—rained down on New Town and Richland Avenue. One of these tank fragments, the six-foot-long pipe (#8), was found as far as about 400 yards away, where it landed in the front yard of another home down Richland Avenue.

Metallurgical tests performed on the ruptured tank car by Battelle Columbus Laboratories revealed that "the yield and tensile strengths of the tank shell material were below the specification values," noting that "this is relatively common in older cars." The NTSB's analysis also stated that the movement of the tank car, from its original derailed location to a position more favorable for offloading the liquid propane, could have exacerbated the damage it had sustained during the derailment:

> Raising one end of the loaded tank car while using the opposite end as a pivot to move the car from the track structure could have provided additional stresses in the damaged area of the tank, causing the crack in the weld area to propagate. Any unequal support of the tank after being moved also could have stressed the damaged area.

Dropping the equivalent of a two-ton barbell on the tank—as witnessed by Toad and several others when the set of wheels fell and hit the tank during cleanup—certainly did nothing to improve the situation.

Sixteen people lost their lives due to the explosion, and when all injuries were taken into account, the final tally of those injured exceeded 200. Of the fatalities, seven were railroad employees and contractors; six were state and local officials; and three were bystanders. Among the state officials killed was Mark Belyew, a communications technician for the Tennessee Civil Defense Agency; he had been providing radio communications coordination onsite when the tank exploded. He was one of the five who was killed instantly. It was the only time, then or since, that an employee of the TCDA or Tennessee Emergency Management Agency was killed while on duty.

The total estimated property damage from the explosion was $1.8 million in 1979 dollars, which translates to over $6.9 million in 2021 dollars. The explosion and resulting fire destroyed 18 buildings, including at least four homes (one of which was the James Adult Group Home, which had been evacuated Wednesday night at the urging of Frank Craver), all of Tate Lumber Company and most of Slayden Lumber Company, an apartment building, the garment factory, and one of Waverly's two taxi companies. It seriously damaged another 20 buildings, both commercial and residential; and destroyed at least 26 motor vehicles, not counting those that may have been sitting in home garages and sustained damage. Fifteen train cars were destroyed and 12 others damaged; approximately 400 feet of railroad track was also in ruins. The explosion blew a crater into Richland Avenue that was 20 feet deep. Had the gas tanks at Carman Oil ruptured or caught fire, another entire section of Waverly would have also been destroyed.

At Slayden Lumber Company, in the building that Sergeant Toad Smith was desperately trying to get behind, the large plate glass windows and most of the concrete block front wall were blown in, and all the inside occupants knocked to the floor. One of the employees happened to be driving a company truck around the building, and was about to turn right onto Willow Avenue, where he would have been facing the wrecked tanker, when it exploded. It blasted his truck to a stop on the corner behind the Slayden building, where he was met by two of the employees scrambling out the back—and by Toad Smith, who asked to be taken to the hospital.

The force of the blast had blown out windows all the way through Waverly's downtown, including at the iconic Mi-De-Ga theater several blocks away. Zach Clayton's father reported looking out the window of his office in the courthouse building across the street, and seeing the flash of the explosion reflected in the black tiles of the Mi-De-Ga marquee.

It took more than four years to resolve all the litigation involving the propane tanker explosion. Attorneys made agreements on the final settlement awards on Friday, May 28, 1982, in Jefferson County Circuit Court in Louisville, Kentucky. The circuit court awarded a total of $10.7 million to the victims and their families.

GIVEN THE MAGNITUDE of the disaster in Waverly, which was the latest in a series of train derailments and hazardous materials accidents on tracks and with trains that were in a state of disrepair across the country—and, unbelievably, less than 48 hours after the propane tanker exploded in Waverly, another freight train derailed 60 miles away in Cades, Tennessee, with a tanker containing caustic lye—alarm bells were ringing at multiple levels of government to hasten major reforms of how hazardous materials were handled and transported.

A year after the Waverly Train Disaster, the manufacturing standards for railroad wheels changed. As a result of its investigation into the disaster, the NTSB made an immediate recommendation (even before the publication of its final report) that, "since the presence of this [high-carbon] wheel creates a high risk for serious accidents," the Federal Railroad Administration (FRA) use its emergency powers "to quickly remove the wheels of this type from service." The FRA did just that, issuing Emergency Order No. 7, "Removal of High Carbon Cast Steel Wheels from Service," on March 27, 1978.

EO No. 7 in its original version restricted the use of freight cars with 70-ton one-percent carbon cast steel wheels, which were often referred to as "70T U-1 wheels." These wheels were to be located, stenciled with the label "Scrap FRA EO 7" in white letters at least two inches high, and removed from freight cars by January 1, 1979. And not only were they to be removed, they were to be destroyed.

The Association of American Railroads (AAR), however, petitioned the FRA to amend its emergency order to limit the inspection and stenciling requirements to freight cars with 33-inch wheels and a nominal capacity of 50 tons, and to exclude Canadian-owned cars from the requirements. The FRA denied this request, citing the "overall high failure rate of '70T U-1 wheels' and the fact that these wheels can readily be substituted for 50-ton wheels that are in short supply because they are no longer in production." The FRA did, however, amend the order to exclude 28-inch wheels from the requirements "because these wheels can be easily distinguished from 33-inch wheels (such as '70T U-1 wheels')." The 28-inch wheels were also generally used only on specialized cars that were not part of the mainstream car fleet.

The FRA also reaffirmed its position that Canadian cars must comply with EO No.7 while they were in the United States, stating:

> FRA estimates that as many as 45,900 '70T U-1 wheels' were installed as maintenance replacements on interchange cars. Since Canadian cars are freely interchanged with U.S. railroad and operate throughout the United States, many Canadian cars may have had '70T U-1 wheels' installed as maintenance replacements by U.S. railroads. Any Canadian car with these wheels is just as much a safety hazard as a U.S. railroad-owned car.

The final Emergency Order No. 7 thus left in place the most stringent requirements regarding the removal of the high-carbon wheels like the one that was a root cause of the Waverly Train Disaster. Specifically, after March 31, 1978—a month after the disaster—any 70-ton or lower capacity freight car "containing any hazardous material" as placarded by requirements of the Department of Transportation Hazardous Materials Regulations was not to be accepted for transportation unless it had been inspected "to ascertain whether it is equipped with any Southern Wheel Company (ABEX) 33", 70-ton, one-wear 1 percent carbon cast steel wheels manufactured during the years 1958 -1969." If such a wheel, even a single one, was found, the hazardous material either had to be offloaded from the rail car at the point of origin, or the car moved "only to the nearest point" where the wheel could be removed. After December 31, 1978, no rail cars of any kind were allowed to remain in service with 70T U-1 wheels.

By the end of 1979, the FRA had released a full set of "Railroad Freight Car Safety Standards," and these included a number of additional qualifications to be met by freight car wheels. For instance, among other requirements, a freight car was not allowed to be placed or continued in service if a wheel flange was worn to a thickness of 7/8 inch or less; if the thickness of a wheel's rim was 11/16 inch or less; if a wheel rim, flange, plate, or hub had a crack or break; or if a wheel on the car had a slid flat or shelled spot greater than 2 1/2 inches in length, or two adjoining flat or shelled spots if each 1 of which were more than two inches in length. Wheels that showed evidence of being loose, such as by oil seepage on the back hub or back plate, or which showed signs of being overheated, were also not permitted to remain in service.

The new safety standards also took aim at numerous other components of the wheel trucks, such as defective axles and defective bearings. They also set out numerous specifications for the identification of defects in couplers, freight car bodies, and cushioning devices. Importantly, the standards made clear that "at each location where a freight car is placed in a train, the freight car shall be inspected before the train departs"—to avoid precisely the tragedy that was set in motion at the intermediate terminal of Colesburg, Tennessee, the evening of February 22, 1978, when the gondola car was added to the train without a brake inspection.

THE FALLOUT FROM the Waverly Train Disaster spurred Congress to act as well, with passage of the Staggers Rail Act on October 14, 1980. The goals of the Act were focused on the rehabilitation of the US rail system in order to "meet the demands of interstate commerce and national defense," and to do so by reforming federal regulatory policies "so as to preserve a safe and efficient rail system."

There had once again been some discussion in the immediate aftermath of the train explosion regarding nationalization of the country's railroads—which had been done before, by President Woodrow Wilson during World War I—but the Staggers Rail Act put this to rest with one of its stated goals, "to assist the rail system to remain viable in the private sector of the economy."

Sponsored by Senator Howard W. Cannon (D-NV), the Staggers Rail Act strove for balance in the regulatory process to try to satisfy the interests of carriers and shippers as well as the general public. While regulators retained the authority to protect consumers and shippers against unreasonable railroad pricing and conduct, Staggers allowed railroads to vary pricing on competing routes and services according to market demand. Railroad companies were also now permitted to choose their own routes, and could now operate over the most efficient routes for the services being provided. In addition, the legislation streamlined the procedures for new short line railroads to buy rail lines.

These and other changes had the effect of allowing railroads to improve financial returns such that they now would have the revenue available to improve their tracks and meet new safety standards. This was in stark contrast to the bankruptcy status that plagued nine carriers and over 21% of the nation's rail mileage during the 1970s and the continually deferred maintenance that went with it, resulting in the abysmal state of both the trains and the tracks at the time of the derailment in Waverly. Since 1980, freight railroads have invested nearly $740 billion of their own funds back into their operations, including new technologies that are meant to improve safety and efficiency.

According to the Association of American Railroads, since 2000, train accident and hazmat accident rates have fallen 33% and 64%, respectively—a feat the AAR attributes to the transformation the nation's railroads have undergone since the Staggers Rail Act. Rail rates have fallen as well. By AAR's calculations, average rail rates, as measured by inflation-adjusted revenue per ton-mile, went down by 44% between 1981 and 2021, allowing the average rail shipper to transport more freight for the same price.

The Staggers Rail Act of 1980 was a rare win for everyone. In a 2011 report on the impact of Staggers, the FRA within the US Department of Transportation concurred with the AAR, concluding that "as a result [of the Act], 30 years after deregulation, the railroad industry's financial health has improved significantly, service to rail customers has improved while overall rates have decreased, and rail safety, regardless of the measure, has improved."

As the FRA report explained, economic regulation prior to 1980 had prevented railroads from implementing any pricing flexibility, making it difficult to remain competitive. Regulations had also prohibited carriers from carrying out a restructuring of their systems, such as abandoning redundant and light density lines, that was necessary for controlling costs. The industry was therefore unable to cover inflation—not only due to these prohibitions but also due to the significant regulatory lag time in rate adjustments. Thus the state of bankruptcy for nine carriers, low return on investment for the entire industry, inability to raise capital, and steadily declining freight market share.

In the 30-year period after Staggers, railroad market share increased to over 40% (from a low of 37.5% before 1980), and return on investment averaged nearly 8% between 1990 and 2009 (as compared with a 2% average in the 1970s). The FRA reported that, "with the industry's improved financial condition, railroads have invested $6 billion a year in roadway, structures, and equipment since the mid-1990s. Between 1981 and 2009, the railroads have expended $511 billion in capital improvements and maintenance of track and equipment."

And these were not the only ways by which the Waverly Train Disaster changed the nation.

In the arena of train car and component manufacturing, another area that saw important changes as a result of the disaster was that involving shelf couplers. Although it may seem a miniature feature compared to the size of the train cars and tankers it holds together, the railroad coupler—the metal connection between the cars—makes the literal concept of the train possible, and its integrity plays an important role in rail safety. In the words of Kevin P. Keefe, former Vice President of Editorial at *Trains* magazine:

> The next time you watch a quartet of six-motor diesels go grinding past with an 11,000-ton unit coal train, consider that all that horsepower is being transmitted by a mere 11-inch-high chunk of steel at the end of each car...the key part of one of railroading's most durable components: the standard coupler.

At the time of the Civil War, when the railroad was being built through Waverly, this coupling was achieved by a link-and-pin design, which, as Adam Burns has noted in the American-Rails.com blog, proved to be extremely dangerous. Eventually, a design known as the knuckle coupler came into use, and its basic plan is what is still in use today.

However, no vertical locking was featured in the first several renditions of the knuckle coupler; only horizontal connection was possible, meaning that when a train derailed, cars could— and often did—separate. This could result in penetration of another car, jackknifing, and the risk of hazardous materials being released from tankers when their shells were damaged or punctured. Additionally, the couplers of adjacent cars could damage the ends of tank cars upon impact. In fact, an accident analysis by the Railway Supply Institute–Association of American Railroads (RSI-AAR) Tank Car Safety Research & Test Project found that one of the leading causes of tank shell punctures was the impact from couplers of adjacent cars.

In the 1970s, the development and use of the Type E shelf coupler was being extensively tested, which would allow for vertical locking as well. Double-shelf couplers (with top and bottom shelves) were developed in 1974, but what was known as the bottom-shelf Type E was not widely adopted until the late 1970s— and the timing was, once again, largely a result of what happened in Waverly. Following the Waverly Train Disaster, coupler requirements changed such that all tank cars carrying hazardous materials had to have double-shelf couplers. The addition of that bottom shelf is meant to provide the support needed to prevent a train car "from falling to the roadbed and presenting a derailment hazard" (McConway & Torley, LLC).

Another feature that became a part of all new tank car construction after Waverly was skid protection in the form of a device attached to the tank's bottom fittings, which include the bottom outlet, washout and/or sump (sometimes referred to as bottom discontinuities). This skid protector is meant to safeguard these bottom fittings from damage in the event of a derailment.

In the words of one former railroad mechanical inspector, the changes in couplers, slid flats, skid plates, and more that resulted from the Waverly Train Disaster "were a very big deal," and had these improvements been in place—and the required inspections performed—on the train that went through Waverly, the derailment might have been prevented; at the very least, the damage to the tank cars might have been avoided. And this former railroad employee, who spent over 20 years inspecting and repairing freight cars, would know this better than most, because his name is Tim Barnett, and his father was Waverly's Chief of Police on February 24, 1978.

CHAPTER SEVENTEEN

One Agency, One Mission

FEBRUARY 28, 1978
TUESDAY

ONE DAY BEFORE GUY BARNETT'S funeral and two business days after the train explosion in Waverly, the National Governors Association (NGA) released a report in which it called for the formation of a federal disaster management agency that would achieve "consolidation of federal emergency preparedness and disaster relief responsibilities into one office [to] make the management and operation of the federal effort more effective and efficient."

The director of this new agency, the NGA urged, should have the "additional responsibility for coordinating the efforts of all federal agencies that deal with emergency prevention, mitigation, and any special preparedness and disaster response activities." This director would ideally have direct access to the President.

This NGA policy document was the result of its Emergency Preparedness Project, a study the NGA had undertaken the year before to review current disaster policy. In its findings, the NGA highlighted the fragmentation of emergency preparedness and response functions at state and federal levels. It was the multi-agency, multi-approach fragmentation witnessed firsthand by

Toad Smith writ large. The NGA's position, therefore, focused on a more comprehensive approach to emergency management. The timing of the report's release indicated that the Waverly Train Disaster had lent fresh urgency to the NGA's recommendations.

At the time of the Waverly train explosion, local disaster management was handled primarily by state civil defense offices, which had their origins in World War II and the early Cold War era. In May 1941, when World War II was underway but prior to the attack on Pearl Harbor and US entry into the war, President Franklin Delano Roosevelt created the Office of Civilian Defense (OCD), which was intended to protect civilians through training programs such as black-out drills and air-raid response procedures. The OCD also provided sponsorship for local daycare and family health services.

The OCD was dismantled in June 1945, but following the war, a number of international events caused the US Congress to revisit the issue of America's civilian defense programs. In August 1949, the Soviet Union conducted a successful nuclear bomb test. On October 1, 1949, Mao Zedong declared the formation of the People's Republic of China, under the control of the Chinese Communist Party. One year later, China was supporting North Korea in the Korean War.

In response to the sense of urgency these events created among US defense planners, members of Congress as well as federal and state administrations, and the American public itself, President Harry S. Truman established the Federal Civil Defense Administration (FCDA) by executive order (EO 10186) on December 1, 1950. Its creation was followed by Congress' passage of the Federal Civil Defense Act of 1950, which, according to President Truman, would provide "the basic framework for preparations to minimize the effects of an attack on our civilian population, and to deal with the immediate emergency conditions which such an attack would create."

In what would become a theme in multi-level disaster preparedness efforts over the ensuing years, the FCDA sought to improve federal and state coordination. The FCDA also led shelter building programs, created stockpiles of supplies, established an attack warning system, and launched a memorable civic education campaign. One of the FCDA's aims with this national campaign was to teach schoolchildren about preparedness, and this resulted in civil defense drills as well as the production of nine civil defense movies that were shown in classrooms across the country.

Perhaps the most famous of these movies was *Duck and Cover*, a ten-minute, animated film that used the main character of Bert the Turtle to demonstrate what children should do if they saw "the flash of an atomic bomb." *Duck and Cover* promotional material showed Bert retreating into his shell when he sees a bomb explode, with text that told children that this was a smart thing for a turtle to do, and to emulate him, they must "learn to find shelter." Millions of schoolchildren saw the film during the 1950s, and it was heralded by media outlets at the time as a positive step toward emergency preparedness. The *New York Herald Tribune* quoted student consensus from the film's premiere that the film was "very instructive," "not too frightening for children," and "interesting and funny in spots."

On April 13, 1952, the Ohio State University's Institute for Education by Radio and Television issued an award to the FCDA's Audio-Visual Division for the radio version of *Duck and Cover*. The film was nominated in the category of Best Civil Defense Film at the fifth annual Cleveland Film Festival in June 1952.

Not everyone was enamored of the film, however. The Levittown Education Association reported receiving numerous complaints from parents that the movie had terrified their children, resulting in nightmares and fears of bright lights and imminent bomb attacks. To this criticism, Forrest E. Corson,

Chief of Public Information for the Nassau County (NY) Civil Defense, responded:

> It is unfortunate that the critics of 'Duck and Cover,' in their misapprehension over the psychological effect of the film on school children, are unwittingly following the Communist party line laid down in their official publications.... I am sure that all thinking parents want their children to be prepared for catastrophe. It is exactly what Civil Defense is trying to do. (as quoted at CONELRAD.com 2007)

In November 1952, members of the Committee for the Study of War Tensions in Children held a special screening of the film with educators, psychiatrists and psychologists, social workers, and parents. The consensus was that *Duck and Cover* was an "actual disservice" to children, more likely to "promote anxiety and tension in children" than to help them prepare for actual response to an atomic bomb attack. It was not until 1959, however, that the film was listed as "obsolete" in the revised version of the Office of Civil Defense and Mobilization's motion picture catalogue. Both the promotion of and response to *Duck and Cover* encapsulated the public debate concerning which methods were truly effective and necessary for disaster preparedness in light of the Cold War tensions of the 1950s.

A CRUCIAL PART of disaster preparedness is a strategy for response, which includes, on the civilian level, coordination of relief and recovery. How this response would be coordinated, however, and who should be in charge, was to become a matter of great political debate and uncertainty. Just two months prior to the creation of the FCDA, Congress had passed the Federal Disaster Relief Act, which allowed the federal government to provide assistance to states at times of dire need due to disaster. This function, as outlined in the bill, was assigned to the Executive Office of the President (EOP).

The Disaster Relief Act of 1950 was the United States' first comprehensive federal disaster relief law and established, for the first time, a permanent source of federal funds for disaster relief. Federal assistance measures outlined in the law included the lending of federal equipment, personnel, facilities, and supplies to states and municipalities in the event of "any major disaster... when directed by the President"; the donation of surplus federal property; the clearing of debris and wreckage; and the distribution "through the Red Cross or otherwise, [of] medicine, food, and other consumable supplies" (64 Stat. 1109). This effectively gave the President the authority to issue disaster declarations that would allow federal agencies to provide direct assistance to state and local governments, setting a precedent that continues to this day.

Then, on December 16, 1950, President Truman used an executive order (EO 10193) to create the federal Office of Defense Mobilization (ODM), the purpose of which was to coordinate federal mobilization, initially for wartime activities. By means of another executive order (EO 10427), dated January 6, 1953—two weeks before Truman left office and Dwight D. Eisenhower assumed office as the 34th President—the ODM inherited responsibilities for disaster relief coordination.

As the Tennessee Department of the Military: Tennessee Emergency Management Agency (TEMA) website so aptly describes the situation generated by these multiple yo-yo moves:

> Confused? No doubt. So was just about everyone else at all levels of government during this period. The distinction between wartime-type civil defense activities and natural disaster relief activities and their attendant

> philosophies would serve to create friction in many dif-
> ferent ways even through the 1980s.... Disaster relief
> was seen by civil defense workers as an unrelated, be-
> nign task best left to others.

After all, as noted above, the original vision for civil defense programs was to develop the capabilities needed to shelter and house civilians in cities that had been attacked, presumably by America's Cold War enemies. Civil defense planners also worked out mass evacuation plans for major cities across the country that might come under attack. For example, the evacuation plan for the city of Memphis, Tennessee, laid out how the entire population of Memphis was to be relocated among approximately 30 other counties in West Tennessee as well as Arkansas, Missouri, and Mississippi. From 1953 through 1958, government authorities at all levels continued to argue over whether evacuation or sheltering was to be the nation's primary civilian response to nuclear attack.

By the late 1950s, however, defense planners had to acknowledge the reality that a missile from the Soviet Union could reach the United States within a few minutes, rather than several hours (as had been the case at the beginning of the decade). There would be no time for long and elaborate evacuations of major cities or even small towns. The focus thus shifted to emergency preparedness and disaster relief.

In 1958, the FCDA and the ODM were combined into a single agency, the Office of Defense and Civilian Mobilization (ODCM), again to be housed in the Executive Office of the President. Congress amended the Federal Civil Defense Act to provide funding toward civil emergency preparedness, supplying 50/50 matching funds to state and local governments for personnel and administration costs in civil defense agencies and thus establishing the concept of joint federal, state, and local responsibility for civil defense and disaster response.

In Tennessee, the Office of Civil Defense that had been created in 1951 continued to have coordinating authority over all other state agencies' activities in the event of an attack, and this policy of central coordination carried over the decades to the time of the train derailment and explosion in Waverly, when the main state agency involvement was directed through the TOCD and its personnel.

THROUGHOUT THE 1960s and early 1970s, the seemingly endless oscillation, on the federal level, between priorities of civil defense (in response to a nuclear attack) and disaster preparedness (primarily in response to natural disasters) continued, with the two functions again being separated into two different agencies during the John F. Kennedy administration, only to be reorganized once more under Richard Nixon. In spite of these federal vacillations, however, the overall policy remained steady in Tennessee, as consecutive governors reinforced the concept of the TOCD, which became known as the Tennessee Civil Defense Agency (TCDA), as the office in charge of coordination and planning efforts in response to emergencies, including potential nuclear attacks, that could involve resource shortages.

Across the country, the 1970s witnessed a rise in the number of natural and manmade disasters resulting in loss of life and significant property damage. In 1972, Hurricane Agnes killed at least 128 people and displaced tens of thousands from Florida to New York; its remnants triggered major flooding in New York and Pennsylvania, where 74 people lost their lives and property damage dollar totals were in the billions. In 1974, violent tornado outbreaks across the Midwest killed hundreds of residents. In January 1977, a blizzard in Buffalo, New York, killed 29 people and stranded tens of thousands while disabling public utilities and bringing regional transportation to a standstill.

Several of these disasters attracting national attention occurred in Tennessee. In 1977, heavy flooding and major dam failures impacted the state. That same year, a tanker truck carrying toxic bromine gas overturned in Rockwood, releasing the hazardous chemical in a gaseous cloud that caused the National Guard to evacuate the town. And then came the Waverly train derailment and liquid propane explosion in February 1978. In the eyes of the National Governors Association, the need for a centralized, federally administrated emergency management agency had become crystal clear, and the train disaster in Waverly served as a final catalyst.

The NGA found a willing listener in President Jimmy Carter, who, since the beginning of his term in 1977, had been pressing for improvements in federal disaster response and a reorganization of the emergency management system. On June 19, 1978, just shy of four months since the Waverly Train Disaster, Carter submitted to Congress the Reorganization Plan No. 3 of 1978. This proposal laid out the merger of five agencies—from the General Services Administration as well as from the Departments of Defense, Commerce, and Housing and Urban Development—into a single, new, independent entity, which would be known as the Federal Emergency Management Agency (FEMA).

On March 31, 1979, Carter issued Executive Order 12127, putting Reorganization Plan No. 3 of 1978 into effect and officially creating FEMA. The new agency's establishment date was April 1, 1979, and at that time, transfer of certain functions took place: fire prevention and control as well as some functions of the Emergency Broadcast System (EBS), from the Department of Commerce; flood insurance from the Department of Housing and Urban Development; and other EBS functions from the Office of the President.

In July of that same year, President Carter issued a second executive order (EO 12148), which transferred further functions to

FEMA, including civil defense, federal disaster assistance, federal preparedness, and earthquake hazards reduction. Once again, the dual functions of civil defense and disaster response were combined in a single agency, as the EO tasked FEMA with coordinating "all civil defense and civil emergency planning, management, mitigation, and assistance functions," "natural and nuclear disaster warning systems," dam safety, and "preparedness and planning to reduce the consequences of major terrorist incidents."

As FEMA's capstone document, Pub 1, explains it, "FEMA's creation in 1979 was the first step in unifying Federal emergency management activity and building a comprehensive approach to national emergency management." Since then, FEMA has responded to all manner of disasters, from floods, hurricanes, tornadoes, typhoons, wildfires, landslides, and earthquakes to water contamination, Ebola, Zika, and COVID-19.

In the process, FEMA transformed emergency management, professionalizing it and improving both disaster planning and personnel training. The example set at the federal level inspired states to create their own offices and agencies for emergency management, and by the 1980s, FEMA had begun to allow states and local agencies to focus on natural and hazardous materials disasters affecting their own communities, rather than prioritizing nuclear attack planning.

In Tennessee, the name of the Tennessee Civil Defense Agency changed to the Tennessee Emergency Management Agency (TEMA) in 1984, and the agency's first civilian director, Mr. Lacy Suiter, was appointed that same year. In November 2001, TEMA established a website dedicated solely to the train explosion in Waverly, introduced with these lines:

> In almost every critical aspect of our daily lives, there
> can usually be found a 'watershed' moment, or a

moment that defines a critical problem or situation that is found in society or the world. An example would be the explosion of the space shuttle Challenger in 1986, which resulted in a top-to-bottom review of the way NASA managed the shuttle program.

TEMA's commentary measures the Waverly Train Disaster as just such an event, given how it resulted in not only a detailed review and revision of all elements of train safety policies and regulations as well as hazardous materials handling, but how it also pushed forward the formation of the nation's agency for emergency management, FEMA—and how, in its wake, TEMA itself came into being.

IN 2003, DURING the George W. Bush administration, FEMA— along with 22 other existing federal agencies—was once again incorporated into another department: the Department of Homeland Security, which had been created in response to the terrorist attacks of September 11, 2001.

On August 29, 2005, Hurricane Katrina slammed into the Gulf Coast, killing 1,833 people and inflicting over $100 billion of property damage (in un-adjusted 2005 dollars). The staggering loss of life and widespread, severe damage across the region made Katrina "one of the most devastating natural disasters in United States history." (Medlin et al., National Weather Service 2016)

It would be a gross understatement to say that the crisis created by Katrina was not handled well by FEMA, and this serious failure to meet the urgent and emergent needs of the victims was well documented by the media, and contributed to the tragically high fatality rate. The agency's response, as Kneeland has described it in *Playing Politics with Natural Disaster,* was "disorganized and dysfunctional," and resulted in "widespread public criticism and ... political fallout that eventually lost [the Republican] party control of the House and Senate in 2006."

As a result of this, Congress passed the Post-Katrina Emergency Management Reform Act of 2006, which reorganized FEMA yet again, making it an independent agency once more, with a director who would report to the secretary of homeland security. The Act did so by reconfiguring FEMA as an autonomous and distinct entity within the Department of Homeland Security (DHS), much like the US Coast Guard and the US Secret Service, and by elevating the status of the FEMA director to the level of deputy secretary.

The Post-Katrina Act also redefined FEMA's mission. As a Congressional Research Service report stated:

> As of March 31, 2007, the Post-Katrina Act will restore to FEMA the responsibility to lead and support efforts to reduce the loss of life and property and protect the nation from all hazards through a risk-based system that focuses on expanded CEM [Comprehensive Emergency Management] components.

All disaster preparedness functions that were previously administered by FEMA remained part of the agency's mandate. Notably exempt from the transfer of functions to the newly reorganized FEMA, however, were those of four Preparedness Directorate units: the Office of Infrastructure Protection, the National Communications System, the National Cyber Security Division, and the Office of the Chief Medical Officer. Thus, activities related to civil defense, protection, and anti-terrorism were once again separated from FEMA's responsibilities and overall mission.

Importantly, the Post-Katrina Act also disallowed "substantial or significant reductions, by the Secretary [of Homeland Security], of the authorities, responsibilities, or functions of FEMA, or FEMA's capability to perform them" (Congressional Research Service 2007). Most transfers of FEMA assets or functions to other sections of DHS were also prohibited. FEMA was to be given the allowance to stand on its own two feet and to focus on its duty of disaster management without interference. Thus was born the mission to which FEMA adheres today: "To help people before, during, and after disasters."

CHAPTER EIGHTEEN

Hazardous Materials

FEBRUARY 2003

TWENTY-FIVE YEARS AFTER THE EVENT, *Firehouse* magazine called the Waverly Train Disaster the "high-water mark of hazardous materials incidents in the United States." Indeed, the federal and local response in the aftermath of the explosion in Waverly changed hazardous materials handling and transportation across the nation.

The NTSB report on the disaster pointed out that "conventional firefighting procedures could not control the fires resulting from the spilled LPG." The Safety Board believed this was an indication "that the knowledge required to make judgment decisions regarding the condition of damaged tank cars is not generally available at the local level in the public or private sectors."

Among the areas in which knowledge on the ground was lacking was the ability to differentiate between an insulated and an uninsulated tank, and the capacity to assess the tank's structural damage with any accuracy. The Waverly fire and police departments, as well as the Tennessee Civil Defense Agency, were under the impression that the tank that exploded was double-walled and insulated—a mistaken impression that, apparently, no one with the L&N Railroad Company corrected prior to the explosion.

Although, according to the NTSB, "the all-volunteer Waverly Fire Department's training sessions regarding the availability and location of the train's consist and waybills show some degree of preparation," there remained an "inability of anyone at the scene to properly assess the mechanical damage sustained by tank cars." The report on the disaster also pointed out that L&N had not obtained assistance from the Association of American Railroads' Bureau of Explosives before the propane ignited—the very experts who *were* trained to evaluate the level of mechanical damage and to handle accidents involving hazardous materials.

In the NTSB's view, the Waverly Train Disaster was another reminder of "the need for training of all persons involved with hazardous materials accidents." The NTSB was not alone in this view. As the TEMA website dedicated to the Waverly explosion described it: "This event would forever change the nature of emergency response to accidents involving hazardous materials."

The Tennessee Civil Defense Agency had developed a draft hazardous materials response plan prior to the disaster in Waverly, in response to the bromine leak in Rockwood the year before, but this plan had yet to be enacted. As a result of the accident in Waverly and several other hazmat accidents that occurred across the country shortly thereafter, the state of Tennessee formulated a new set of standards for hazardous materials handling, and established a training program for hazmat responders. Governor Ray Blanton, who was present in Waverly that Friday night while the fires were still burning, created the Tennessee Hazardous Materials Institute by executive order in 1980.

The Institute's training programs and courses were quickly adopted as models for the development of hazmat training programs in several other states as well as by the federal government, and continue to be referenced across the country as well as internationally. In fact, as early as the week after the explosion,

Waverly received visits from fire chiefs who came from all over the nation—Florida, Connecticut, Pennsylvania—and even Scotland, to learn what to do if such an event ever happened in their towns or municipalities.

The hard-learned lessons from the Waverly Train Disaster became part of hazmat training from coast to coast. A section of the training manual for the California Specialized Training Institute's Hazardous Materials Section, a part of the California Emergency Management Agency (CalEMA), references the Waverly Train Disaster as a case study of a boiling liquid expanding vapor explosion (BLEVE) without flame impingement. As Robert Burke explained in *Firehouse*: "The explosion in Waverly was unusual because it did not involve flame impingement on the tank. When the derailment occurred in Waverly, there were no leaks, fires, or explosions. This might have been a primary factor that led to disaster two days later." According to Burke, the explosion in Waverly also changed how firefighters across the nation respond to LPG fires, particularly those that originate in containers.

THE PUBLIC SAFETY issues surrounding hazardous materials had been a growing concern on the national level in the years leading up to the Waverly Train Disaster—even their manner of classification, and who held the authority for that classification, had been a matter of debate. In 1975, the Hazardous Materials Transportation Act gave the Secretary of Transportation the authority to designate as hazardous material any "particular quantity or form" of a material that "may pose an unreasonable risk to health and safety or property."

Currently, there are nine classes of hazardous materials: explosives (Class 1); compressed gases (Class 2, which includes LPG); flammable liquids (Class 3); flammable solids (Class 4); oxidizers and organic peroxides (Class 5); toxic materials (Class 6, which includes poisonous and infectious agents); radioactive material (Class 7); corrosive material (Class 8); and miscellaneous (Class 9).

On February 7, 1979—less than a year after the Waverly Train Disaster—the Federal Railroad Administration, one of ten agencies within the US Department of Transportation concerned with intermodal transportation, issued Emergency Order No. 11. This placed restrictions on the movement of railroad freight cars carrying hazardous materials, known as "placarded hazardous materials cars," by the Louisville & Nashville Railroad Company and any other railroads using L&N-owned or leased track. The EO stated that the FRA would consider "gradual removal of its restrictions dependent upon the L&N's progress in rectifying its safety deficiencies."

In the reasons given for its action, the FRA stated it had found "substantial evidence that the L&N had inadequately dealt with a number of factors that had led, or contributed, to train derailments on its system during the 37 months preceding issuance of [Emergency Order No. 11]." This included, of course, the derailment in Waverly on the night of February 22, 1978.

The FRA said that "one of the purposes of the Order was to call the L&N's attention to the safety hazards created by its actions and omissions with the expectation that the L&N would take appropriate remedial action to improve the safety of operations over its system." However, the L&N continued to make separate requests—on March 1, March 23, March 28, April 20, and May 7, 1979—that the Order be modified to exclude coverage of 1,350 miles of track (in multiple segments), including the line running through Waverly.

The FRA conducted an investigation of all railroad operations over each track segment in question, and concluded that only 204 miles of the L&N's system, between Flomaton, Alabama and Chattahoochee, Florida, met the requirements necessary for the FRA to remove the Order, which it did on April 6, 1979—but only for those 204 miles of track.

L&N requested an administrative hearing seeking injunctive relief, which was granted on June 18, 1979, in the US District Court for the District of Columbia, Judge Gerhard Gesell presiding.

Judge Gesell, by that time, had already overseen the Pentagon Papers case, delivering a ruling in 1971 that allowed the *Washington Post* to publish the leaked classified documents on the origins of the Vietnam War. He had also presided over some of the Watergate-era trials, which resulted in another of his memorable rulings: that the playing of President Nixon's tape recordings during a Watergate trial placed those recordings in the public domain. Yet another of his many Watergate-related rulings concerned Nixon's attempt to fire the first Watergate special prosecutor, Archibald Cox; Gesell ruled this attempt illegal.

In the case of *Louisville & Nashville R.R. v. Sullivan,* Gesell agreed with L&N's complaint that the EO failed to specify the standards under which relief could be obtained and the Order lifted. The FRA amended EO No. 11 to specify that the requirements to be met included "substantial compliance" with all of the following Department of Transportation regulations: Track Safety Standards, Freight Car Safety Standards, Power Brake Regulations, and the standards set forth in the Locomotive Inspection Act. However, the effect of Gesell's ruling was to invalidate EO No. 11 entirely, forcing the Federal Railroad Administrator, John M. Sullivan, to declare that the Order was "not an operative document affecting the rights or liabilities of any party."

The federal fight to secure the safe handling and transportation of hazardous materials was far from over, however, and extended next to the oversight of hazardous wastes. On December 11, 1980, Congress enacted the Comprehensive Environmental Response, Compensation, and Liability Act (CERCLA) of 1980, better known as the Superfund law, which authorized a direct federal response to the release or threatened release of hazardous materials. This law primarily focused on the regulation of hazardous waste sites like the defunct Hooker Chemical site at Love Canal in Niagara Falls, New York, where 22,000 tons of mixed chemical waste that had been dumped into Love Canal between 1942 and 1953 began oozing to the surface in the mid-1970s, and no government agency had the authority or funding to address the situation. However, the law also grew out of the more general national concern regarding how hazardous materials were being handled from beginning to end, and what safeguards could protect the communities where these substances were being transported and stored.

CERCLA also allowed for revision of the National Oil and Hazardous Substances Pollution Contingency Plan, known as the National Contingency Plan (NCP). According to the US Environmental Protection Agency (EPA), the NCP continues to be "the federal government's blueprint for responding to both oil spills and hazardous substance releases," and is "the result of efforts to develop a national response capability and promote coordination among the hierarchy of responders and contingency plans."

The Superfund law continued to grow through amendments and further legislation. By 1987, the National Institute of Environmental Health Sciences (NIEHS), one of the institutes of the National Institutes of Health (NIH), had established the NIEHS Worker Training Program based on the Congressional mandate set forth in the Superfund Amendments and Reauthorization Act of 1986 (SARA). As specified in the Act, the purpose of the Worker Training Program was to provide grants "for the training and education of workers who are or may be engaged in activities related to hazardous waste removal or containment or emergency response."

SARA also required the Occupational Safety and Health Administration (OSHA) to become involved by promulgating standards "for the health and safety protection of employees engaged in hazardous waste operations." This, in turn, led to

OSHA's issuance of the Hazardous Waste Operations and Emergency Response (HAZWOPER) standard. This standard, along with standards set by the EPA, guides curricula development and training programs throughout the nation, supported by the NIEHS Worker Training Program, in order to help employers meet the requirements and train workers in the safe handling of hazardous wastes.

As for the Louisville and Nashville Railroad Company, it ceased to exist on December 31, 1982, when it officially merged into the Seaboard System Railroad, bringing an end to a 132-year-old era. CSX Transportation then absorbed the Seaboard System in 1986. CSX trains continue to run through Waverly to this day.

THE CHANGES IN hazardous materials transportation safety that followed the Waverly Train Disaster did have the desired effect of reducing loss of life due to rail accidents involving these materials. According to the Federal Railroad Administration, during the 12 years from 1994 through 2005, railroad accidents involving hazardous materials resulted in a total of 14 fatalities—less than the 16 fatalities in Waverly from the accident of a single afternoon. In the same period, hazardous materials released in highway accidents accounted for a total of 116 fatalities.

The FRA notes that the "continuous sponsored industry and government improvements in rail equipment, tank car and container design and construction, and inspection and maintenance methods"—which were all put in place after Waverly and continued to see improvements over the years since—"have resulted in reducing derailments, spills, leaks, and casualties while the volume of traffic increases."

The FRA even goes so far as to say that "rail transportation of hazardous materials in the United States is recognized to be the safest method of moving large quantities of chemicals over long distances." This does not mean that accidents never happen, of course, but they are fewer in number and better handled. In addition, the FRA's hazardous materials research program continues to encourage innovation throughout the railroad industry, developing new regulations and setting new design standards to improve the safety and integrity of tank cars.

THE ONGOING ATTENTION to the improvement of hazardous materials handling, storage, and transportation is appropriate, because the devastating and far-reaching impact—both literal and figurative—of hazardous materials accidents cannot be overstated. This is particularly true in areas that are already struggling or are otherwise ill prepared to cope with the destruction and the aftermath.

In August 2020, well into the COVID-19 pandemic and across the world from Waverly, an estimated 2,750 tons of ammonium nitrate blew away a major part of the port of Beirut, Lebanon, and damaged over half of the structures in the city, in what has been called the "largest non-nuclear blast in modern history" (El Sayed 2020). The blast killed at least 200 people and injured over 6,000 more. Infrastructure and property damage—including severe damage to the city's grain elevator, multiple hospitals, museums, cultural heritage sites, embassies, shoreline, 90% of its hotels, and housing for up to 300,000 people— has been estimated to exceed $10 billion. Occurring against the backdrop of the pandemic, food shortages, and an already serious financial crisis, the fallout led to the collapse of the Lebanese government and eventually, to the economic collapse of the entire country.

The catastrophes following the releases of radioactive hazardous materials from the nuclear power plants in Chernobyl in 1986 (again threatened with disaster by the Russian invasion of Ukraine in 2022) and in Fukushima in 2011 have been well documented.

Nations are changed forever on multiple levels by major accidents like these, but most importantly, the people involved are changed forever, too.

In Waverly, the town itself was never quite the same after the propane explosion of February 24, 1978; the New Town section never recovered from the totality of the destruction. A few years after the disaster, plans to build a bypass around Waverly, by widening US Highway 70 and diverting it around the town's business districts, were put forward by external authorities, and a fair portion of the former New Town area was subsumed in the construction of the bypass. Longtime Waverly residents feared that the bypass, by diverting traffic away from Waverly's downtown area, would lead to the demise of local businesses and result in an overall downturn for the local economy. And as things turned out, they were right. By the late 1980s, the commercial side of Waverly that Dr. McClure remembered in its heyday was no more, and many family-owned businesses closed, helped along in their demise by the opening of a big-box retailer on the west side of town.

The community remained strong and tightly knit, however, and showed an uncommon resilience. Small but significant museums were established, tourist attractions were featured in local and regional magazines, new and varied shops and businesses started to pop up in numerous sections of town. As the third decade of the 21st century approached, Waverly's commercial district appeared to thrive again. The Mi-De-Ga theater looked forward to celebrating its 85th year in business. Even the hospital, which had changed hands multiple times since the explosion and at one point was under such financial stress that closure was considered, had found new ownership and a new path forward.

CHAPTER NINETEEN

The Struggle of the Rural Hospital

NOVEMBER 1, 2019
FRIDAY

BOTH PROFESSIONAL PHOTOGRAPHERS AND TRAUMA surgeons refer to the "golden hour," but with very different meanings. For the surgeons, the golden hour is the approximate duration from time of injury in which therapeutic interventions have the best chances of success. It's the time available to achieve the best possible outcomes; success rates start to drop with every minute that passes after that hour is up. When the tanker exploded in Waverly, having a hospital one mile away with a trauma surgeon on staff allowed for the successful triage of all critically injured patients within that golden hour.

In fact, the NTSB report on the train disaster in Waverly had only one mention of unconditional praise, and this was given to Nautilus Memorial Hospital and to the town of Waverly for their joint disaster plan, "which, when correlated with the State Civil Defense Agency, provided excellent care for the public following the accident."

The NTSB further concluded that "quick implementation of the nearby hospital's [Nautilus Memorial] emergency plan and preliminary treatment and classification of the injured [triage], along with a well coordinated transportation effort by regional military units, worked to minimize loss of life."

Thus, one of the striking features of the successful medical response to the Waverly train explosion was the relative robustness of Nautilus Memorial Hospital and the depth and breadth of its capabilities in serving its community at the time. Like so many rural community hospitals across the country, Nautilus Memorial provided thousands of residents from multiple surrounding counties with access to essential inpatient, outpatient, and emergency medical services.

Rural hospitals like Nautilus also contributed significantly to their local economies, attracting new businesses and generating employment. In fact, rural community hospitals are often one of the largest employers in the area. And for a new business or industry looking to establish itself in a certain location, quick access to high-quality healthcare is one of the most appealing features a community can offer.

NAUTILUS MEMORIAL HOSPITAL was established with the help of funding provided by the Hill-Burton Act of 1946, formally known as the Hospital Survey and Construction Act, and signed into law by President Harry S. Truman. The bipartisan bill was co-written by Alabama Senator J. Lister Hill and Ohio Senator Harold H. Burton, and was designed to fund healthcare services in underserved areas of the country—particularly in the rural South.

The Hill-Burton Act provided loans and grants for the construction of new hospitals where they were deemed to be both needed and sustainable. However, the law infamously codified the notion of "separate-but-equal," even in hospitals, allowing segregation of Black and White patients. Over the ensuing years, and with momentum building in the Civil Rights Movement, the

NAACP filed several lawsuits aimed at eliminating this discrimination, and in 1963, the US Supreme Court struck down the "separate-but-equal" clause of Hill-Burton.

The success of Hill-Burton in building access to healthcare across the rural South led to other federal government programs that increased funding for health, education, and welfare, and then extended to infrastructure like new roads and airports. As historian Karen Kruse Thomas has noted, this made "prosperity possible in the Sun Belt while allowing southern states to maintain low taxes."

In 1975, the legislation of Hill-Burton was incorporated into the more expansive, existing Public Health Service Act, in an extensive amendment introduced by Senator Edward "Ted" Kennedy and passed by Congressional override of President Gerald Ford's veto. The new legislation extended the programs of Hill-Burton across the country while revising and extending other programs as well, including health revenue sharing, family planning, community mental health centers, nurse training, and the National Health Service Corps.

HILL-BURTON WAS A milestone in American public health efforts. Early public health activities in the late 1700s were primarily urban endeavors focused on containment of specific diseases like cholera, smallpox, tuberculosis, malaria, typhoid fever, and yellow fever. The rapid growth of industrialization in the late 19th and early 20th centuries resulted in a continued urban focus for public health, but with a demographic focus as well: the urban slums. Thus, until the passage of Hill-Burton, rural public health remained largely neglected and unfunded.

The renewed focus on geography that continued with and after the success of Hill-Burton provided an important context for public health efforts in non-metropolitan areas across the nation. However, as Charles D. Phillips and Kenneth R. McLeroy have so eloquently written:

> It is important to realize how deceptive perceptions of geography and place can be. The images conjured up by the term "rurality" in the minds of the general population are quite consistent. . . . Metropolitan dwellers believe that rural folk have freely chosen their location and lifestyle because farming, ranching, and the interconnectedness of rural or small-town life are important values for them. This consensus captures as much of the reality of rural life in modern America as does Grant Wood's iconic image of rurality in his painting American Gothic.

Thus, the definition of "rural" is not "pastoral." In fact, the US Census Bureau and the Office of Management and Budget (OMB), which define rural areas for government agencies and government programs, consider "rural" to include "all people, housing, and territory that are not within an urban area. Any area that is not urban is rural."

Furthermore, the Census divides the definition of "urban" into two categories: Urbanized Areas of 50,000 or more people, and Urban Clusters of 2,500 to 49,999 people. By this definition, then, Waverly was and still is an Urban Cluster. However, according to the American Hospital Association (AHA), hospitals that are not located within a metropolitan area as defined by the OMB—which uses the definition of an urban core of 50,000 or more people—are considered to be rural hospitals. This includes more than half of all hospitals in the United States, including many rural community hospitals that started out like Waverly's Nautilus Memorial. So, due to these (somewhat confusing) differences in definitions, while the City of Waverly itself is not rural, its hospital is considered rural for all purposes related to health-care funding, classifications, and discussions—including those pertaining to public health.

THROUGHOUT THE 1980s, hospitals like Nautilus Memorial continued to thrive, but by the end of the 1990s, a combination of managed care reforms, administrative burdens created by multiple government regulations, reimbursement changes modeled by Medicare and Medicaid, and the rise of advanced medical technologies affordable only to large healthcare systems, were beginning to put the squeeze on small hospitals everywhere. The Great Recession of 2008, coupled with hospital mergers, reduced demand for inpatient services, and the choice made by several states to refuse Medicaid expansion, further deepened the financial challenges faced by rural hospitals.

By 2019, the hospital in Waverly had changed ownership multiple times, and was struggling to keep its doors open. On November 1, 2019, Nashville-based newspaper the *Tennessean* ran an article declaring it "on the brink of collapse." Front and center in the photo that accompanied the article was Nancy Daniel, RN, at a patient's bedside—still her favorite place to be.

Waverly's hospital was far from alone in its struggles. According to the North Carolina Rural Health Research Program (NCRHRP), 138 rural hospitals closed between January 2010 and February 2, 2022. These closures occurred disproportionately in the South, due to financial distress exacerbated by "multiple factors . . . including a decrease in patients seeking inpatient care and across-the-board Medicare payment reductions," as the US Government Accountability Office (GAO) noted in its 2018 report on rural hospital closures. In this report, the GAO's analysis revealed that 64 of these closures occurred in the five-year period from 2013 through the end of 2017, representing approximately 3% of all the rural hospitals in existence in 2013 and more than twice the number of closures as during the previous five-year period. The GAO also commented that these closures affect certain populations most—particularly those who are most vulnerable, such as the elderly and those with low income.

Given the vibrancy of Nautilus Memorial Hospital at the time of the Waverly train explosion and its critical importance in the disaster response and to the community at large, it should come as no surprise that the NCRHRP has found that "closure of a rural hospital has a direct effect on the individuals within that hospital's service area, decreasing the health and economic well-being of that community."

Counted among NCRHRP's rural hospital closure statistics are both abandoned hospitals and hospital conversions. Abandoned hospitals, as the term implies, are "those that no longer provide any form of health service," while hospital conversions are those that "remain a healthcare facility but do not provide any inpatient care." In NCRHRP's breakdown of the numbers, during the five-year period from 2010 through 2014, approximately 800,000 people were living in rural healthcare markets with abandoned hospitals. Another 700,000 people lost access to local inpatient care due to rural hospital conversions.

To what sorts of facilities are rural hospitals converted? The three most common care models, again according to NCRHRP, are urgent care or emergency care facilities; outpatient or primary care services; and skilled nursing or rehabilitation.

Rural hospitals that were abandoned entirely were more likely to have a higher proportion of their patient base that was non-White (33%) than were converted hospitals (17%). NCRHRP also found that abandoned hospitals were more likely to serve populations with higher poverty rates and lower per capita income, and were at greater distances from the next nearest hospital, making their loss even more keenly felt and contributing further to the sense of isolation felt by rural residents when it comes to healthcare access.

In an attempt to address the failing financial performance of rural hospitals, Congress enacted legislation authorizing Medicare to provide higher payments to such hospitals, through the development of reimbursement models that assess rural hospital claims by different eligibility criteria, adjustment factors, and timeliness of data. Not all rural hospitals faced the same financial pressures; hospitals designated as Medicare-Dependent Hospitals and Standard Prospective Payment Systems Hospitals were at higher risk than those classified as Critical Access Hospitals or Sole Community Hospitals.

In this classification scheme, as of 2015, the majority of rural hospitals (61%) fell under the category of Critical Access Hospital (CAH), with no more than 25 beds and a location that is at least 35 miles by primary road or 15 miles by secondary road from the next nearest hospital, or otherwise deemed a "necessary provider" by the state in which they were located. Seventeen percent of rural hospitals qualified for the Sole Community Hospital (SCH) designation; these hospitals are located at least 35 miles from the nearest similar hospital (excluding CAHs), or meet other federal criteria as the community's only source of acute care. These hospitals, the CAHs and SCHs, were those that tended to have marginally better financial performance than the remaining two categories.

Medicare-Dependent Hospitals (MDHs) represented 8% of rural hospitals and were those with no more than 100 beds, not classified as an SCH, and having at least 60% of their inpatient days or hospital discharges due to Medicare patients. Finally, the Standard Prospective Payment System Hospitals (PPSs), a designation that encompassed 15% of rural hospitals, were those that were paid under Medicare's traditional PPS rates—where payment is made based on a predetermined, fixed amount; these included Rural Referral Centers not otherwise classified.

Although the new legislation hoped to save the MDHs and PPSs in particular, as researchers for NCRHRP have noted, certain factors of consequence—such as average daily patient census, average distance from a patient's residence to the hospital, and local unemployment rate—were not reflected in Medicare's payment methods. Furthermore, some of the variables that were identified as important cost predictors for hospitals tended to be more associated with Medicare program eligibility than with actual reimbursement.

As the numbers from 2015 onward show, the slide of rural hospitals into oblivion has continued across the country, with grave consequences for the communities they served. One has only to consider the case of the Waverly Train Disaster to understand these consequences. Had Nautilus Hospital not existed in Waverly, the death toll for the disaster would have been much higher.

These closures have dire economic implications as well. As one journalist in California, Elizabeth Zach, put it: "The very economic decline that contributed to [rural hospitals'] closure is likely to be worsened by their disappearance."

Zach's reporting highlighted the challenges faced by the small town of Kingsburg, California, since its hospital closed in 2010. The original hospital, Kingsburg Medical Center, was converted to a mental health clinic, and "the lack of a hospital is making life difficult for many of the 11,000 residents," as Zach reported in 2016. Importantly, "the lack of a hospital can also erode a community's sense of security and affect its economy," since "potential job-creators are more inclined to set up shop closer to hospitals, especially in urban areas, where doctors are more likely to set up practice."

The economic ripple effect of rural hospital closures has now been documented in recent research. In an analysis published in March 2022 by Tyler L. Malone and colleagues at the University of North Carolina at Chapel Hill, of the 1,759 non-metropolitan counties in their study sample from 2001 to 2018, 109 experienced hospital closures—and these closures significantly reduced the size of the labor force in each county by an average of 1.4%.

And although rural hospitals have been closing at record rates across the country, the majority of closures since 2010 have been in the South. According to data compiled by Dr. Arriana Marie Planey and colleagues for the NCRHRP, in the 2010s, closures were 3.5 times more common in the South than in the Midwest, and 9 times more common in the South than in the Northeast or the West, such that the South accounted for two-thirds of all rural hospital closures nationally. Thus, the brunt of the problem has been borne by the very region and populations that Hill-Burton initially sought to champion.

IRONICALLY, COVID-19 MAY have saved some rural hospitals (though not all—19 rural hospitals closed nationwide in 2020, unable to endure the added strain of the pandemic). It certainly did so for the one in Waverly, which was given a new lease on life at the end of 2021 when a large healthcare system, Ascension Saint Thomas, signed an agreement to purchase it. By that time, Three Rivers Hospital (the former Nautilus Memorial) was a Critical Access Hospital, and as the *Tennessean* reported, its bed capacity had shrunk by roughly half, to 25 beds; it "was poised to become the next casualty of Tennessee's rural hospital crisis."

One of the many unforeseen consequences of the pandemic was the renewed demand for community hospitals everywhere to step up and bolster the beleaguered healthcare system in the face of the overwhelming patient care needs presented by the illness and complications caused by the virus. This, in turn, increased financial revenue for these hospitals, enough for them to meet their payrolls and stay open. The pandemic also fostered a boom in telemedicine services—and reimbursement for them—which has enabled rural hospitals to access specialists, like neurologists and psychiatrists, remotely.

The work-from-home phenomenon imposed by the pandemic may also turn out to be more than a temporary circumstance. The ability to work remotely enables knowledge workers to log on from anywhere with broadband internet access, and even before the pandemic, there had been signs in the real estate market of a move out of the cities to locations, often suburbs and small towns, with more land and more living space. Tennessee, for example, has seen an influx of homebuyers from New York, California, and other more densely populated states in recent years. This could encourage greater use of the rural hospitals that do manage to hold on and survive.

Direct legislative responses to the pandemic on the federal level, particularly in the form of the Coronavirus Aid, Relief, and Economic Security (CARES) Act of 2020, also provided rural hospitals with much-needed funding lifelines that have the potential to help them endure current challenges. The CARES Act made available $100 billion in new funding for healthcare professionals to reimburse healthcare-related expenses or lost revenue due to COVID-19. These funds, made available on a rolling basis, assisted rural hospitals in addressing COVID-19-related patient care costs as well as lost revenue due to putting elective treatments and procedures on hold.

The CARES Act also provided loans (many of which were forgivable) to small businesses through the Paycheck Protection Program, and this included both for-profit and not-for-profit hospitals with fewer than 500 total employees. As the American Hospital Association has noted, this provision offered critical financial support to small rural hospitals to pay salaries and benefits. The Act made changes pertaining to Medicare payments that also affected rural hospitals favorably, especially Critical Access Hospitals (CAHs). Included in these changes was a 20% add-on to the Diagnosis Related Group rate for patients with COVID-19 treated in rural and urban inpatient Prospective Payment System (PPS) hospitals.

Nearly a year after the CARES Act was signed into law, Representatives Tom Reed (R-NY) and Terri Sewell (D-AL) introduced the Rural Hospital Support Act, which would make permanent the Medicare-Dependent Hospital (MDH) program and enhanced low-volume Medicare adjustment for small rural PPS hospitals. These changes would help provide further funding for these rural hospitals. As of this writing, the bill remains in referral status, referred to the House Subcommittee on Health.

Another piece of legislation aimed at helping rural hospitals was Section 125 of the Consolidated Appropriations Act of 2021, which created the Rural Emergency Hospital (REH) model as a new Medicare provider type. The designation will become effective on January 1, 2023, and will give current CAHs and rural PPS hospitals with fewer than 50 beds the opportunity to convert to REH status. Such a conversion would allow these hospitals to deliver certain outpatient hospital services, including emergency department and short-term observation admission services, in rural areas. And as has been seen, hospital conversions, while not the most ideal of outcomes, are still better for the communities they serve than are outright closures (abandoned hospitals). As the National Rural Health Association stated in its support of the legislation, "NRHA believes the REH model will be an opportunity for vulnerable rural communities to maintain an essential access point for health services."

In Waverly, the transaction to buy Three Rivers Hospital was completed in the spring of 2022. If the hospital can continue to endure—and by all indications, it can—it will be yet another example of Waverly's resilience.

Epilogue

IN THE BARBER SHOP ON the corner of West Main Street and Highway 13, Toad Smith stands behind the chair, scissors in hand. Sitting in that chair is Waverly's only resident surgeon, Dr. Subhi D. Ali, who comes once a month to have his hair cut by the man whose hands he degloved on the night of February 24, 1978.

Not long after returning home from Parkview Hospital, Toad went back to work with the police department as a dispatcher. As his hands got better, Dr. Frist told him that he needed to exercise them more and use them whenever possible. So in his free time, he helped his wife's cousin remodel the interior of his home. Then he helped him put up a cattle fence, driving in steel posts with a ten-pound sledgehammer. He could grip it enough to swing it, and that was how he gave his hands the exercise he believed they needed.

On his follow-up visits with Dr. Frist, the surgeon would tell him, "Well, I don't know what you're doing, but whatever it is, you just keep doing it!"

Dr. Frist also told him, "I don't believe you'll ever cut hair anymore."

Toad responded, "Well, I don't know, Doc; we'll cross that bridge when we get to it."

Since then, Toad has worked not only as a barber but also as bailiff at the courthouse on Waverly's town square, across Main Street to the south of his shop. He also runs a small sawmill, but still considers barbering to be his master trade.

More than a decade after the train disaster, Toad was serving as bailiff during a child abuse case, and a psychiatrist was called in to testify. It was none other than the psychiatrist who had met with Toad when he was in the hospital at Parkview. After court, Toad walked over to him. He said, "Doc, you don't remember me, do you?"

The doctor squinted at him. "You look familiar."

"You remember the fella who told you about walking across the desert?"

"Oh-ho! There you are!"

Toad was proud that the doctor had never forgotten his story, and he was proud to show him how well his hands had healed. "You know, Dr. Frist once said to me that I may never cut hair again. Well, guess what?" He pointed at the barber shop across the street and laughed wholeheartedly.

His thumbnails never grew back, so he still has trouble buttoning a shirt with buttonholes down the front; he'd never realized before how integral thumbnails were to push those buttons on through. It can take three or four tries per button, so shirts with buttons that snap together under pressure are preferred.

It can also be difficult trying to pick up something small or flat from the floor. And though he can still feel the sensation of pressure in his hands, there will be times when he bumps his hand against something, and looks down to find blood running down his hand, with no feeling at all. With his hands, it is as though he can feel but he can't feel.

But he is alive, and doing all the things he wants to do. He can still cut hair, and he does wood carving as a hobby, and all in all, feels quite fortunate in life. He still has the impression of the walkie-talkie burned into the palm of his left hand, and every time he looks at it, he remembers. How bad things were, and how much worse they could have been, and how good they are now.

FOR HIS PART, Dr. Ali went on to become Surgeon General for the Tennessee Defense Force (later known as the Tennessee State Guard) and a Brigadier General in the Tennessee State Guard. He was diagnosed with Stage IV non-Hodgkin lymphoma the week after his 51st birthday in March 1994. The physician who read his CT scan in Nashville, confirming metastasis, was none other than the radiologist who had called him about the slit throat in the ER of Nautilus Memorial Hospital all those years earlier.

He was given a 5% chance of survival, but Dr. Ali had made a life out of beating the odds, and after undergoing grueling rounds of chemotherapy as well as stem-cell therapy, he was declared to be in remission. During his chemotherapy, Toad offered to make him a hairpiece. Although Dr. Ali declined, he still remembers Toad's kindness throughout the most difficult time of his life.

Dr. Ali went on to become President of the State Guard Association of the United States from 2000 to 2001, serving in this capacity when the tragedy of 9/11 occurred. He became President of the Tennessee Medical Association (TMA) in 2003, and has served on the Tennessee Board of Medical Examiners (BME), the licensing board for all Tennessee physicians, since 2004. In 2012, he was honored by the TMA with its Outstanding Physician Award. He continues to serve prominently—often as Chair—on various boards, including those of the Tennessee Medical Education Fund and the Physicians Foundation, a national nonprofit organization that he helped found in 2003 to empower physicians to lead in the delivery of high-quality, cost-efficient healthcare. He also continues to serve as President and Treasurer of the LaSalle D. Leffall Jr., MD, Surgical Society Foundation, which he co-founded with Dr. Maysoon on February 23, 2001, to help fund the education of residents and students at their alma mater, Howard University Medical College in Washington, DC.

In the wake of the train explosion, the L&N Railroad offered compensation to the physicians at Nautilus Hospital who treated patients injured in the disaster: a flat $350, total, per physician. Dr. Ali told L&N's representatives: "L&N cannot pay me for the work I did. No one can. There is no payment, no way to pay me for that."

The other physicians on staff, however, told him that if he refused the money, they would feel compelled to do so as well, so he finally agreed to accept. The moment the check was handed to him, in a medical staff meeting with everyone present, he turned it over on the table and wrote on the back of it, then handed it to the hospital administrator with the announcement that he had reassigned it to Nautilus Memorial Hospital, as a donation to build a hospital chapel, with more to follow. Dr. Maysoon did the same, on the spot.

And thus it came to pass that the installation of the hospital chapel in Waverly, Tennessee, was sponsored by the Drs. Ali.

DIRECTLY ACROSS THE street to the east of Toad's barber shop, in a corner office of the Waverly City Hall, sits the Mayor of Waverly, Buddy Frazier. His landslide victory in the May 2015 mayoral election was merely seen as a blessing to continue his lifetime career in public service. Following the train disaster, Officer Frazier continued to serve with distinction on a police force reeling from the trauma of the explosion and its aftermath. He was promoted to sergeant, then did criminal investigation for a number of years. He eventually became Assistant Police Chief and, finally, Chief of Police—a position he held for 18 years. In 2002, he became Waverly's City Manager, a post in which he served for the 13 years before he was elected Mayor.

From the four patrol cars that were in service when Buddy and his brother met the westbound L&N train that fateful Wednesday night in 1978, the Waverly police department has now more than tripled in size, with 14 patrol cars on hand. Thanks to Buddy, all officers now cross-train to be firefighters too; in 2004, he finally convinced the mayor at that time of the merits of his idea to create the Waverly Department of Public Safety, which would incorporate both the police and fire departments into a single entity.

This cross-training had been an idea of Buddy's for years, but it didn't become a reality until one day when he was meeting with the mayor at City Hall, and a fire call came in. The mayor stood at the window of Buddy's office, watching and waiting for the fire truck to leave from the fire station next door. And he waited, and he waited, and he waited.

Finally, the mayor turned to Buddy and asked, "What's wrong?"

"Our volunteer firemen have jobs," Buddy replied. "You know, at one time, most volunteer firemen lived right here and worked in the downtown area. But now people work everywhere."

It took about 15 minutes to get that truck out of the fire hall.

The mayor turned to Buddy and said, "We gotta beat this."

"Absolutely we gotta beat this," Buddy said. "There's a way. Lemme tell you about it."

Now that all officers are cross-trained, fire response is three minutes or less. The city is also able to pay its public safety officers better wages because of their higher level of training.

The Waverly Train Disaster is never far from Buddy's mind; in many ways, it has defined his career as a public servant. Nearly two decades after the explosion, he happened to be attending a state conference on disaster management and emergency response. The speaker was a Mr. John White, newly appointed Director of the Tennessee Emergency Management Agency. Buddy noticed something about him as he spoke and gestured.

Following Mr. White's talk, Buddy approached him and pointed at his hands. "You were there in Waverly when the train exploded, weren't you?"

"Yes, I was! And were you—why, you were the police officer who took me up to the hospital when my hands were burned!"

"That's right. You were one of the first people I picked up. You were beside me in the front seat of my patrol car. I knew you were a Civil Defense employee, but I did not know your name. I sure am glad to see you doing so well."

Buddy Frazier still thinks about how a matter of a few minutes or seconds can make all the difference between life and death, injury and health. About how it gives new meaning to your life forever after. About what might have happened had Chief Barnett not asked him to leave the derailment site to pick up Officer Tarpley when he did, or what might have happened had he been a few minutes later in reporting for duty that day.

Such good fortune, in Mayor Frazier's words, "makes you want to do good," and he has dedicated his entire life to public service, grateful for every healthy minute. He has dedicated himself to preserving the records and archives related to the train disaster and honoring the memory of those who lost their lives as a result of the explosion—those who, not as fortunate as he, were in the wrong place at the wrong time. Those whose time ran out at 2:55 P.M. on February 24, 1978.

On the one-year anniversary of the train explosion, he and many others helped set up a memorial and dedicated a monument at the site of the derailment. It is still there to this day, and as long as Buddy Frazier is around, there will always be a fresh wreath of flowers at the monument.

On the 25th anniversary of the disaster, while Buddy was City Manager, he and city officials dedicated a red L&N caboose adjacent to the monument, on the former site of the James Adult Group

Home, and opened it to the public as the Waverly Train Explosion Memorial Museum. Buddy frequently visits the museum himself to check on things, and while he is there, he always picks up the sign-in book and looks at the last page or two just to see the names, just to see who's come to visit. He is amazed every time he does so; people come from all over the country and even the world to check out the little museum in the small town of Waverly.

He was also surprised to discover that another Tennessee-based organization, one with which he had been familiar for years, can trace its roots to the Waverly Train Disaster. In the immediate aftermath of the disaster, the brotherhood director of the Tennessee Baptist Convention (TBC), Archie King, visited Waverly's First Baptist Church and delivered a $2,000 check to assist families affected by the explosion. This marked the TBC's first "official" disaster relief response, and from it, Tennessee Baptist Disaster Relief was born. Since then, its members have responded to disasters both at home and around the globe.

To Buddy's mind, the scope of the Waverly Train Disaster may well have been both the worst thing and the only good thing about it. As he puts it:

> That's how far-reaching this thing was. You know, you think, we're off down here, and the rest of the world has no idea what we're doing. But even in 1978, with communications and technology what they were then, the whole world knew, in just a little while, what happened here. And what happened here should have never happened. There's no good reason for it happening. And I guess if there's one good thing about what happened, it's that there's no telling how many lives have been saved over the years because of the lessons that were learned here.

206 — WALK THROUGH FIRE

It is not uncommon, even this many years later, when a train derailment happens elsewhere in the country—especially one involving tank cars carrying hazardous materials—for Mayor Frazier to receive a call, forwarded to him from the Waverly Police Department. Invariably, on the other end of the line is a concerned official from the location of the fresh derailment or disaster, and he or she wants Buddy's advice on what to do. They want to know about what happened in Waverly, and Buddy is the only person left in Waverly City Hall who can tell them from memory exactly what happened, and what they must do differently.

Sometimes those who want to know are, in fact, those closest to home. Not long after Buddy became City Manager, he happened to be away on vacation when he received a call late at night. It was from none other than the mayor of Waverly, who said to him, "You'll never guess what we're doin'." The mayor proceeded to tell him about a train derailment on the east side of town.

"Get away from there," Buddy told him. "Get everybody away from there. If you think the perimeter's safe, whatever it is, however wide it is—double it."

And now he brings the many hard lessons he's learned with him into the mayor's office, the office, both physical and titular, with which the people of Waverly have entrusted him. On his bookcase in this office in City Hall, there rests a red box. It is the old fire alarm box that was downtown, the very one he remembers from his childhood; he had it restored and now keeps it in his office as a tribute to his old friend, the late Fire Chief Wilbur York. It also serves as a reminder of all the small-town heroes he has been privileged to know, both living and fallen. A reminder of what he was too young to know when it first captured his imagination as a little boy: how life can change forever in an instant.

———

DOWN THE STREET to the east of City Hall, Dr. Maysoon S. Ali sits in an exam room of a building directly across from the train tracks on East Main Street where Buddy Frazier and his brother first saw the westbound L&N on the night of February 22, 1978. In her exam room in Waverly Clinic, PC, she sits at a desk with a stack of charts piled higher than her head, dictating notes on the day's patients. She was the first and is still the only resident gastroenterologist in Humphreys County, and has served several terms as President of the Benton-Humphreys County Medical Society.

Since the disaster, Dr. Maysoon has gone on to become a Fellow of the American College of Physicians (FACP), Secretary of the Leffall Foundation, and a member of the Board of Trustees of the Tennessee Medical Education Fund. Like her husband, she also became a member of the Tennessee State Guard and served a term as Surgeon General for the State Guard Association of the United States.

She never talks about the disaster, and tries never to think about it either. She puts her head down and works, and prides herself on excellence of medical care and caring for the whole patient. She has been seeing many of the same patients— including Toad Smith—and their families for nearly 40 continuous years now.

She has never forgotten how Mrs. Jennie Lee Monroe became one of her most memorable patients. Mrs. Monroe would bring her mother to Waverly Clinic to see Dr. Maysoon for follow-up visits, and on one of these visits, Mrs. Monroe surprised her mother's physician by saying, "Now, Dr. Maysoon, why should I switch doctors to come see you?"

"No one has asked you to switch doctors, Mrs. Monroe. You are free to see anyone you want."

"Well, I know you're good, but my doctor is good too."

"I'm sure he is."

The next time Dr. Maysoon saw Mrs. Monroe, she was there as a new patient. She had "switched doctors," and she remained a loyal patient of Dr. Maysoon's—and of Dr. Ali's, when she needed a surgeon—until she died. Along the way, she designated herself "adopted grandmother" to Dr. Maysoon's three daughters, and looked after them with great love and affection, as if they were her own granddaughters. In January 2013, Dr. Maysoon, along with Dr. Ali and Toad Smith, served as honorary pallbearer at Mrs. Jennie Lee Monroe's funeral at the McEwen Church of Christ—fulfilling the request Mrs. Monroe herself had made before her death.

IN THE HOUSE next door to Waverly Clinic, a stone's throw away from Dr. Maysoon, Nurse Carolyn Tucker has returned home from work. After the train disaster, Sam continued to serve with dynamism and verve as OR Supervisor and as Dr. Ali's scrub nurse and right-hand assistant. She was diagnosed with multiple sclerosis in 1999, and, never one to let anything get in her way, has continued to come to work at Waverly Clinic every single day. She has trained generations of nurses—and at least one physician; saved countless lives; and immeasurably enriched countless more.

Sam's good friend and partner-in-crime, Nancy Daniel, comes by about once a week to check in, give a report on the latest happenings at the hospital, and sometimes reminisce. She continues to be an avid (and vocal) supporter of St. Patrick School in the neighboring town of McEwen—still the only Catholic school in all of Humphreys County, the school built by the Irish immigrants who, in the mid-nineteenth century, laid down the railroad itself.

Now when Nancy is at church, sometimes, in the quiet moments of prayer, the horn of the passing train on the tracks behind the church will blow, distracting the parishioners in their moments of silence. Unlike the others, Nancy, her head bowed over her folded hands, is not annoyed at all; rather, she smiles to herself, and thinks, "If it weren't for that railroad, we wouldn't be here."

ZACH CLAYTON STILL pauses at railroad tracks and keeps his car several feet farther back than necessary when a train is coming through. He never pulls up close to the crossing. And he always watches the cars going by to see if there are any of those white tankers on the train. The sound of helicopters still brings back memories of the explosion. In fact, for years afterward, he and others he knew in Waverly would flinch or shudder whenever they heard a helicopter.

Zach has never been able to bring himself to go inside the caboose that houses the train museum. His kids have been there, but he has never gone with them. He doesn't know why.

Zach's good friend, Tim Barnett, spent over 20 years chasing the railroad. He went from a job in Florida cleaning up welds at five bucks an hour to working for CSX as a mechanical inspector, where he started looking at tank cars. For a long time, that was all he did: look at tank cars. He started out at entry level and worked his way up to Local Chairman for CSX in Florida.

Tim had learned not only how to inspect freight cars, but how to repair them as well. He inspected them before they left each rail yard; he inspected them when they came back in. As a mechanical inspector and repairman, he was, as he puts it, "tearing them up, every little thing that was wrong with them."

He was so unrelenting in his inspections, it got to the point where he would get called in to the head office. "Hey, man, you gotta calm down," they would tell him. "Whaddaya think you're doin'?"

But he knew that they must know what he was doing, and why he was doing it. When he had been sent to Philadelphia for four weeks to learn his trade, the instructors took him aside one day and said, "We're gonna show this film. We understand that your dad's in it." They were worried about showing it to Tim, but he had a different reaction.

Wow! Tim thought. He was proud of his dad, and proud that he could now do something to help others, so that maybe his dad's sacrifice would not be in vain. So that maybe another little boy somewhere wouldn't have to lose his daddy too soon.

AND FRANK CRAVER? He went back to being the quintessential jack-of-all-trades after spending years in recovery, and, in latter years, has been a commercial bus driver, driving all over the region and the country with busloads of tourists, students, and others from all walks of life. Although he can't make a complete fist, he can bend all his fingers, and can do anything he wants to do. He still has the Timex watch he was wearing when the explosion literally blew him out of his shoes. It is still ticking.

Coda

ON A SATURDAY MORNING IN August during the second year of the COVID-19 pandemic and while I was still writing this book, my sister watched in horror from the front door of our family home in Waverly as flood waters rushed over the front steps and up to the front porch on the second floor. After being trapped in the house for several harrowing hours, she and other family members eventually made it out safely. As it turned out, they were among the lucky ones in Waverly that day.

Nearly 21 inches of rain were reported to have fallen in areas of Humphreys County within the 24-hour period between Friday and Saturday, exceeding all previous Tennessee records for 24-hour rainfall. That Saturday morning, the downpour came at a rate of three inches per hour for several hours, creating the devastating flooding that took 20 lives and much of Waverly's infrastructure with it.

The main tributary of the Tennessee River that winds through the town of Waverly, Trace Creek, was reported to have risen by one foot every 30 seconds, reaching four feet within two minutes and leaving almost no time for victims to evacuate. The waters of the Creek, as it is known in Waverly, engulfed the Waverly Elementary and Junior High Schools in totality as well as the sports

211

fields and parts of Waverly Central High School, the only grace being that the date and time was a Saturday morning, and school was not in session.

The Creek swept away home after home, clearing them from their foundations, never to be found in one recognizable piece again. Along Waverly's beautiful and iconic Main Street, many homes and businesses were a total loss. According to the *Tennessean*'s report of August 25, 2021, 523 homes in Humphreys County were affected by the flooding, including 272 that were completely destroyed—Barbara Horner's among them. In a town with a population of just over 4,000, this easily represented at least a quarter to a third of all of Waverly's residents. And this is believed to have been an underestimate.

Along another of Trace Creek's curves, Waverly's shopping district was completely destroyed. Throughout town, at least 44 businesses sustained damage. The situation was truly apocalyptic. Roads cratered beneath the flood waters and bridges were torn apart. All utilities and most services—electricity, water treatment, cell phone, landlines, internet, and 911 services—went down, as call centers and transformers and power lines and utility buildings succumbed to the deluge. Rail traffic through Waverly halted as several sections of the railroad bed lay under water and once again, the area where the L&N train had derailed in 1978 became part of a disaster zone. For a number of hours on Saturday, August 21, the only way into and out of Waverly was by boat.

Reflecting upon the flood, Cooter Bowen echoed the thoughts of many when he felt the impact on the community at large to be even greater and more traumatic than that of the train disaster. The train explosion occurred in a relatively confined area, in Waverly's New Town section, but the floodwaters washed over areas from the east of the county to the west of Waverly. For too many, there was no escape from the water, which was tsunami-like in its swiftness and filled with mud, so that even the best swimmers couldn't navigate it. One of the women who was killed was found in her little workshed, knocked around inside of it; the Creek had taken the shed and all, carried it away with her in it. In perhaps the most heartbreaking incident, twin infants were ripped out of their father's arms as he tried to hold on to all four of his children while his wife clung to a tree. The water rushed over him, and when he came back up, his wife saw that only their older two children remained in his arms.

And so the creek named after Natchez Trace, the very one where, over 40 years before, Cooter witnessed those on fire throwing themselves in—the very one from which surrounding fire departments drew water to put out the flames of New Town—had proved itself foe as well as friend, a reminder of the delicate balance of nature and the consequences of its upset.

As THEY ALWAYS do, the people of Waverly pulled together to help one another. Tales of heroism came to light after the fact. How a woman, Mary Luten, saved her neighbors' lives by knocking on their doors and convincing them to leave their homes, only to run out of time to save herself. How two brothers, Mark and Brian Bohanon, with no previous training in water rescue, saved 15 people and at least six dogs from their upper-story windows, rooftops, and even treetops—using nothing more than a jet ski that had, earlier that morning, failed to start due to wiring in need of repair and then ran out of gas; the pair used gas from a chain saw to power it.

Shelters were opened, emergency supplies were gathered and donated, fundraisers were held. Volunteers came from all over the state and the country to assist the flood victims and offer what they could to support the town's recovery. In the weeks that followed, donations poured in from all over the world. Millions of dollars were raised for flood relief, including close to two million dollars from the Community Foundation of Middle Tennessee and nearly a million from the star-studded Grand Ole Opry benefit concert organized by country music legend Loretta Lynn, who calls Humphreys County home and lives 10 minutes from the site of the 1978 train disaster. Her good friend and fellow Tennessean, Dolly Parton, also donated a portion of ticket sales from her East Tennessee businesses to the United Way of Humphreys County.

Buddy Frazier, first on the scene to the train disaster, was now Mayor of Waverly, and was called upon to help steer his city through yet darker days. Mayor Frazier is someone who understands the importance of reliable infrastructure and the need to learn from disaster. He had, in fact, been working for years to secure funding for water infrastructure improvements for the city of Waverly, and in a cruel twist of irony, less than four weeks before the devastating August flood, Waverly had been granted a $580,000 loan for this very purpose from the State of Tennessee's Clean Water State Revolving Fund Loan Program.

And once again, Waverly and FEMA were connected, spoken together in a single breath. FEMA officials began assessing damages in Waverly that Monday, when President Joe Biden approved Tennessee Governor Bill Lee's disaster declaration, paving the way for federal assistance. Less than a month later, FEMA had provided over $4 million in disaster assistance. And so it was that FEMA, the agency whose establishment was catalyzed by the Waverly Train Disaster, would be there to help in Waverly's worst time of crisis.

Unfortunately, on an individual level, FEMA's funding assistance to individuals and households is limited when it comes to home repair and replacement costs, and has applied only to losses not covered by insurance. The Waverly flood added further weight to the discussion in Washington regarding the National Flood Insurance Program, and a need for its overhaul, with Congress considering subsidies for those unable to afford the insurance.

In the days and weeks after the flood, Waverly once again became the center of a national conversation about infrastructure. This time, the questions revolved around adaptations to climate change and enduring solutions to issues of stormwater drainage and management, floodplain mapping, and land use regulation.

Many have wondered how a landlocked state like Tennessee could experience the type of flooding normally associated with coastal areas, but as I have noted before, Tennessee is a land of rivers. And feeding those rivers are streams and creeks and countless unnamed tributaries, many of which are unmapped. The complete mapping of these tributaries and assigning to them the importance that is their due would be a good beginning to getting a handle on the situation, and would recognize more areas and properties as existing within flood-prone areas, with the necessary infrastructure changes that should be attendant to that.

Numerous creeks and streams have also become clogged with debris over the decades, reducing their depth and capacity to handle these heavier and more frequent major rainfall events. Much more will be needed, of course, but knowing and understanding the scope of the problem, and acknowledging that these sorts of floods are no longer once-in-a-lifetime or once-in-a-century events, is a must.

The wheels of change can be slow to turn, but when spurred by crisis and united by will, how much we as a country and as a society can accomplish in a relatively short time span can be formidable. There is precedence for this sort of thing, for taking the necessary lessons from disaster to make the world a better place. The Waverly train disaster set such a precedent back in 1978, and there is no good reason why the Waverly flood disaster of 2021 cannot do the same.

ALTHOUGH I LIVE nearer to Nashville now, I was personally heart-broken over the flooding of Waverly and the devastation in my hometown. No matter where I go or what I do, I find that, in my heart and soul, I always come back to Waverly.

It was in Waverly, after all, that I learned how to walk and then how to run. How to read, how to write, how to fish, how to swim, how to play the piano, harmonica, and recorder. It was in Waverly and its environs that I learned how to play basketball and how to play chess, how to give public speeches—eventually becoming, through the 4-H series of speaking competitions, the winner of the state public speaking contest.

It was in Waverly and Humphreys County that I learned how to ride horses, play tennis and golf, train my voice for singing, and judge interior design (again through 4-H). In Waverly I learned to cross-stitch, basket-weave, crochet, and do needlepoint. I learned how to identify trees, flowers, and the edge of the Milky Way Galaxy in the night sky; how to diagram sentences; how to wash a car. How to drive, how to write for the newspaper, how to speak French, how to file medical records and perform electro-cardiograms.

It was in Waverly that I practiced my tae kwon do forms into the wee hours of the morning, driving my parents crazy while putting myself on the path to winning championships and eventually becoming a fourth-degree black belt.

It was in Waverly and Humphreys County that I learned how to learn. Thanks to my mother, I must have attended every children's story hour at the Humphreys County Public Library, and worked my way through every book in the children's section. From the safety of Waverly, I read and I read, about everything; and I fell in love with science, and music, and history, and words—in just about any language, but especially in English.

Before attending high school at Waverly Central, I had the good fortune of going through the first eight grades at St. Patrick

School in McEwen. And so I, the child of immigrants, got to attend the Catholic school that was built for the children of the Irish immigrants who, in turn, built the railroad.

I may have been the only person in my class—maybe the only person in the entire school, even—who loved grammar lessons. Both at St. Patrick and at Waverly Central High, I was blessed with fantastic teachers who encouraged and advanced my learning in any way possible. They supported my participation on the science and math teams, in the high school band, in quiz bowl competitions across the state. My English teachers let me sit in their classrooms after school and write quotes on their chalkboards, stories and essays in their composition notebooks. They gave me books to read that were considered college-level. They even let me raid their old textbook closets.

As a high school senior, I won the state Beta Club English competition. The trophy still sits on one of my bookshelves.

Waverly was also where I began my career in medicine, first as a medical records clerk at the age of 13, and then as a certified nursing assistant (CNA) by the age of 16—a certification I earned through the health occupations classes offered at Waverly's vocational school. Being a CNA allowed me to see clinical medicine up close for the first time, and I learned from the best, at the side of nurses like Carolyn Tucker and Nancy Daniel, Roberta Marrs and Barbara Horner, Dot Smith and Cheryl Wunderlin.

Long before I went to medical school, Sam (always "Ms. Tucker" to me) and my father taught me the sizes of sutures, the names of surgical instruments, how to put together a suture kit, how to maintain a sterile field, and how to tie a surgical knot. My mother and Roberta Marrs taught me how to take vital signs, with a particular emphasis on accurate blood pressure measurements using Korotkoff sounds. Cooter Bowen's wife, Carol, taught me the right vials to use for blood draws, and how to prepare microscopy specimens. And it was there at Waverly Clinic, sifting through the electrocardiograms (ECGs) on my mother's desk, that I first fell in love with cardiology.

My parents, to my mind, exemplified all the finest qualities of the model physician; I had the tremendous privilege of watching them practice medicine in a way that I hoped to emulate one day. What is today labeled "patient-centered care," as though it were a novel idea, was what was taken for granted then. Their focus was always—*always*—on the patient in front of them, the patient who was inherently at the center of all care, the raison d'être. As my parents and the nurses who worked with them would not hesitate to remind me: "The patient is the reason we're here," and "Watch the patient, not the chart."

When my mother opened the door to a patient room—always with her trademark, "HELLO, Mr./Ms. So-and-So!!"—her entire face showed how happy she was to see them, and she took as long as it took to get to the bottom of their ailments. Being a doctor was all she ever wanted to be, and doing her very best for her patients was what she lived for. And from what I could tell, her patients knew it, too.

It was not unusual for her to see every member of a family over the decades, and she did everything she could to give her patients the best quality of life for the longest period of time. When a patient's time was running out, though, she was there for them too. I'll never forget how, whenever possible, she would call terminally ill patients in their final days (sometimes their final hours), and thank them for allowing her the privilege of being their physician for all those years.

Watching my father perform surgery was like watching an artist at work. The graceful movements of his fingers when suturing, the meticulous attention to detail, the supreme focus on the surgical field and the anatomy within, was like a carefully choreographed dance, every operation, every time, no matter how minor.

All this happened in Waverly.

But most of all, in Waverly I learned about decency, and compassion, and the goodness of neighbors. Mrs. Jennie Lee Monroe designated herself my "adopted grandmother," and taught me more life skills than I can count, from letter writing to gardening to Southern cooking and more. Much, much more. Frank Craver drove the bus for our school field trips, and managed to keep a cool head and a sense of humor even with a load of rowdy junior-high and high school students carrying on to, literally, beat the band.

Our friends and neighbors were there for us in the good times and in the bad times—even when we didn't know them by name. On an icy hilltop in Waverly one winter, when I was around 13 years old, a pickup truck stopped beside our car, which my mother was unable to navigate down the steep hill because every time she tried to advance, the wheels spun and we slid. In the truck were a man and his wife, and they asked if we were okay. My mother told them she didn't think she could get our car down the hill, and she thought we needed help.

"You've got help now, ma'am," the woman reassured her as her husband climbed out of the truck.

The movement of my mother out of the driver's seat to turn over the steering wheel to the man was enough to set the car sliding down the hill, with me in the passenger's seat. The next thing I knew, my mother was screaming and the man was jumping into the car, grabbing the wheel even as the door still hung open. Down the hill we went, building up momentum with no traction at all, but somehow, he was able to steer the car safely to a stop at the bottom. I didn't know that man or his wife, and I still have no idea who they were, but I remain indebted to their kindness and to his bravery. He saved me from serious injury and possibly death that day.

When my father was going through the worst rounds of chemotherapy as well as a stem cell transplant for his stage IV non-Hodgkin lymphoma, it was the people of Waverly and the surrounding towns—including many of his own patients—who donated the plasma needed to help save his life. It was his scrub nurse, Sam, who fed him daily through his feeding tube, and sat with him in hospital and treatment rooms while the two of them, in a time before internet, took to naming the squirrels outside the windows just to pass the time.

I believe I was in my thirties the first time I watched the Jimmy Stewart classic, *It's a Wonderful Life*, from beginning to end, and when I did so—in Waverly—it was a revelation. In addition to it being a truly wonderful film, there was much in that final scene, when all the people whose lives have been touched by George Bailey show up to save him in his moment of greatest need, that reminded me of Waverly. That, for me, is Waverly.

I cannot imagine a better childhood or upbringing. Living in Waverly, I had a wealth and diversity of opportunities I doubt I would have found as easily—or as open to me—in a major metropolis. I have found that it is not uncommon, even fashionable in some quarters, for residents of urban areas to look askance at the ways of small towns, finding them easier to dismiss than to understand. And I am sometimes asked—almost always by folks who were not raised in the South—if I experienced discrimination in Waverly, if I was somehow made to feel inferior or less capable, but nothing could be farther from the truth.

In Waverly I learned that if you work hard and do your best, no matter where you're from, people will notice and respect that. And if you stay humble enough to learn, there are people who will teach you. I know that isn't everyone's experience everywhere, but it was mine in Waverly.

In Memoriam

The 16 Lives Lost in the
Waverly Train Disaster of 1978

WILLIAM EARL BAKER, 57, of Waverly, died on Saturday, March 11, 1978, at University Hospital in Birmingham, Alabama. He had been an employee of the L&N Railroad, and was a World War II veteran.

GUY OAKLEY BARNETT, SR., 45, of Waverly, died on Sunday, February 26, 1978, at University Hospital in Birmingham, Alabama. He had been Waverly's Chief of Police since 1972, and prior to that had served as an officer in the Tennessee Highway Patrol and was a Korean War veteran.

DONALD MARK BELYEW, 24, of Jackson, TN, died on Friday, February 24, 1978, in the explosion. He was an operations officer for the Tennessee Civil Defense Agency.

JAMES E. CRAWFORD, 55, of Nashville, TN, died on Saturday, February 25, 1978, at Vanderbilt University Medical Center in Nashville. He had been employed by the L&N Railroad, and was a US Navy veteran of World War II.

DANIEL LEE ENGLE, 24, of Dickson, TN, died on April 15, 1978, at Cincinnati General Hospital. He had been an enforcement officer for the Tennessee Public Service Commission. His son was born after his death.

CHARLES WESLEY EWING, 44, of North Bend, OH, died on March 6, 1978, at St. Thomas Hospital in Nashville, TN. He had been a truck driver for Liquid Transport Co. and had earlier served in the US Armed Forces.

LLOYD FLOROW, 70, of Waverly, died on Friday, February 24, 1978, in the explosion. He was a retired fireman from Pasadena, TX, who had relocated to Waverly with his wife for their retirement.

REX LEON GAUT, 21, of Sterrett, AL, died on Friday, February 24, 1978, in the explosion. He was an employee of Steel City Erection Co., Inc.

JAMES ERVIN HAMM, 58, of Waverly, died on Sunday, February 26, 1978, at the Veterans Affairs (VA) Hospital in Nashville. He was an employee of Tate Lumber Company in Waverly.

TERRY LYNN HAMM, 20, of Waverly, died on Wednesday, March 15, 1978, at University Hospital in Birmingham, AL. He was the son of James E. Hamm, also killed by injuries sustained in the explosion, and was an employee of Tate Lumber Company.

MELVIN BURLEIGH HOLCOMBE, 43, of Nashville, TN, died on Friday, February 24, 1978, in the tanker explosion. He was a railroad claims adjustor.

TOMMY HORNBURGER, 19, of Waverly, died on Friday, February 24, 1978, at Vanderbilt University Medical Center in Nashville, TN. He was in the second semester of his senior year at Waverly Central High School, and was an employee of Waverly's Mi-De-Ga theater.

ROBERT HUFF, 31, of Hendersonville, TN, died on Friday, February 24, 1978, at Meharry-Hubbard Hospital in Nashville, TN. He was an L&N Railroad employee.

MELVIN WAYNE MATLOCK, 45, of Centerville, TN, died on Friday, February 24, 1978, in Waverly, killed instantly in the explosion. He was an employee of Thermo Kool Insulating Company and a volunteer member of the Waverly Fire Department.

HERBERT WASSING, 34, of Fulton, KY, died on Sunday, February 26, 1978, in Louisville Hospital from injuries sustained in the February 24 train explosion. He was an employee of Liquid Transport Co.

WILBUR J. YORK, 65, of Waverly, died on Friday, February 24, 1978, at Vanderbilt University Medical Center in Nashville, TN. He was Waverly's Fire Chief.

Acknowledgments

SOMETIME IN THE SUMMER OF 2011, a tall, stately man with the nickname of "Toad" stopped me in the hallway of my parents' clinic in Waverly, Tennessee. He initially stopped me just to say hello and see how I was doing, as I was down from Nashville to visit for the day. Then my father, Dr. Subhi Ali, came out of an exam room and saw us in the hallway, and called out to Mr. Smith: "Toad, show her your hands." From that moment and the story that ensued (for Toad Smith is a marvelous storyteller), I became utterly fascinated, and then somewhat obsessed, by the tragedy that occurred in my hometown in February 1978, and the heroic roles played by people whom I had known—or thought I had known—all my life.

So thank you, Mr. Smith, for the story that started it all, for your countless hours spent in answering all my questions, for reviewing the manuscript, and for your constant encouragement throughout the entire process.

It must also be said that this book would never have been possible without the tireless efforts of Carolyn "Sam" Tucker, who, quite amazingly, took it upon herself to become my de facto research assistant, putting me in touch with nearly everyone I interviewed. Thank you, Sam, for supporting all my efforts on this book from the very beginning—and indeed, all my efforts throughout my life. Thank you for always believing in me.

So many pieces from so many people had to fall into place for this project to come to fruition. To everyone who did me the profound honor of entrusting me with your stories, sharing some of the worst, most difficult memories of your lives and relying on me to get it right: the debt I owe you all can never be fully repaid. But if with this book you feel I've done right by you, feel I've done you proud, then that would be a start. In fact, as far as I'm concerned, that's the only measure of success that really matters.

Thanks in particular:

To Buddy Frazier, for giving me the interview of a lifetime. For painstakingly preserving so many of the documents, photos, and artifacts related to the train disaster. For getting me what I needed even while overwhelmed with flood recovery, and for remaining supportive of my efforts on this project for so many years.

To Frank Craver, for not only sharing such a personal story but also for supplying me with so many important details and archival information, for giving me a tour of the accident site, for taking me through every available map and picture (more than once!), and for hanging in there through the long and arduous publishing process.

To Sue Craver, for also sharing some difficult memories with me and for supporting this entire project.

To Nancy Daniel, for being such a good friend to me and my family, for modeling the fundamentals of good nursing, and for letting me pick her brain on countless occasions, on this project and much more.

To Barbara Horner, for also being such an incredible friend to me and my family for so long, for sharing so many personal details and memories, for always being such an inspiration, and for helping me to understand a bygone era in nursing.

To Cheryl Allen, for providing an important piece of the puzzle that was this project at the beginning, for sharing so many details from memory, and for being there for my parents throughout their careers.

To Cooter Bowen, who has a memory like a trap, for sharing his own story and so many important details with me in a way that really brought part of the narrative to life.

To Julie Bowen Einerson, for putting me in touch with her father, Cooter, and for verifying some key details of Luff-Bowen history for me.

To Dr. Joe McClure, for so kindly allowing me to interview him in his own home, and for being so candid in sharing his memories of Waverly and of the disaster.

To Dr. Arthur W. Walker, may he rest in peace, for allowing me to interview him regarding his recollections of the disaster.

To Mrs. Jennie Lee Monroe, may she rest in peace, for adopting me as her granddaughter, for teaching me so much about life, and for sharing her and her mother's story the day of the disaster. Thanks also go to Wendell Monroe, who has always been there for me, and has been so supportive of all my projects, including this one.

To Zach Clayton, for taking an interest in and responding to my newsletters, which led to such a great interview with not only Zach himself, but also with Tim Barnett, with whom Zach put me in touch.

To Tim Barnett, for sharing some of the hardest memories of his entire life, and for helping me to see and understand so many of the human aspects of his father, Guy Barnett, for which the Chief was so beloved by his friends and colleagues. Tim also provided invaluable assistance in fact-checking the most technical aspects of the manuscript with regard to rail safety changes, and for that, too, I am most grateful.

To Andy Daniels, past president of the Waverly Exchange Club, for granting me permission to use many of the photos that appear in this book, and for being such a good friend to my family over the years.

To Leon Alligood, longtime Tennessee journalist and Middle Tennessee State University professor, for so generously sharing with me all his notes on the Waverly Train Disaster and its connection to the establishment of FEMA. In fact, it wasn't until I came across a line in a 2008 article by Mr. Alligood that I even realized the FEMA connection myself. I owe Mr. Alligood a tremendous debt of gratitude for his diligence.

To Bob Holliday, park manager of Johnsonville State Historic Park, for stopping to chat by happenstance while I was visiting the park in 2021, and then telling me the story of the Battle of Johnsonville. Mr. Holliday also made me aware of the existence of the excellent book by former park manager Jerry T. Wooten, which provides every detail of the battle and the role of Johnsonville. Additionally, Mr. Holliday was the first to mention to me the connection with Sherman's March to the Sea. All of this informed and led me to further research for chapter 5, "From the River to the Rail."

To Dr. Kelly Moore, my dear friend, for listening for soooo long to me and all my angst about this book and my authorial aspirations with other books, yet never wavering in her support and encouragement.

To Dr. Holly Urban, for looking at a very early draft and giving valuable feedback, and for staying so supportive of my writing.

To Vicki Harden and Jann Einfeld, for being such fantastic friends and cheerleaders for this and so many other projects, for agreeing to be part of my launch team, and for always being so authentically encouraging.

To Dr. Heather Fork of the Doctor's Crossing, whose friendship I so cherish, for cheering me on with such gusto the whole time—but most importantly, for teaching me how to live in my True Self.

To Dr. Phill Cuculich, who appeared like a guardian angel at a time when I was deeply in doubt, and told me I must finish this book. It was just the kick in the pants I needed, at just the time I needed it. I will be forever grateful.

To my close friends Janell Pendergrass, Ben Papa, and Brad Bullock, for keeping the excitement alive for this project from the very beginning and for adding such richness to my life in so many ways and for so many years—I am the lucky one.

To Dr. Stacy Davis, for her constant support, enthusiasm, and encouragement—before, during, and after the writing of this book.

To Missy Rodriguez Brower, for reminding me of the importance of having a room of one's own—and helping me get it.

To Liz May, Jackie Dinas, Lynn Cully, Sherry Wasserman, and the entire team at Kensington, for helping to publish this book.

To my AMAZING agent, Amy Elizabeth Bishop, who kept the faith even as I was losing it. This book may never have come to light had it not been for her insistence and persistence.

To Reema and to Melissa Manning, for saving so many important documents from the flood, including the earliest newspaper clippings of my parents at Nautilus Hospital.

To Nadia and Khaled, who always had (and still have) a book in their hands, and who were my best role models for so many things, with reading, self-education, and pushing the boundaries of the imagination foremost among them.

To Samar, for cheerleading and support in the earliest stages of this project and in the most difficult times always.

To my parents, Drs. Subhi and Maysoon Ali, who taught me the value of lifelong learning by their example, and who made everything possible.

To my lifelong friend, Shannon Tolene...where do I even begin? Without you, this book would have been so much less than it is. From our weekly brainstorming conversations to your constant moral support, you helped in so many ways to uplift both me and this work. The chapter "From the River to the Rail" would not exist had you not convinced me to check out Johnsonville

State Historic Park and dive deep into its history and the history of the Battle of Johnsonville. Thank you also for helping me track down the permissions for many of the photos used in this book, and for directing me to important resources regarding the flood. This book might not have made it across the finish line without you—thank you for invaluable feedback on the manuscript and for helping me strategize. But most of all, thank you for always being there for me, rain or shine.

To my four-legged family members, who are, quite literally, the reason I get out of bed in the morning.

And, finally and always, to my darling Keith, love of my life and brilliant soulmate, who puts up with far more than his fair share, and whose sage advice was an integral part of moving this project along from beginning to end. I can never thank you enough for all your patience, encouragement, and unrelenting support. You lift me up and make me whole.

References

Interviews with survivors coupled with my personal knowledge inform the narrative across multiple chapters. Otherwise, sources that are chapter-specific are listed in order of use by chapter. Direct quotes are attributed in the text, with full source information listed here.

The following archival sources also inform multiple chapters:

Discovery Deposition of Frank Craver, July 17, 1979. In the United States District Court for the Middle District of Tennessee Nashville Division. In Re: Waverly Accident of February 22–24, 1978. No. 78-3119-NA-CV, et al. Offices of Waller, Lansden, Dortch and Davis, Nashville, TN. (Taken down by Associated Reporters, Ray L. Walker—Jack Jeske—Audrey Jeske, General Stenographic Reporters.)

The Exchange Club of Waverly, Tennessee. *Waverly Propane Disaster: Explosion in Waverly Tenn.* Edited by Tony A. Chapman. Dallas, TX: Taylor Publishing Company, 1982.

Chapter One: Derailed

Luff-Bowen Funeral Home. "Who We Are: Our Story." luffbowen.com /history.

Castner, Charles B. "A Brief History of the Louisville & Nashville Railroad." Louisville & Nashville Railroad Historical Society. lnrr.org/History.aspx.

Association of American Railroads. "A Short History of U.S. Freight Railroads." AAR Newsletter. April 2021. aar.org/wp-content

/uploads/2018/05/AAR-Short-History-American-Freight-Rail roads.pdf.

Wurtele, Lolla. "The Origins of the Louisville and Nashville Railroad." *Electronic Theses and Dissertations*. Master's thesis, University of Louisville, 1939. doi.org/10.18297/etd/1857.

Clark, Thomas Dionysus. *The Beginning of the L & N Railroad: The Development of the Louisville and Nashville Railroad and Its Branches from 1836 to 1860*. Louisville, KY: Standard Printing Company, 1933.

National Transportation Safety Board. NTSB-RAR-79-1. February 8, 1979.

Macrotrends. "Nashville Metro Area Population 1950–2021." macro trends.net/cities/23077/nashville/population.

Chapter Two: Morning Rounds

Berry, Frank B. "The Story of 'the Berry Plan.'" *Bulletin of the New York Academy of Medicine* 52, no. 3 (March–April 1976): 278-82.

Mailer, John S. Jr., and Barbara Mason. "Penicillin: Medicine's Wartime Wonder Drug and Its Production at Peoria, Illinois." *Illinois History Teacher* 8, no. 1 (2001). Published by Illinois Historic Preservation Agency. lib.niu.edu/2001/iht810139.html.

The Tennessean. "John Seigenthaler, Longtime *Tennessean* Editor, Dies at 86." Last modified July 12, 2014. tennessean.com/story /news/2014/07/11/john-seigenthaler-dies/12529753.

Chapter Three: Nautilus Memorial Hospital

United States Naval Academy. "Notable Graduates: William Robert Anderson." usna.edu/Notables/congress/1943anderson.php.

Vanderbilt University Medical Center. "Vanderbilt LifeFlight: History." Last modified 2022. vumc.org/lifeflight/history.

Freemon, Pam. "Diagnostic Tool Purchased by Nautilus Hospital Recently." News-Democrat, September 22, 1976.

Julian, DG. "Treatment of Cardiac Arrest in Acute Myocardial Ischaemia and Infarction." *Lancet* 2, no. 7207 (October 1961): 840–4.

Khush, Kiran K, Elliot Rapaport, and David Waters. "The History of the Coronary Care Unit." *Canadian Journal of Cardiology* 21, no. 12 (October 2005): 1041–5.

Pirmohamed, Munir. "Warfarin: Almost 60 Years Old and Still Causing Problems." *British Journal of Clinical Pharmacology* 62, no. 5 (November 2006): 509–11.

Sikri, Nikhil, and Amit Bardia. "A History of Streptokinase Use in Acute Myocardial Infarction." *Texas Heart Institute Journal* 34, no. 3 (2007): 318–27.

Wessler, Stanford, and Laurence A. Sherman. "Antiplatelet Aggregate Agents and Thrombolytic Compounds in Myocardial Infarction: Current Status." *Circulation* 45, no. 4 (April 1972): 911–18.

Chatterjee, Paula, and Karen E. Joynt Maddox. "US National Trends in Mortality from Acute Myocardial Infarction and Heart Failure: Policy Success or Failure?" *JAMA Cardiology* 3, no. 4 (April 2018): 336–40.

Barton, Matthias, Johannes Grüntzig, Marc Husmann, and Josef Rösch. "Balloon Angioplasty—The Legacy of Andreas Grüntzig, M.D. (1939–1985)." *Frontiers in Cardiovascular Medicine* 1 (December 2014): 15.

Chapter Five: From the River to the Rail

Binkley, Trina L. "Humphreys County." Tennessee Encyclopedia. The Tennessee Historical Society. Last modified March 1, 2018. tennesseeencyclopedia.net/entries/humphreys-county.

Whitfield, John H. "History of Waverly." The City of Waverly, Tennessee. waverlytn.org/history.

The Goodspeed Histories of Montgomery, Robertson, Humphreys, Stewart, Dickson, Cheatham, Houston Counties of Tennessee. Columbia, TN: Woodward & Stinson Printing Co., 1972. Reprinted from

Goodspeed's History of Tennessee. Chicago: Goodspeed Publishing Company, 1886.

Associated Press. "Today in History, February 25: Nashville First Confederate State Capital Occupied by Union in Civil War." *Tennessean*. February 25, 2020. tennessean.com/story/news/2020/02/25/today-history-february-25-nashville-occupied-union-civil-war/4790282002.

Van Hooser, David, and Ken Tucker, producers. *The Battle of Johnsonville: A Success That Failed*. DVD. Dickson, TN: TRC Media, 2009.

Wooten, Jerry T. *Johnsonville: Union Supply Operations on the Tennessee River and the Battle of Johnsonville*, November 4–5, 1864. El Dorado Hills, CA: Savas Beatie, 2019.

Cox, Jacob D. *The Battle of Franklin, Tennessee, November 30, 1864: A Monograph*. New York: Charles Scribner's Sons, 1897.

Hudson, Myles. "Battle of Atlanta: American Civil War [1864]." Britannica. britannica.com/event/Battle-of-Atlanta.

American Battlefield Trust. "Atlanta." battlefields.org/learn/civil-war/battles/atlanta.

Kalmoe, Nathan. "The Fall of Atlanta and Lincoln's Reelection: 'Game-Changer' or Campaign Myth?" *Washington Post*. September 2, 2014. washingtonpost.com/news/monkey-cage/wp/2014/09/02/the-fall-of-atlanta-and-lincolns-reelection-game-changer-or-campaign-myth.

Secrist, Philip Lee. "Cobb County in the Atlanta Campaign." American Battlefield Trust. battlefields.org/learn/articles/cobb-county-atlanta-campaign.

History.com Editors. "The Destruction of Atlanta Begins." History.com. Last modified November 10, 2020. history.com/this-day-in-history/the-destruction-of-atlanta-begins.

History.com Editors. "Nathan Bedford Forrest." History. Last modified July 15, 2019. history.com/topics/american-civil-war/nathan-bedford forrest.

"Johnsonville State Historic Park." Tennessee State Parks (brochure). October 2014.

Chapter Six: Minding the Perimeter

Cox, Bob. "Memphis-to-Bristol Highway Once Part of 'Broadway of America.'" Bob Cox's Yesteryear. Last modified January 2, 2019. bcyesteryear.com/node/9594.

Roadnow. "Tennessee State Route 1." roadnow.com/us/tn/road_de scription.php?road=Tennessee-State-Route-1&id=r10019131.

Tennessee Virtual Archive. "Route of the Memphis-Nashville-Bristol Highway (1911)." Tennessee State Library and Archives. teva.contentdm.oclc.org/digital/collection/p15138coll23/id/53.

Pioneer LNG. "LNG vs. LPG—What's the Difference?" July 19, 2018. pioneerlng.com/lng-vs-lpg.

U.S. Department of Energy. "Propane: Liquefied Petroleum Gas (LPG)." fueleconomy.gov/feg/lpg.shtml.

Chapter Eight: The End of the World

Reiman, Matt. "The Largest Non-Nuclear Explosion in U.S. History Destroyed Most of a Texas Town, Killing Hundreds." Time line. June 2, 2017. timeline.com/texas-city-explosion-grand camp-6c08615fc898.

Burke, Robert. "The Kingman Rail Car BLEVE." Firehouse. July 1, 1998. firehouse.com/rescue/article/10544591/the-kingman-rail -car-bleve.

Propane 101. "About Propane—Characteristics, Properties and Com- bustion." propane101.com/aboutpropane.htm.

Chapter Ten: Triage in a Two-Room ER

Weber, Mark. "Residents Inside a COVID-Plagued Retirement Home Discuss Their Hopes, Fears and Worries." *Daily Mem- phian*. May 22, 2020. dailymemphian.com/article/14088/coro navirus-makes-retirees-question-future.

Lollar, Michael. "Despite Detractors, Ex-Medical Examiner Defends Elvis Conclusions." *Commercial Appeal*. August 10, 2008. archive .commercialappeal.com/entertainment/despite-detractors-ex

-medical-examiner-defends-elvis-conclusions-ep-396157868
-324276121.html.

Williamson, Joel. "The Elvis Presley Coverup: What America Didn't
Hear about the Death of the King." *Salon.* November 16, 2014.
salon.com/2014/11/16/the_elvis_presley_coverup_what_america
_didnt_hear_about_the_death_of_the_king.

Cole, James P., and Charles C. Thompson. "The Death of Elvis: The
Fascinating Tale of How the *Commercial Appeal* Got—and
Lost—One of the Biggest Stories of the Seventies." *Memphis
Magazine.* August 2, 2017. memphismagazine.com/elvis/the
-death-of-elvis.

Chapter Eleven: The Day After

Tennessee Emergency Management Agency (archives). "The Waverly
Explosion: The Response." November 23, 2001. tnema.org/Ar
chives/Waverly/Waverly4.htm.

Chapter Twelve: The Greatest Sacrifice

Bikle, Daniel D. "Vitamin D and the Skin: Physiology and Pathophys-
iology." *Review in Endocrine and Metabolic Disorders* 13, no. 1
(March 2012): 3–19.

Brown, Thomas M., and Karthik Krishnamurthy. "Histology, Dermis." *StatPearls.* November 19, 2021. ncbi.nlm.nih.gov/books
/NBK535346.

Yousef, Hani, Mandy Alhajj, and Sandeep Sharma. "Anatomy, Skin
(Integument), Epidermis." StatPearls. November 19, 2021.
ncbi.nlm.nih.gov/books/NBK470464.

WoundSource. "Burns, Full-Thickness (Third- and Fourth-Degree)."
2021. woundsource.com/patientcondition/burns-full-thickness
-third-and-fourth-degree.

Warby, Rachel, and Christopher V. Maani. "Burn Classification."
StatPearls. September 5, 2021. ncbi.nlm.nih.gov/books/NBK
539773.

Church, Deirdre, Sameer Elsayed, Owen Reid, Brent Winston, and Robert Lindsay. "Burn Wound Infections." *Clinical Microbiology Reviews* 19, no. 2 (April 2006): 403–34.

Chapter Thirteen: For Whom the Bells Tolled

"Sen. Bill Frist Has Many Chattanooga Family Ties." *Chattanoogan.* December 21, 2002. chattanoogan.com/2002/12/21/30512/Sen. -Bill-Frist-Has-Many-Chattanooga.aspx.

Chapter Sixteen: A Force for Change

Waverly TN Department of Public Safety. "The Waverly Tank Car Explosion: Investigation." waverlypublicsafety.com/what-hap pened/investigation.

National Transportation Safety Board. NTSB-RAR-79-1. February 8, 1979.

Inflation Tool. "Value of 1979 US Dollars Today." inflationtool.com /us-dollar/1979-to-present-value?amount=1800000.

Forge. "Full Steam Ahead: Railroad Wheel Manufacturing." May 9, 2016. forgemag.com/articles/84479-full-steam-ahead-railroad -wheel-manufacturing.

Stagl, Jeff. "Technology Update: Tread-Conditioning Brake Shoes." Progressive Railroading. November 2008. progressiverailroad ing.com/mechanical/article/Technology-Update-Tread-Con ditioning-Brake-Shoes—18557.

Railway Supply Institute. "Tank Car 101." tankcarresourcecenter .com/tankcar101.

U.S. Department of Transportation: Federal Railroad Administration. "Emergency Order No. 7: Removal of High Carbon Cast Steel Wheels from Service; Interim Restrictions on Their Use." *Federal Register* 43, no. 59 (March 27, 1978): 12691. govinfo.gov/content/pkg/FR-1978-03-27/pdf/FR-1978-03-27.pdf.

U.S. Department of Transportation: Federal Railroad Administration. Emergency Order No. 7. 43 FR 12691. March 27, 1978.

U.S. Department of Transportation: Federal Railroad Administration. 44 FR 77340. December 31, 1979.

S.1946 - Staggers Rail Act of 1980. 96th Congress (1979–1980). Congress .gov. https://www.congress.gov/bill/96th-congress/senate-bill /1946.

Mall, Scott. "FreightWaves Classics: U.S. Railroads Were Nationalized in World War I." FreightWaves. June 9, 2021. freight waves.com/news/freightwaves-classics-us-railroads-were-na tionalized-in-world-war-i.

Association of American Railroads. "Freight Railroads & The Staggers Rail Act of 1980." July 2021. aar.org/article/freight-rail roads-the-staggers-act-of-1980.

Winston, Clifford. "The Success of the Staggers Rail Act of 1980." Brookings Institution. October 15, 2005. brookings.edu/research /the-success-of-the-staggers-rail-act-of-1980.

Palley, Joel. "Impact of the Staggers Rail Act of 1980." U.S. Department of Transportation: Federal Railroad Administration. March 2011. railroads.dot.gov/elibrary/impact-staggers-rail -act-1980.

Maty, Allen D. *Field Guide to Tank Cars*. Association of American Railroads/Bureau of Explosives. Third edition. February 6, 2017. ethanolresponse.com/wp-content/uploads/2017/02/2017-Field -Guide-for-Tank-Cars.pdf.

Keefe, Kevin P. "Couplers: The Durable Link." *Trains*. May 1, 2006. trains.com/trn/train-basics/abcs-of-railroading/couplers.

Burns, Adam. "Railroad Couplers." American-Rails.com blog. Last modified January 2, 2022. american-rails.com/couplers.html.

Byrne, John. "RSI-AAR Railroad Tank Car Safety Research and Test Project." FRA Hazmat Seminar, Houston, TX, August 2018. railroads.dot.gov/sites/fra.dot.gov/files/fra_net/18097/HZ1802 _AAR%20RSI%20Safety%20Project.pdf.

McConway & Torley, LLC. "Freight Couplers." mcconway.com/cata log/freight-couplers.

Railway Supply Institute. "RSI Celebrates 50th Anniversary of RSI-AAR Tank Car Safety Research & Test Project." September 7,

2021. rsiweb.org/rsi-celebrates-50th-anniversary-of-rsi-aar-tank-car-safety-research-test-project.

Chapter Seventeen: One Agency, One Mission

Hogue, Henry B., and Keith Bea. "Federal Emergency Management and Homeland Security Organization: Historical Developments and Legislative Options." CRS Report for Congress. Congressional Research Service – The Library of Congress. Updated June 1, 2006.

National Governors' Association. "National Governors' Association Policy Position A.-17: Emergency Preparedness and Response." *1978 Emergency Preparedness Project: Final Report.* Washington: GPO, 1979.

Alligood, Leon. "Lessons Linger from '78 Tenn. Rail Explosion." *Journal of Emergency Medical Services.* February 21, 2008. jems.com/operations/lessons-linger-78-tenn-rail-ex.

Delaney, David G. "Federal Civil Defense Act of 1950." Encyclopedia.com. encyclopedia.com/history/encyclopedias-almanacs-transcripts-and-maps/federal-civil-defense-act-1950.

Tennessee Department of Military. "TEMA: History 1950s." tn.gov/tema/the-agency/agency-history/history-1950s.html.

Kneeland, Timothy W. *Playing Politics with Natural Disaster: Hurricane Agnes, the 1972 Election, and the Origins of FEMA.* Ithaca and London: Cornell University Press, 2020.

Cohen, Wilbur J., and Evelyn F. Boyer. "Federal Civil Defense Act of 1950: Summary and Legislative History." *Social Security Bulletin* 14, no. 4 (April 1951).

FEMA. "Emergency Management Authorities Review." emilms.fema.gov/is_0230e/groups/356.html.

Office of Policy Development and Research, U.S. Department of Housing and Urban Development. "History of Federal Disaster Policy." *Evidence Matters.* Winter 2015. huduser.gov/portal/periodicals/em/winter15/highlight1_sidebar.html.

Homeland Security National Preparedness Task Force. "Civil Defense and Homeland Security: A Short History of National Preparedness Efforts." September 2006. training.fema.gov /hiedu/docs/dhs%20civil%20defense-hs%20-%20short%20 history.pdf.

Brown, JoAnne. "A is for Atom, B is Bomb: Civil Defense in American Public Education, 1948 – 1963." *The Journal of American History* 75, no. 1 (June 1988): 68–90.

CONELRAD. "Duck and Cover." Last modified 2007. conelrad.com /duckandcover/cover.php?turtle=04.

"10-Min. 'Duck and Cover' a Hit at Class Premiere: Every School to See It." *New York Herald Tribune.* March 7, 1952.

Tennessee Emergency Management Agency (archives). "The Waverly Explosion." web.archive.org/web/20060516064527/http://www .tnema.org/Archives/Waverly/Waverly1.htm.

Tennessee Department of Military. "TEMA: History 1970s." tn.gov /tema/the-agency/agency-history/history-1970s.html.

Kneeland, Timothy K. *Declaring Disaster: Buffalo's Blizzard of '77 and the Creation of FEMA.* Syracuse, New York: Syracuse University Press, 2021.

Runner, Gerald S., and Edwin H. Chin. "Flood of April 1977 in the Appalachian Region of Kentucky, Tennessee, Virginia, and West Virginia." *United States Geological Survey Professional Paper 1098.* Washington, DC: Superintendent of Documents, U.S. Government Printing Office, 1980.

ABC Evening News. "Tennessee/Toxic Gas Emergency/Truck Safety." July 13, 1977.

The President. "Executive Order 12127 of March 31, 1979: Federal Emergency Management Agency." *Federal Register* 44, no. 65 (April 3, 1979): 19367. govinfo.gov/content/pkg/FR-1979-04-03/pdf/FR -1979-04-03.pdf.

The President. "Executive Order 12148 of July 26, 1979: Federal Emergency Management." *Federal Register* 44, no. 143 (July 24, 1979); 43239–43. govinfo.gov/content/pkg/FR-1979-07-24/pdf/FR-1979 -07-24.pdf.

Federal Emergency Management Agency. *Publication 1*. fema.gov /sites/default/files/2020-03/publication-one_english_2019.pdf.

Peterson, Mark. "Disaster Planning." *Before, During & After* (podcast). FEMA. March 2020. fema.gov/sites/default/files/audio-tran scripts/2020-03/fema_disaster-planning.docx.

FEMA. "Federal Government's Procurement and Distribution Strategies in Response to the COVID-19 Pandemic." June 10, 2020. fema.gov/fact-sheet/federal-governments-procurement -and-distribution-strategies-response-covid-19-pandemic.

FEMA. "COVID-19 Funeral Assistance." Last modified May 25, 2022. fema.gov/disaster/coronavirus/economic/funeral-assistance.

Tennessee Department of Military. "TEMA: History 1980s." tn.gov /tema/the-agency/agency-history/history-1980s.html.

Medlin, Jeffrey, Ray Ball, and Gary Beeler. Updated by Morgan Barry, Jason Beaman, and Don Shepherd. "Extremely Powerful Hurricane Katrina Leaves a Historic Mark on the Northern Gulf Coast: A Killer Hurricane Our Country Will Never Forget." National Weather Service. Last modified November 2016. weather.gov/mob/katrina.

Keith Bea. *Federal Emergency Management Policy Changes after Hurricane Katrina: A Summary of Statutory Provisions*. CRS Report for Congress. Congressional Research Service. March 6, 2007.

Chapter Eighteen: Hazardous Materials

Burke, Robert. "Tennessee Propane Blast: A Turning Point for Hazmat." Firehouse. January 11, 2013. firehouse.com/rescue/article /10852275/fireservicehazmatincidents.

National Transportation Safety Board. NTSB-RAR-79-1. February 8, 1979.

United States Department of Labor: Occupational Safety and Health Administration. "Transporting Hazardous Materials." osha.gov /trucking-industry/transporting-hazardous-materials.

Northeastern University Office of Environmental Health and Safety. "Hazardous Material Definition." Accessed March 1, 2022.

northeastern.edu/ehs/ehs-programs/research-material-ship ping/hazardous-material-definition.

U.S. Department of Transportation: Federal Railroad Administration. Emergency Order No. 11. 44 FR 8402. February 7, 1979.

"Notices: Federal Railroad Administration: Amendment of Emergency Order Limiting Movement of Hazardous Materials; Louisville & Nashville Railroad Co." *Federal Register*. Vol. 44, No. 128. July 2, 1979.

Levy, Claudia. "District Judge Gerhard Gesell Dies at Age 82." *Washington Post*. February 21, 1993. washingtonpost.com/archive /local/1993/02/21/district-judge-gerhard-gesell-dies-at-age -82/e08549c6-2bfb-4d36-a2eb-cd99dabde842.

Altschuler, Bruce. "Pentagon Papers." *The First Amendment Encyclopedia* (presented by the John Seigenthaler Chair of Excellence in First Amendment Studies). Last modified 2009. mtsu.edu /first-amendment/article/873/pentagon-papers.

"Louisville and Nashville Railroad Co.; Emergency Order Limiting Movement of Hazardous Materials; Partial Removal of Order." *Federal Register*. Vol. 44, No. 114. June 12, 1979.

U.S. Department of Transportation: Federal Railroad Administration. "Hazardous Materials Transportation." Last modified December 1, 2021. railroads.dot.gov/program-areas/hazmat -transportation/hazardous-materials-transportation.

United States Environmental Protection Agency. "Superfund: CERCLA Overview." Last modified February 14, 2022. epa.gov/su perfund/superfund-cercla-overview.

United States Environmental Protection Agency. "National Oil and Hazardous Substances Pollution Contingency Plan (NCP) Overview." Last modified March 25, 2022. epa.gov/emergency -response/national-oil-and-hazardous-substances-pollution -contingency-plan-ncp-overview.

Bennett, Vance. "Hazmat History." California Emergency Management Agency/California Specialized Training Institute: Hazardous Materials Section. 2012.

"Superfund Sites." NIH: National Institute of Environmental Health Sciences. tools.niehs.nih.gov/wetp/index.cfm?id=2563.

United States Department of Labor: Occupational Safety and Health Administration. Standard Number 1910.120—Hazardous Waste Operations and Emergency Response. osha.gov/laws -regs/regulations/standardnumber/1910/1910.120.

El Sayed, Mazen J. "Beirut Ammonium Nitrate Explosion: A Man-Made Disaster in Times of the COVID-19 Pandemic." *Disaster Medicine and Public Health Preparedness* 18 (November 2020): 1–5.

John, Tara, Melissa Macaya, Mike Hayes, Veronica Rocha, Meg Wagner, Joshua Berlinger, Adam Renton, Zamira Rahim, and Ed Upright. "Beirut Explosion Rocks Lebanon's Capital City." CNN. August 6, 2020. edition.cnn.com/middleeast/live-news /lebanon-beirut-explosion-live-updates-dle-intl.

Regencia, Ted, Linah Alsaafin, and Farah Najjar. "Beirut Explosion Death Toll Rises to 135 as 5,000 Wounded: Live." Al Jazeera English. August 5, 2020. aljazeera.com/news/2020/8/5/beirut -explosion-death-toll-rises-to-135-as-5000-wounded-live.

Castner, Charles B. "A Brief History of the Louisville & Nashville Railroad." Louisville & Nashville Railroad Historical Society. lnrr.org/History.aspx.

"CSX Merger Family Tree." *Trains.* June 2, 2006. trains.com/trn/rail roads/history/csx-merger-family-tree.

Chapter Nineteen: The Struggle of the Rural Hospital

"Hill-Burton Act." Harvard Medical School: Perspectives of Change. Last modified 2020. perspectivesofchange.hms.harvard.edu /node/23.

Thomas, Karen Kruse. "Hill-Burton Act." Encyclopedia of Alabama. Last modified August 2, 2021. encyclopediaofalabama.org/ar ticle/h-1439.

U.S. Congress. Senate. "S.66—94th Congress (1975–1976): An Act to Amend the Public Health Service Act and Related Health Laws to Revise and Extend the Health Revenue Sharing

Program, the Family Planning Programs, the Community Mental Health Centers Program, the Program for Migrant Health Centers and Community Health Centers, the National Health Service Corps Program, and the Programs for Assistance for Nurse Training, and for Other Purposes." January 15, 1975. congress.gov/bill/94th-congress/senate-bill/66.

Phillips, Charles D., and Kenneth R. McLeroy. "Health in Rural America: Remembering the Importance of Place." *American Journal of Public Health* 94, no.10 (2004): 1661–63.

Starr, Paul. *The Social Transformation of American Medicine: The Rise of a Sovereign Profession and the Making of a Vast Industry.* New York, NY: Basic Books, 1982.

"Fast Facts: U.S. Rural Hospitals Infographic." American Hospital Association. May 24, 2021. https://www.aha.org/infographics/2021-05-24-fast-facts-us-rural-hospitals-infographic.

"Rural Hospital Programs." Health Resources & Services Administration. Last modified March 2022. hrsa.gov/rural-health/rural-hospitals.

Rural Health Information Hub. "Rural Hospitals." Last modified February 10, 2022. ruralhealthinfo.org/topics/hospitals#challenges.

U.S. Government Accountability Office. "Rural Hospital Closures: Number and Characteristics of Affected Hospitals and Contributing Factors." GAO-18-634. August 29, 2018. gao.gov/products/gao-18-634.

Rural Health Research Gateway. "Rural Health Research Recap: Effects of Rural Hospital Closures." December 2017. ruralhealthresearch.org/alerts/145.

Thomas, Sharita R., Brystana G. Kaufman, Randy K. Randolph, Kristie Thompson, Julie R. Perry, and George H. Pink. "A Comparison of Closed Rural Hospitals and Perceived Impact." Findings Brief, NC Rural Health Research Program. April 2015. ruralhealthresearch.org/publications/966.

Moss, Kristin, G. Mark Holmes, and George H. Pink. "Do Current Medicare Rural Hospital Payment Systems Align with Cost Determinants?" Findings Brief, NC Rural Health Research

Program. February 2015. ruralhealthresearch.org/publications
/958.

Zach, Elizabeth. "What Hospital Closures Mean for Rural California." *High Country News.* September 5, 2016. centerforhealth
journalism.org/fellowships/projects/what-hospital-closures
-mean-rural-california.

Planey, Arriana Marie, Julie R. Perry, Erin E. Kent, Sharita R.
Thomas, Hannah Friedman, Randy K. Randoph, and G. Mark
Holmes. "Since 1990, Rural Hospital Closures Have Increas-
ingly Occurred in Counties That Are More Urbanized, Diverse, and Economically Unequal." Findings Brief, NC Rural
Health Research Program. March 2022. ruralhealthresearch
.org/publications/1481.

Malone, Tyler L., Arriana Marie Planey, Laura B. Bozovich, Kristie
W. Thompson, and George M. Holmes. "The Economic Effects of Rural Hospital Closures." *Health Services Research* 57,
no. 3 (March 2022): 614–23. doi.org/10.1111/1475-6773.13965.

Kelman, Brett. "Ascension Saint Thomas to Buy Struggling Three
Rivers Hospital." *Tennessean,* December 15, 2021. tennessean
.com/story/news/health/2021/12/15/ascension-saint-thomas
-buy-struggling-three-rivers-hospital-waverly/8893108002.

Patino, Marie, Aaron Kessler, and Sarah Holder. "More Americans
Are Leaving Cities, But Don't Call It an Urban Exodus."
Bloomberg CityLab. April 26, 2021. bloomberg.com/graphics
/2021-citylab-how-americans-moved.

American Hospital Association. "CARES Act: Provisions to Help
Rural Hospitals." Fact sheet. April 2020. aha.org/fact-sheets
/2020-03-31-cares-act-provisions-help-rural-hospitals.

American Hospital Association. "AHA-Supported Bill Would Aid
Small Rural Hospitals." March 12, 2021. aha.org/news/head
line/2021-03-12-aha-supported-bill-would-aid-small-rural
-hospitals.

U.S. Congress. "H.R.1887—117th Congress (2021–2022): Rural Hospital
Support Act." Introduced in House March 12, 2021. congress
.gov/bill/117th-congress/house-bill/1887.

Olson, Alex T. "NRHA Outlines New Rural Emergency Hospital Model." NRHA: Rural Health Voices. April 15, 2021. rural health.us/blogs/ruralhealthvoices/april-2021/nrha-outlines -new-rural-emergency-hospital-model.

Epilogue

Wilkey, Lonnie. "Tanker Explosion Still Remembered." *Baptist and Reflector.* July 24, 2018. baptistandreflector.org/tag/missions /page/12.

Coda

Staff reports. "Tennessee Flooding Updates: Final Death Toll at 20; Gov. Bill Lee Declares State of Emergency." *Tennessean.* August 25, 2021. tennessean.com/story/news/2021/08/25/waverly -tennessee-floods-updates-residents-recovery-clean-up-con tinues.

Davis, Chris. " 'She's a Hero.' Woman Dies Saving Neighbors from Waverly Flooding." NewsChannel5 Nashville. Last modified August 25, 2021. newschannel5.com/news/shes-a-hero-woman -dies-saving-neighbors-from-waverly-flooding.

Horan, Kyle. "Brothers on Jet Ski Rescue 15 People from Waverly Floodwaters." NewsChannel5 Nashville. Last modified August 25, 2021. newschannel5.com/news/brothers-on-jet-ski-res cue-15-people-from-waverly-floodwaters.

Young, Amelia. "Community Foundation of Middle Tennessee Raises $1.7 Million for Flood Relief and Recovery." NewsChannel5 Nashville. September 10, 2021. https://www.newschan nel5.com/news/community-foundation-of-middle-tennessee -raises-1-7-million-for-flood-relief-and-recovery.

Hauari, Gabe. "Loretta Lynn's Opry Benefit Concert for Waverly Flood Victims Raises Nearly $1 Million." *Tennessean.* September 17, 2021. tennessean.com/story/entertainment/2021/09

/17/how-much-money-loretta-lynn-benefit-concert-raised
-waverly-flood.

Tennessee Department of Environment & Conservation. "Lee, TDEC Announce $580,000 Loan for Waverly Water Improvements." July 28, 2021. tn.gov/environment/news/2021/7/28/lee--tdec-announce--580-000-loan-for-waverly-water-improve ments.html.

FEMA. "A Guide to the Disaster Declaration Process and Federal Disaster Assistance." https://www.fema.gov/pdf/rrr/dec_proc.pdf.

Horan, Kyle. "Flood Victims Are Finding That Federal Aid Isn't Enough." NewsChannel5 Nashville. September 14, 2021. news channel5.com/news/flood-victims-are-finding-that-federal -aid-isnt-enough.

The Editorial Board. "A Step toward Flood Insurance Fairness." *Wall Street Journal*. June 24, 2021. wsj.com/articles/a-step-toward -flood-insurance-fairness-11624573955.

Mitchell, Damon. "Tennessee Mayors Want Lawmakers to Invest in Flood-Proof Infrastructure." 90.3 WPLN News, Nashville Public Radio. September 13, 2021. wpln.org/post/tennessee-mayors -want-lawmakers-to-invest-in-flood-proof-infrastructure.

Carr, Julie. "Mayor Buddy Frazier of Waverly, Tennessee Talks August 21st Flood Damage, Recovery, and Ongoing Response." *Tennessee Star*. January 11, 2022. tennesseestar.com/2022/01/11 /mayor-buddy-frazier-of-waverly-tennessee-talks-august-21st -flood-damage-recovery-and-ongoing-response.

Matisse, Jonathan, and Travis Loller. "Flooded Tennessee Town Wrestles with How, Where to Rebuild." Associated Press. October 2, 2021. abcnews.go.com/US/wireStory/flooded-tennes see-town-wrestles-rebuild.